# Human Centered Methods in Information Systems: Current Research and Practice

Steve Clarke
University of Luton Business School, UK

Brian Lehaney
University of Luton Business School, UK

 **IDEA GROUP PUBLISHING**
Hershey USA • London UK

Senior Editor:        Mehdi Khosrowpour
Managing Editor:      Jan Travers
Copy Editor:          Maria Boyer
Typesetter:           Tamara Gillis
Cover Design:         Connie Peltz
Printed at:           BookCrafters

Published in the United States of America by
        Idea Group Publishing
        1331 E. Chocolate Avenue
        Hershey PA 17033-1117
        Tel: 717-533-8845
        Fax: 717-533-8661
        E-mail: jtravers@idea-group.com
        Website: http://www.idea-group.com

and in the United Kingdom by
        Idea Group Publishing
        3 Henrietta Street
        Covent Garden
        London WC2E 8LU
        Tel: 171-240 0856
        Fax: 171-379 0609
        http://www.eurospan.co.uk

Library of Congress Cataloging-in-Publication Data

Human centered methods in information systems : current research and practice / [edited
by] Steve Clarke, Brian Lehaney
        p. cm.
    Includes bibliographical references.
    ISBN 1-878289-64-0 (pbk.)
        1. Information technology. 2. Information technology--Social aspects. 3. Human
    engineering. I. Clarke, Steve, 1950- II. Lehaney, Brian, 1953-

    T58.5 H58 2000
    025.04--dc21                                              99-088689

British Cataloguing in Publication Data
A Cataloguing in Publication record for this book is available from the British Library.

# Human Centered Methods in Information Systems: Current Research and Practice

## Table of Contents

## PART 2: SOCIO-TECHNICAL AND CRITICAL SYSTEMS

# Preface

The effective use of information systems (IS) is an essential factor in the successful operation of organisations, but for many this is all too readily translated into the efficient use of information technology. Such an approach is, in our view, only partial, and fails to recognise the influence that human factors have on IS development and management.

The purpose of this book is therefore to present for discussion those issues which practitioners and researchers have found to be critical to understanding and progress within the domain of information systems. This seems to have led quite naturally to the study of IS from three perspectives: technology, organisations, and people. Chapter 1 reflects this position, aiming to set the scene for this book by categorising IS as technical, social, socio-technical, or critical. This chapter seeks to introduce the human-centered focus of the text by casting light on the commonly encountered 'human-centered' versus 'technology' debate in information systems. Information systems are discussed as complex, adaptive, human activity systems, enabled by information technology (IT), giving rise to a view that a purely technical approach to such systems, focusing on fixed and definable objectives is insufficient. Instead, an approach is required which sees the whole system through the views of the human participants.

In Chapter 2, Andrew Wenn describes some aspects of the development of VICNET, an open system in use in the state of Victoria, Australia. Andrew sees the system as difficult to characterise, being dynamic both in geographical and onto-logical scope, size and usage. The chapter describes VICNET, an Internet information provider established in 1994 as a joint venture between the State Library of Victoria and Royal Melbourne Institute of Technology, as an open system: it is being used by a large number of people and public libraries, yet simultaneously it is evolving and being shaped by the technology, the users and the environment of which it is part. VICNET, argues Andrew, may be characterised both in terms of the social and technical worlds embedded within it, and the part it plays in a much larger sociotechnical system—the Internet. By studying the transformations around the VICNET development, it is argued that we can reach an enriched understanding of how open systems come into being and evolve.

In Chapter 3, Gordon Hunter's review of the IS domain reveals people, process, and technology as the key components of an IS, of which the first component, people, is seen to have the greatest relative impact. The chapter outlines a research project which has focused on this people component, aiming to develop an understanding of the specific skills and personal characteristics which systems analysts contribute to IS development and maintenance. What do 'excellent' systems analysts do that is different from other systems analysts? The answer may contribute to a better understanding of the functions performed by systems analysts and to the overall effectiveness of the IS development and maintenance function.

In Chapter 4, Bill Hutchinson's 'bottom-up management and system design,' puts forward the proposition that IS development techniques almost always use top-down approaches to develop software and business systems. Humans, Bill argues, need to simplify the external world by using cognitive models to build a boundary around a problem: a boundary which, whilst helping us to cope with the complexity of the problem at hand, nevertheless produce dilemmas, as they lead to misconceptions about the real behavior of systems, and the people in them. The chapter offers a preliminary methodology to approach system design using 'bottom-up' thinking, a view which is not promoted as the opposite of top down thinking, but as a supplement to it.

Jonathan Lazar and Anthony Norcio's chapter on end-user error presents definitions of error, as well as a taxonomy of user error in order to unravel the causes of error, and different approaches for assisting the end user. The chapter discusses two general approaches for assisting the end user in responding to errors: system design and training design, the aim being to describe the current situation of end-user error and suggest ways to improve the end-user experience.

Ruth Small and Marilyn Arnone focus on a domain ever growing in relevance: the Internet. Their evaluation of the effectiveness of Web sites looks at the business problem of attracting, interesting and motivating Web 'surfers'. They argue that, whilst guidance on the structure and content of Web interfaces is available, these typically concentrate on content, with few having a theoretical foundation, offering diagnostic methods for assessing and interpreting results, or providing detailed feedback for improvement. Furthermore, few, if any, emphasize the motivational aspects of Web sites, i.e. those features that stimulate curiosity, and engage the user's interest, while providing relevant content and an easy-to-use interface. These features help to motivate customers to visit, explore, and return to a Web site. The chapter specifies essential criteria that can be used by both web designers as guidelines for creating 'motivating' Web sites, and by businesses interested in evaluating their existing Web sites.

In Chapter 7, Simon Bell, begins from a position where he sees information technology (IT) projects as more prone to failure than other technology-based interventions. The IS practitioner, he argues, given the responsibility to manage the change process by analysis and design and other mediating strategies, can end up as the victim of technology failure, organisational inability to make up its mind, and half-developed applications. This chapter uses reflective discourse to develop the theme of the vulnerability and power of the action research IS practitioner. Using current case study material drawn from working in transitional economies the chapter indicates lessons learned in the value of the action research approach to analysis and design and the real benefits and powers which can arise from vulnerability, such as autonomy and viability.

Elayne Coakes and Dianne Willis, in their chapter on collaborative working, use the example of a collaborative venture between three members of the Sociotechnical group of the British Computer Society, resulting in a book which gathered together a series of modern sociotechnical experiences. The wide geographical distribution of the editors and contributors dictated a need for enabling technology to support the process. Major options considered for the project were the telephone, fax or electronic mail, the international perspective finally determining email as the best option. The chapter describes the problems encountered and lessons learnt.

Gill Mallalieu's discussion of information systems as 'Wicked Problems' is very much in line with the theme of the book, as a means of conceptualising the relationships between people, organisations and information technology. The chapter outlines a major IS project undertaken in the United Kingdom (RAMESES: Risk Assessment Model: Evaluation Strategy for Existing Systems), using a grounded theory approach. The overall objective of RAMESES was 'to provide a strategic model for the risk assessment of legacy software systems within small-to-medium enterprises considering business process change.' Thus the relationship between the organisation, the way its staff carried out its processes, and their legacy IT systems was at the centre of the project's concerns. This chapter describes how the broad conceptualisation of the problem led to a detailed method to address it, and the results available to date.

In Chapter 10, Vance Wilson and Joline Morrison describe the development and initial testing of an instrument to measure the perceived effectiveness of computer-mediated communication systems based on task type (PE measure). They argue that, although research findings repeatedly suggest that the fit between task and computer-mediated communication technology is important, researchers have not yet been able to comprehensively describe or measure the dimensions of appropriate fit. The PE measure extends prior research in several ways. First, it operationalizes the four major dimensions of McGrath's task circumplex, a model frequently used as a conceptual framework for studying group support systems and computer-mediated communication systems: thus, it will be straightforward to integrate findings from studies that use the PE measure into the existing literature. Second, all four task types are incorporated into the PE measure, where prior research has focused primarily on generation tasks and, to a lesser extent, choice tasks. This comprehensive view of the overall task construct should benefit the process of theory-building as well as prediction in practical applications. Finally, the PE measure has been tested successfully within heterogeneous task domains, suggesting that the instrument has validity and is relatively robust.

Liz Davidson, in Chapter 11, looks at metaphor, using it to enrich understanding of data warehousing. Metaphors have long pervaded the discourse around information technology design, helping developers to conceptualize technological features and functions, to design human-computer interfaces, and to articulate application requirements. Data warehousing is one such metaphor, drawn from practices for materials management in manufacturing and distribution operations, which has been used to conceptualize organizational processes for gathering, storing, and distributing firm-wide data for business analysis and to define the applications of technologies such as multi-dimensional and relational databases and on-line analytic processing software in these processes. However, this metaphor has implications for the meaning and utility of data used by business analysts and for end users' relationships with IS staff, that have not been fully explicated and debated; as more companies commit to a data warehousing strategy, it becomes increasingly important to balance the technological design perspective with a human-centered perspective. Liz therefore aims in this chapter to explore data warehousing from the human centered perspective, first by examining the data warehousing metaphor and its implications for organizing IT support of business analysis activities. Then, the consequences of relying on the data warehousing metaphor as a conceptual model for designing the social aspects of business analysis processes are considered in a review of findings from a field study of a data warehousing project. Finally, the chapter considers the limitations of the data warehousing metaphor and explores alternative metaphors to highlight the human dimensions of this IT innovation.

Lorraine Warren's chapter pursues the idea of Critical Thinking in Information Systems. Lorraine begins from the position that the permeation of IT into wider social environments has meant that the range of people now closely involved with IT on a regular basis has expanded far beyond the white-coated experts in the early DP departments, with terms such as 'the information society' in common parlance. The discipline of information systems (IS), she argues, is now evolving to meet the challenge of analysis and design in these complex and dynamic social contexts, moving on from its early emphasis on highly structured formal methods of analysis and design, to a far softer, human-centered focus. Focusing first on examples of IS failure, it is suggested that problems are rarely caused by the technology itself, but instead by the lack of attention paid to the people who have to use the technology and by broader organizational factors. All of this has led those working in IS to draw on the disciplines of psychology, linguistics, sociology and anthropology for theoretical sophistication to guide and inform the human-centered design agenda. The trawl for useful strands of theory has been wide: the first part of this chapter begins by presenting an overview of how this is changing research and practice in IS; the second discusses an information systems design project where one particular strand of social theory, critical systems thinking, was applied.

Finally, in Chapter 13, Jose Rodrigo Córdoba, Diego Ricardo Torres, and Gerald Midgley review some theoretical constructs on the IS planning problem, which they bring to life through a study at a Colombian University. They argue that the majority of methodologies fail to consider the diversity of users' social contexts, and that IS planning should involve the participation, right from the start, of a variety of stakeholders, each of whom inhabit multiple domains of action. Each domain of action involves people playing a different 'language game', which brings forth specific concerns about other people as human beings. For example, a person may play one language game when interacting with her family, and then switch to another at work. The two language games will imply different expectations and duties of both the self and others. Indeed, within the work context alone, people may be able to identify several domains of action, and several different language games (or rationalities) that they draw upon. Even many of the IS planning methodologies based on user involvement define involvement in terms of a single, pre-set purpose to be pursued by the participant group, usually set by senior management. However, the experience of many people is that they have to juggle multiple (sometimes conflicting) purposes and rationalities in the course of managing their lives.

It is therefore contended that stakeholders (including IS 'experts') should not be confined to a single role within IS planning, or be expected to conform to a single rationality. Rather, the spectrum of their (sometimes contradictory) lives should be swept in. Within an extended IS planning process, founded upon genuine stakeholder involvement (that is, sweeping in a range of stakeholders and their multiple concerns, with only minimal constraints from an organisational agenda), a variety of questions about what is meaningful in different domains of actions can arise. These questions can be dealt with by considering the different values and boundaries that are assumed in different domains of action, and debate can be fostered between stakeholders on the implications of choosing any one boundary, or set of boundaries, for IS planning. They argue that working like this will ensure that IS planning deals with the effects of change on as many as possible of the domains of action that people participate in, and that IS implementation will be improved, because the factors that cause user resistance will be accounted for from the start.

In conclusion, it is, of course, impossible in a book of this length to represent the diversity of views and approaches to information systems from a human perspective. We just hope that the variety represented by this volume goes some way to explaining the domain, and if nothing more, whets your appetite for further study.

**Steve Clarke and Brian Lehaney**
**Editors**

## Acknowledgements

*The editors would like to acknowledge the help of all involved in the collation and review process of the book, without whose support the project could not have been satisfactorily completed.*

*A further special note of thanks goes also to all the staff at Idea Group Publishing, whose contributions throughout the whole process from inception of the initial idea to final publication have been invaluable.*

## Chapter I

# Introduction: Information Systems as Constrained Variety — Issues and Scope

Steve Clarke and Brian Lehaney
University of Luton Business School

## INTRODUCTION

This chapter seeks to cast light on the commonly encountered 'human-centred' versus 'technology' debate in information systems (IS: Clarke and Lehaney, 1998; Clarke and Lehaney, 1999; Lehaney, Clarke et al., 1999). It takes as its starting point a view which sees information systems as complex, adaptive, human activity systems, enabled by information technology (IT). Two approaches dominate in trying to understand such systems. The first redefines them as purely technical systems, for which a fixed and definable objective can be determined: from this point, the problem becomes one of design. The second approach sees the whole system through the views of the human participants: here, the problem initially is one of debate, aimed at determining a consensus view of the system of concern before moving on to designing relevant solutions.

The technical view outlined above might be seen as an attempt to reduce the system's complexity, by removing the voluntaristic, probabilistic behaviour which the human actors bring to the system. Once this is done, more technologically focused IS managers are on comfortable ground, having redefined the system as one which is highly deterministic, and for which a solution can be achieved through the design of a new or improved system. Similarly, the human-centred view may be seen as excluding technical considerations in order to reach agreement on the part of participants before proceeding further.

To try to understand these and other possible, positions, this chapter looks at the IS domain through the concept of constrained variety (Ashby, 1956). In the section which follows, we will first look at the theoretical grounding which casts light on this problem. Subsequent sections then discuss how IS may be constrained, and what this means for understanding such systems. Examples are given of systems for which the variety constraint has been drawn differently, and some reflections and conclusions are drawn.

## THE LAW OF REQUISITE VARIETY

Ashby's (1956) 'Law of Requisite Variety' is a *systems* concept, and, in so far as an information system may be seen generally as a *system*, the 'Law' may be related directly to information systems. Ashby (1956) introduced the idea of variety as, in one respect, the number of possible states in which a system can exist. Ashby's work addressed the idea of probabilistic systems, and used the concept of variety to express the number of different ways in which a system may be configured before the system itself is no longer able to survive.

Think, for example of the system of traffic lights. The colours red, amber and green have six possible colour variations or 'variety' (using a maximum of two colours and a minimum of one colour at any one time): red; green; amber; red and amber; red and green; amber and green. As an example, only four of these are used in the United Kingdom, but should more be required, the two currently possible but unused combinations could be actioned within the existing variety of the system. If seven colour combinations were required, the system would no longer be able to cope, and would need to be redesigned, at substantial cost.

Added to this concept of 'constrained variety' is Ashby's further assertion that only variety can destroy variety. For a manager to control a system, this infers that the manager must have at his or her disposal at least as much variety as the system has. This 'rule' has far-reaching consequences when dealing with systems for which complexity stems from both technology and human activity.

The conclusion to be drawn from this is that control in systems depends on either reducing the variety in the system (variety reduction), or increasing the variety we have at our disposal to manage the system (variety amplification). This has implications for those engaging in the development and management of human-centred information systems. In the following sections, four types of variety constraint are considered (technical, social, socio-technical, and critical), and are critiqued from the perspectives of variety reduction and variety amplification.

## CONSTRAINT 1: TECHNICAL

### The Human-Centred Position

Any study of the theory and practice of information systems from a technical perspective soon reveals the domain to be problematic. The most important single reason for this is that, whilst information systems management may often be pursued as a predominantly technical endeavour, it nonetheless has to work within a given social framework.

This adherence to technical problem solving leads to tensions when the system

---

**CASE EXAMPLE: Wessex Area Health**

The computer problems of Wessex Area Health (a major provider of hospital and health services in the United Kingdom) are well documented. During the 1980s and early 1990s, Wessex drew up a plan to integrate the information systems provision for all of the Area Health Authority, linking hospitals, general practitioners and community healthcare within one system. From the beginning the project was beset by major problems. Ultimately the project failed, providing little of the originally intended system, but at an estimated cost of up to £64 million.

From the perspective of those involved in the development, one of the main failings was a lack of participant involvement: care staff, it is reported, referred to the computer systems developers as 'Androids', because their terminology was such that they might have been from another planet. Certainly there is no doubt that the system failed; and certainly there is equally no question that it was undertaken as a predominantly technical solution to a problem that was subject to change in a highly socio-cultural environment.

---

or systems to be managed require significant user input. The need for discovering the requirements of users is not disputed, but is typically achieved by including a user analysis stage within an existing problem-solving approach. This approach, inherited from computer systems development, relies on the systems development life cycle (SDLC: Wetherbe and Vitalari, 1994, p.211; Kendall and Kendall, 1992, p.7) as the primary method.

The systems development life cycle is a stagewise or waterfall approach, whereby each stage is undertaken in a linear sequence, generally requiring the completion of a stage before the next is commenced. So, for example, work on system design would not be authorised until the system specification was written and approved. User requirements specification fits uncomfortably into this process, since such requirements are seldom fixed, but vary over the life of a project. System developers demonstrate varying success in coping with this, and many become very adept at accommodating user prompted changes. However, the tension is not removed, since it derives from the fact that an iterative element (user needs) is being incorporated into a fixed, sequential schedule. The very reason for the term 'waterfall method' is the recognition that, whilst movement downward is the norm, movement back up the development stages is not part of the methodology.

---

**The Systems Development Life Cycle**

Feasibility Study
User Requirements Specification
System Specification
System Design
Testing
Implementation
Maintenance

The argument for an alternative to these technology-based approaches is further supported by the findings from a number of studies of systems failure. Examples range from simple failure to meet performance goals (the Organisational Aspects of IT Special Interest Group (OASIG) of the Operational Research Society (OASIG, 1996)) concludes that up to 90% of information technology (IT) investments do not meet the performance goals set for them) to catastrophic failure of the type evidenced in the London Ambulance Service and Taurus, the London Stock Exchange System. OASIG regard the technology-led nature of the process, and the lack of attention to human and organisational factors as key factors in this lack of success.

Through a thorough review of the information systems literature, Lyytinen and Hirschheim (1987) make a compelling case for the argument that few information systems can be considered a success. The reason for claiming success is, they argue, largely based on an erroneous classification of how such success should be measured, which usually focuses on the extent to which the completed system meets the requirement specification laid out in advance. Lyytinen and Hirschheim promote the notion of expectation failure, or the failure of the system to meet the expectations of the key stakeholder groups, as conveying a more pluralistically informed view, and forcing a dynamic perspective of computer-based information systems.

## Strengths and Weaknesses

Information systems management pursued as a purely technical endeavour is littered with examples of failure: a failure which it has been widely argued stems largely from the exclusion of the views of human participants in the system. It is therefore difficult to escape the conclusion that the application of such an approach must be restricted to systems in which human activity is not an important factor. The main weakness lies in the belief that including a 'user requirements' phase within the development life cycle of such systems effectively deals with human activity within the system. Empirical and theoretical evidence denies this, and point to the need for more human-centred methods in such cases.

---

### CASE EXAMPLE: Information Systems Failure
### The London Ambulance Service

The London Ambulance Service (LAS) computer-aided dispatch system failed on October 26, 1992, its first day in operation. From its inception, the system had been treated as a technical problem, to which a viable solution could be found. But LAS exhibited social and political dimensions which the technologically based approach proved ill-equipped to address.

Following this initial failure, a new computer-aided dispatch system was successfully implemented, but only through an approach which paid heed to the whole system of concern, of which the technical system was just one interactive part.

---

# CONSTRAINT 2: SOCIAL

### The Human-Centred Position

The human-centred approach to IS has given rise to the so-called 'soft' methods (for example, Lewis, 1994; Stowell and West, 1994). It is argued that traditional 'engineering' approaches are 'hard' or functionalist, being based on a view of the world which sees it as composed of determinable, rule-based systems. 'Soft' methods, by contrast, take an interpretivist, ideographic stance: the world is seen as determinable only from the viewpoints of human participants.

It is widely argued that whilst 'hard' methods give rise to a systematic approach to IS, 'soft' methods typically rely on a more holistic, systemic view, which, it is maintained, are more representative of the domain. In general terms the purpose is to form a view of the system of concern through the eyes of participants, and use this to manage the process. The key issues emerging from this approach are: 1) the problem domain is seen as a system; 2) the system is one of human activity, not technical parts in interaction.

### Human-Centred Methods

The view that is represented by human-centred methods can be seen by reference to methodologies in general usage. A brief summary is therefore given below of four such methodologies: soft systems methodology, strategic assumption surfacing and testing, interactive planning, and strategic options development and analysis.

Soft systems methodology (SSM) was developed by Checkland (1981) and Wilson (1984), and enables the people involved in running a system (Actors), those responsible for controlling it (Owners), and those who receive its benefits (Customers), to participate in the process of developing a system model. SSM uses a debating approach to build a representation of the system of concern in the form of 'rich pictures' and 'root definitions,' the latter using the mnemonic, CATWOE, for Customer, Actors, Transformation process, Weltanschauung, Owner, and Environmental constraints. SSM uses the concepts of 'real world' and 'systems thinking world' to differentiate those activities which involve the participants and their normal, everyday language, and those modelling activities which could be undertaken solely by the analyst. The debate inherent within SSM is used to explore three systems dimensions: intervention (roles of participants), social, and political. This exploration helps highlight actions which are deemed both systemically desirable and culturally feasible.

Strategic assumption surfacing and testing (SAST: Mason and Mitroff, 1981) is designed for use with complex systems of highly interdependent problems, where "problem formulation and structuring assume greater importance than problem solving using conventional techniques" (Jackson, 1991). The approach is aimed at groups lacking a common set of values or goals, and in use focuses on forming sub-groups, drawn from as wide a participant base as possible, and each holding a position on which they have consensus. Techniques are then used to 'surface' the assumptions underlying their position and to enable the sub-group to become aware of these and the ontology that makes them meaningful. Debate between the sub-groups is then encouraged, in which each position is attacked and defended, it being a key point that this debating should be adversarial in nature: this is intended to clarify for each group the differing perspectives and enable a synthesis of viewpoints, albeit temporary, which can be used as a basis for decision making. The underlying ethos is that organisations are unable or unwilling to challenge seriously the accepted policies and procedures. By providing a forum in which sympathy is extended to ideas that diverge considerably from current practice, the underlying assumptions of that current practice can be 'surfaced' and more fully considered.

Strategic options development and analysis (SODA) was developed as a means to cope with both the qualitative and quantitative aspects of complex, messy, problems (Eden and Graham, 1983; Eden, 1985). SODA focuses on individual's interpretations of situations, eliciting personal constructs by means of cognitive maps, in a participatory fashion, during one-to-one interviews (Kelly, 1955). The individual maps are merged to help facilitate the process of team negotiations which take place in workshops. A SODA workshop aims to achieve a consensus commitment to plans of action. SODA uses a framework of four areas: the 'individual', whom it recognises as having a personal interpretation of the situation; a view of the 'nature of organisations' (in particular, it attempts to consider power structures and relationships concerning individuals); 'consulting practice', in which negotiations and commitment, relative to the problem area, are highlighted; and finally 'technology and technique.' The SODA approach is encapsulated in that it seeks consensus and commitment, rather than compromise and agreement.

In interactive planning, Ackoff (1981) argues that purposeful behaviour cannot be value free. Hence, if one regards an organisation as a purposeful system itself, containing another purposeful part (the individual), but itself part of a larger purposeful system (the environment), then all three need to be served by managers, and this is best done by acknowledging their input to a decision process and the accompanying values. Three principles provide the basis for interactive planning. The first is the 'participative' principle. It encompasses a belief that the process of planning is more important than the plans themselves. It is through the process that individuals come to a greater understanding of the organisation and their part in it. All those affected by the planning should be involved. The second principle is that of 'continuity'. This acknowledges the changing role of individuals and their changing values. Hence any plans should be constantly revised to facilitate them. The last principle is that of the 'holistic.' Planning should span simultaneously and interdependently the various strata of an organisation. The methodology is actioned through five phases. These are 'formulating the mess' (analysing threats and opportunities to provide a reference scenario); 'ends planning' (specify the objectives and goals and produce an idealised design); 'means planning' (generate policies to draw together the reference scenario and the idealised design); 'resource planning' (facilities, equipment, personnel and money) and 'design of implementation and control' (how and by whom are the decisions made to be executed?). This is a systemic process and hence the order is not fixed. Amongst the advantages of this methodology, cited by practitioners, are the involvement of all stakeholders generating consensus and commitment and the ability of the methodology to release suppressed creativity and harness it to individual and organisational development.

### Strengths and Weaknesses

The appeal of 'soft methods' in IS management is easy to understand. A richer view is gained of participants' needs, enabling a deeper understanding of the system of concern. However, such approaches are not without their problems. Two issues are particularly problematic. Firstly, where is the guarantee that the understanding reached is a true representation of participants' views? Secondly, once a common understanding is achieved, how is this then turned into a working (often technical) system? These problems are addressed in the two sections below.

# CONSTRAINT 3: SOCIO-TECHNICAL

### The Human-Centred Position

Loosely, the aim of socio-technical approaches may be seen as blending the soft and technically constrained methods outlined above. The perceived need for such methods stems from the contention that neither socially nor technically constrained approaches will, by themselves, offer a valid approach to managing information systems.

The socio-technical domain in IS has been dominated by methodology, the most widely used of which have been ETHICS, multiview, and client-led design.

ETHICS (Mumford, Hirschheim et al., 1985): Effective Technical and Human Implementation of Computer-based Systems is a socio-technical methodology, developed in the 1970s to combine organisational, administrative and quality-of-working-life factors. Although essentially a goal-directed methodology which retains a technological system as its primary target, ETHICS nonetheless gives much greater concentration to the micro-social impact of IS management.

Multiview (Wood-Harper, Antill et al., 1985) is based on the assertion that at any stage of information systems development, the approach is contingent on the circumstances met at that stage. It differs from traditional systems development life cycle (SDLC)-based methodologies in that it is not seen as step-by-step problem solving, but as an iterative process in which different approaches may be used at different times. Multiview accepts the view that no one methodology can be seen to work in all cases, and that the methodology to be chosen cannot be decided in advance of the problem situation being known. There is explicit recognition within multiview of the need for participation.

Client-led design (CLD: Stowell, 1991) was developed as a result of the argument that, since information systems result from social interaction, participants in that interaction ought to be central to systems analysis and design. CLD is therefore a genuine attempt at perceiving ISD as a primarily social process. Information systems development from this perspective needs to be *driven* by interpretivism: at the technical development stage, functionalism should not be allowed to take over.

### Strengths and Weaknesses

The socio-technical perspective may be criticised for giving rise to essentially *methodological* arguments. By focusing on methodology, both the 'hard' and 'soft' schools exhibit shortcomings resulting from the lack of investigation of underpinning theory. Flood and Ulrich (1990), for example, categorise 'hard' (technical) and 'soft' (social) methods respectively as 'non-reflective positivistic {and} non-reflective interpretivistic'. They argue that the 'hard' school is predominantly pragmatic, dominated by technique with limited reference to underlying theory at any level; functionalist methods prevail, giving rise to frequent challenges when applied within social contexts. The 'soft' school attempts to deal with these social issues, but mostly operates at a methodological level, with little reference to underlying theory.

## CONSTRAINT 4: CRITICAL

### The Human-Centred Position

Critical systems thinking (CST) accepts the contribution of both social and technical approaches and, through critique, enhances awareness of the circumstances in which such approaches can be properly employed. The pragmatism of the technical approaches and the lack of theoretical reflection in the social approaches allow CST to expose both as special cases with limited domains of application. Figure 1 summarises this position through an expansion of the Burrell and Morgan grid (after Oliga, 1991).

This perspective further supports the view that traditional approaches to IS largely emerge as serving the technical interest, with labour applied as purposive-rational action to achieve transformation by application of the means of production: information technology and functionalist planning methods. The alternative, evident in these domains since the 1970s but still limited in acceptance, is the service of the practical interest from the interpretative paradigm, relying on the communication of perceptions and consensus forming.

A theoretically and practically informed framework for IS must therefore embrace a number of issues. Firstly, any investigation must be conducted with technical, social and critical intent. The latter involves examination and re-examination of assumptions and material conditions (the conditions according to which those assumptions have been made), within an emancipatory framework. The investigation must be sensitive to the given organisational climate, and will demand a diversity of methods. All of this should take place within a cycle of action and learning, in which all involved and affected are included. A diagrammatic representation of such a framework is given in Figure 2.

The first consideration in using this critical framework is the need to set a boundary for any investigation. Since the system is to be seen in social terms, this boundary should consider primarily those involved in and affected by the system. The core of the study is then seen in terms of the 'critical cycle of learning and action', whereby a mix of interpretative and structured analysis may take place within the determined boundary, having regard to the given organisational con-

*Figure 1: The Social Validity of Hard, Soft and Critical Approaches*

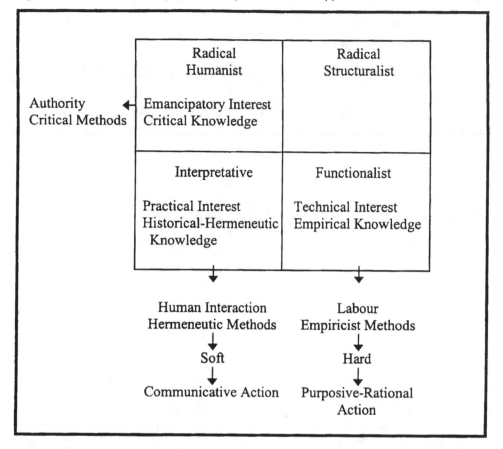

text. Our view is that we should not be prescriptive about the approach taken to this, but recent research points to a number of possible approaches. Firstly, forms of action research, in particular cooperative inquiry (Reason and Heron, 1995) offer an action learning cycle which has open participation as a primary aim. The initial objective is to creatively investigate the system through interpretative analysis with a critical intent. Methods available to specifically facilitate this task include brainstorming, lateral thinking, the use of metaphor, Ackoff's idealised design, and Checkland's soft systems methodology stages one to five.

### Strengths and Weaknesses

Critical analysis within IS offers much that is lacking in technical, social or socio-technical approaches. Its strength lies in the theoretical ability to combine technical and social analysis within a critically reflective, iterative framework. Methods have been developed to apply this in a practical setting, primary among which has been Total Systems Intervention (TSI: Flood and Jackson, 1991; Flood, 1995). Arguably, the main weakness of the critical approach stems from its strength.

*Figure 2: A Critical Framework for Information Systems Strategy*

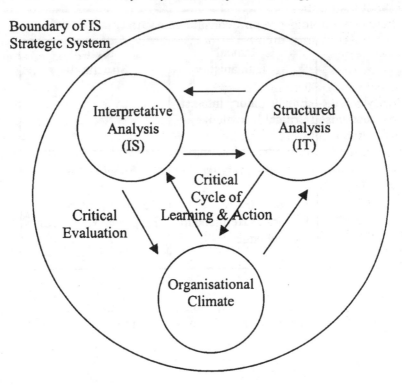

Founded as it is on a branch of critical social theory which promotes human emancipation, it has little means to bring about emancipatory conditions in circumstances characterised by severe coercive influences. The result is that many argue its conception of emancipation in human affairs to be flawed.

## REFLECTIONS AND CONCLUSIONS

The Law of Requisite Variety offers a perspective from which to understand the variety of approaches to IS management.

This chapter has argued that the most common approach, focusing on technical issues, may be seen as the most constrained, and largely excluding human participants from the area of study. Its domain of applicability may therefore be seen as constrained to those systems where human activity is of little importance. It relies on variety reduction in order to make the area of concern more amenable to human intervention.

The inadequacy of a technically constrained approach in certain problem contexts initially gave rise to social or 'soft', human centred methods. Much has been learned from their application, and the IS domain has benefited from the development of a number of human centred methodologies, some of which are outlined in this chapter. Certainly, these approaches have demonstrated an ability to bring about richer understanding of human centred contexts in IS, but again are not without their critics.

These methodologies require considerable variety amplification on the part of interventionists, in order to embrace the complexity of human behaviour alongside a system's technical complexity. But, as is the case with the technical approach, system variety is still constrained, in this case to technical issues together with a consensual view of its human participants.

Socio-technical methodologies might be expected to combine the best of both technical and socially based methods, and to an extent this is what they do. However, the socio-technical methodologies developed rely on considerable variety amplification on the part of interventionists, whilst still seeing the problem context as constrained to an unreflective viewpoint within commonly a pragmatic, contingent approach.

The deeper analysis of social theory used to underpin a critical view of IS gives it a potential unavailable to technical, social or socio-technical methods. Whilst there are unresolved issues with this approach, it could be argued that this is *all* the result of a need for variety amplification. The complexity of a system seen as 'critical' is such that, even now almost 20 years after the early application of this thinking within business and management, practitioners and theorists have difficulty grasping all its facets. This is evidenced, it may be argued, in the strong basis in emancipatory critical theory, to which only recently have alternative perceptions been sought.

Perhaps the future lies in this latter view of IS. If so, we should be seeking less to constrain the variety of the systems of concern, and more to amplify the variety available to IS practitioners.

# REFERENCES

Ackoff, R. L. (1981). *Creating the Corporate Future*. New York, Wiley.

Ashby, W. R. (1956). *An Introduction to Cybernetics*. London, Chapman and Hall.

Checkland, P. B. (1981). "Rethinking a Systems Approach." *Journal of Applied Systems Analysis* 8(3): 3-14.

Clarke, S. A. and B. Lehaney (1998). Information Systems Intervention: A Total Systems View. *Modelling for Added Value*. R. Paul and S. Warwick. London, Springer-Verlag: 103-115.

Clarke, S. A. and B. Lehaney (1999). "Human Centered Research and Practice in Information Systems." *Journal of End User Computing* 11(4): 3-4.

Eden, C. (1985). "Perish the Thought!" *Journal of the Operational Research Society* 36(9): 809-819.

Eden, C. and R. Graham (1983). "Halfway to Infinity: Systems Theorizing for the Practitioners?" *Journal of Operational Research* 34(8): 723-728.

Flood, R. L. (1995). "Total Systems Intervention (TSI): A Reconstitution." *Journal of the Operational Research Society* 46, 174-191.

Flood, R. L. and M. C. Jackson (1991). *Creative Problem Solving: Total Systems Intervention*. Chichester, Wiley.

Flood, R. L. and W. Ulrich (1990). "Testament to Conversations on Critical Systems

Thinking Between Two Systems Practitioners." *Systems Practice* 3(1): 7-29.

Jackson, M. C. (1991). *Systems Methodology for the Management Sciences*. New York, Plenum.

Kelly, G. A. (1955). *The Psychology of Personal Constructs*. London, Weidenfeld and Nicholson.

Kendall, K. E. and J. E. Kendall (1992). *Systems Analysis and Design*. Englewood Cliffs, New Jersey, Prentice Hall.

Lehaney, B., S. A. Clarke, et al. (1999). "The Human Side of Information Systems Development: A Case of an Intervention at a British Visitor Attraction." *Journal of End User Computing* 11(4): (TBA).

Lewis, P. (1994). *Information Systems Development*. London, Pitman.

Lyytinen, K. and R. Hirschheim (1987). Information Systems Failures: A Survey and Classification of the Empirical Literature. *Oxford Surveys in Information Technology*. Oxford, Oxford University Press. 4, 257-309.

Mason, R. O. and I. I. Mitroff (1981). *Challenging Strategic Planning Assumptions: Theory, Cases and Techniques*. New York, Wiley.

Mumford, E., R. Hirschheim, et al., Eds. (1985). *Research Methods in Information Systems*. Amsterdam, Elsevier.

OASIG (1996). "Why do IT Projects so often Fail?" *OR Newsletter* 309, 12-16.

Oliga, J. C. (1991). Methodological Foundations of Systems Methodologies. *Critical Systems Thinking: Directed Readings*. R. L. Flood and M. C. Jackson. Chichester, Wiley: 159-84.

Reason, P. and J. Heron (1995). Co-operative Inquiry. *Rethinking Methods in Psychology*. J. A. Smith, R. Harre and L. V. Langenhove. London, Sage.

Stowell, F. A. (1991). *Client Participation in Information Systems Design*. Systems Thinking in Europe (Conference Proceedings), Huddersfield, Plenum.

Stowell, F. A. and D. West (1994). "'Soft' systems thinking and information systems: a framework for client-led design." *Information Systems Journal* 4(2): 117-127.

Wetherbe, J. C. and N. P. Vitalari (1994). *Systems Analysis and Design: Best Practices*. St. Paul, MN, West.

Wilson, B. (1984). *Systems: Concepts, Methodologies and Applications*. Chichester, Wiley.

Wood-Harper, A. T., L. Antill, et al. (1985). *Information Systems Definition: The Multiview Approach*. London, Blackwell.

# Part 1

# End User Issues

**Chapter II**

# Topological Transformations: The Co-Construction of an Open System

Andrew Wenn
HPS University of Melbourne and
Victoria University of Technology

The kind of systems we envisage will be open-ended and incremental – undergoing continual evolution. In an open system it becomes very difficult to determine what objects exist at any point in time.

Hewitt, C., and de Jong, P. (1984)
*Open Systems*

... VICNET provides an information "shopping mall" giving ease of access and a convenient user-friendly approach to a wide range of information "shops"—databases and networks, among which customers can browse, inspect, try out, avail themselves of free demonstrations and offers, and, if they choose, purchase from commercial outlets.

http://www.vicnet.net.au/vicnet/abtvic.html

## INTRODUCTION

This chapter describes some aspects of the development of VICNET, an assemblage of computers, cables, modems, people, texts, libraries, buildings, dreams and images. It is a system that is difficult to characterise, it is dynamic both in geographical and ontological scope, size and usage. I have attempted to capture some of its nature through the use of several vignettes that may give the reader a small insight into parts of its being, then using some of the techniques and explanatory and exploratory mechanisms available from the field of science studies such as heterogeneous engineering and Actor Network Theory (ANT), I reveal some of the ways that VICNET came into existence. Many computer systems are undergoing continual evolution and it is extremely difficult to discern their configuration and what objects have agency at any given point in time; they can be thought of as open systems as described by Hewitt and de Jong (1984). VICNET, an Internet information provider established in 1994 as a joint venture between the State Library of Victoria and Royal Melbourne Institute of Technology, is one such system; it is being used by a large number of people and public libraries, yet simultaneously it is evolving and being shaped by the technology, the users and the environment of which it is part. Consider the system, VICNET as it is called, as a node of a much larger network. I have attempted to unfold this node to reveal the social and technical worlds contained therein, but I also fold the VICNET node in itself so that it becomes part of a much larger sociotechnical system – the Internet. This process of folding I refer to as a topological transformation and it is by studying transformations of this type that may help us understand how open systems come into being and evolve.

In what follows, I provide a brief background to VICNET and the data collection method I used. Next, I discuss some the analytical techniques that are available for those who wish to study the development of technological systems. Following this all-too-brief comment I then present a selection of vignettes that show the varied nature of this socio-technical system. Presenting these then allows me to develop further the idea of social topologies introduced in the section on analytical techniques. In the final section there is some discussion as to why this way of looking at socio-technical systems may be useful.

## BACKGROUND

In 1995, the Premier of Victoria officially launched VICNET, Victoria's Network. VICNET is a collaborative project between the Royal Melbourne Institute of Technology (RMIT) and the State Library of Victoria (SLV), funded from the Community Support Fund by the State Government of Victoria as part of its commitment, as the Office of the Minister for the Arts (OMA) News Release said, to "restore Victoria's library system and develop its capability to take full advantage of modern technology" (OMA, 1994). After many months of negotiations, during which time a pilot scheme was established to test the feasibility of the project, VICNET had finally gone public. In simple terms, VICNET is an information provider[1] connected to the global Internet, which in a less global sense aims to provide access for all Victorians to the world of electronic information.

The public launch was simply the "coming out" of the results of many months of work during which time: equipment was purchased, installed, configured and tested; staff were hired; documents formatted using HTML (the standard markup language for web documents) and published; and negotiations between a variety of organisations took place. The launch however did not mean that VICNET was complete—far from it—all that it indicated was that it was ready to enter the public arena and start to discharge its responsibilities.

Many readers, when encountering discussions of Internet systems, will think first and foremost of them as collections of computers, cables, network cards, modems, software of various types (operating system software, communications, text editing and so on) and a multitude of other technical peripherals. However, this view is rather limiting as I show both here and elsewhere (Wenn, 1996a; 1996b). Within VICNET there are a number of subgroups who attempt to operate cooperatively and run the system. There are the central staff whose salaries are paid out of the government grant; volunteer workers who donate their time to mark up documents; sponsors who have provided either money, discounted equipment or both; people from outside who provide information to be stored on the primary computer or links from the VICNET site to their own pages, the libraries that will provide public access terminals; and the people who will search for information. In short, VICNET is a heterogeneous collection of computers, cables, modems, people, texts, libraries, rules, regulations, policy documents, images and dreams that are undergoing continual and incremental change—an open system. The major hardware location is in the State Library of Victoria's PABX/computer room whilst the editorial staff are located in the west wing of the State Library of Victoria in Melbourne's Central Business District.

In much of the above, the way I have referred to VICNET implies that it operates from a central site, this being the State Library of Victoria. The use of the word 'central' is problematic in that it makes it appear that this place is the important one, it is the one to study, it is where all the action is. However, this turns out to be not altogether true. The word 'central' may be the correct one to use when referring to the site where the main computer is situated, it may be justifiable to use it when referring to the very early days of VICNET, it may also be correct when talking about the place that people contact when they wish to join VICNET or provide sponsorship. But, as my research shows, it is not correct to think of it as where all the action takes place. The problem is though how do I refer to the macro VICNET? The word central is too strong, the word exchange tends to imply that all that happens here is information flows from one route to another, this is where connections are made. Yet it is more than this. Without the central computer VICNET would not exist, yet as we will see, without the widely distributed access points VICNET would be quite useless because no one would be able to use it and the government would be reluctant to provide funding. So, although in some circumstances I may call it the central site, this should be understood to mean nothing more than the artifacts located at the SLV site.

In what follows, I will reveal VICNET as an assemblage, a large-scale system (Hughes, 1987) of technical and social actors that is constructed through cooperation and negotiation. Before moving on to describe some aspects of this system and the mode of analysis it would be appropriate to comment on the means of data collection and presentation.

## A Note on Method

The material used in this chapter is a small part of that which I collected whilst undertaking a qualitative study of the early days of VICNET. Qualitative research is a valuable method to use if one wishes to study the underlying culture and emergence of a system. I was interested in the way things came about, not just in the numbers of users or counts of the various types of equipment being used, although this doesn't preclude the use of quantitative data where it helps build a picture of the system's development.

Much of the material came from unpublished documents kindly lent to me by the VICNET staff; other sources included interviews and e-mail discussions with people whom I have never met but who chose to answer all my questions via the medium of the Internet. Although some might criticise the use of material obtained via e-mail interviews, especially from people whom I have never met, by comparing information obtained by e-mail with events that actually happened or materials from other sources, one can validate the data and hence establish the reliability of the material. In fact as Van Maanen reminds us "qualitative research is marked more by a reliance upon multiple sources of data than by its commitment to **any one source alone**"[2] (1982, p. 15, my emphasis). I feel that using electronic media, provided suitable care is taken to verify the material obtained, makes it possible to obtain a richer set of data than would otherwise be possible, from a larger range of geographically disparate sources.

By its very nature qualitative research tends towards the holistic, trying as it does to reveal as many influences as possible on the "thing" being studied (Myers, 1995). In a work of this length and type, it is very hard to present, and for you the reader to make sense of, that whole. I have chosen to discuss just four aspects of VICNET to give you a glimpse of the complexity of and to underline some of the difficulties that arise when trying to describe a system that is both open and heterogeneous. The first vignette shows how quickly the equipment inventory of the VICNET site at the SLV grew in the 18 months since it was first established as a trial scheme and offers some reasons for this growth. Vignette Two offers a glimpse of how VICNET and a remote organisation coalesced to change the nature of both participants – a fluid topology in the sense used by Mol and Law (1994). The third vignette attempts to illustrate how VICNET can be seen as a vehicle for bringing remote information back to Victoria. In fact the system seems to fold the space occupied by the Internet bringing the remote points closer together in a sense – in this way VICNET transforms the space occupied by the Internet. Systems may also encounter resistance to their development or reconfiguration, and this is illustrated in the last vignette where difficulties are encountered with the equipment being used, lack of confidence on the part of the user and a clash of cultures. In choosing these vignettes I am acutely aware of the fact that we have to understand large-scale infrastructure projects from a multiplicity of views which will include "work practices of designers and users, the emergence of large-scale technical systems, and the encoding and decoding of information" (Neumann and Star, 1995) but also acknowledge that is not possible to cover all aspects of the system in this chapter. Here, VICNET is revealed as infrastructure, as an organisation within the SLV community, and as the people or external organisations using it to gather or publish information as they attempt to become part of an ever-widening system — in short networks of the social and technical.

## Theoretical Perspectives

Articulating a large infrastuctural project within a globally changing electronic infrastructure is no easy matter. The challenge for us is no less than simultaneously to understand the work practices of designers and users, the emergence of large-scale technical systems, and the encoding and decoding of information, including its heterogeneity and disputed character as well as its conventional aspects.

Neumann, L.J. & Star, S.L. (1995)
*Untitled Paper given at the Society for the Social Studies of Science*

How do we understand the development of technological systems that are both simultaneously global in scope and yet localised, that are messy yet structured, socially ordered yet socially shaping? These systems may also be continually changing and open ended, leading to even greater problems for those who wish to describe their emergence. One of the first to study large-scale systems was Thomas Hughes who argued, that at least for the Electric Power Systems he studied, there were phases of development with each phase showing certain characteristics (Hughes, 1983, p. 14). "System builders are no respecters of knowledge categories or professional boundaries", they mix the economic, technical, scientific, organisational, geographical and managerial with elements of power and politics in their efforts to construct their technological artifacts (Bijker et al, 1989, p. 9). In short, the artificial boundaries used to create the dichotomies of technology/science, pure/applied, internal/external, social/technical do not exist for the constructors of networks and systems. They work within, see a seamless Web, which they manipulate and are in turn manipulated by. It is the dissolution of these boundaries and the move towards viewing technologies as heterogeneous webs which I wish to take from Hughes' work.

While Hughes was able to successfully reveal the sociotechnical heterogeneity of large-scale systems, it is Langdon Winner amongst others who highlights the moral ramifications that construction of such systems may hold (Winner, 1986; 1989, p. 301). As Hughes writes of Edison we follow him (Edison) as he lobbies politicians, performs his economic calculations and does his research; we see the world through his eyes and things that are of no concern to Edison fall from view - they become invisible (Law, 1991, p. 11). Thus, if Edison is not concerned with issues of race or equality and so on, then these moral stories are not told. On the other hand, Winner shows how Moses constructed overpasses on Long Island so that they would exclude certain sections of the population – the poor and the blacks – from travelling there as the buses they would normally use for transport were too tall to cope with the overpass – the artifacts have a political dimension (Winner, 1986, p. 23).

Heterogeneous engineering borrows much from Hughes, in particular the idea that systems are built through the interrelationships between dissimilar entities that offer varying degrees of cooperation. This argues that the systems so produced can be seen as a *"network"* of juxtaposed elements (Law, 1987, p. 113). That is the heterogeneous entities that come to make up the network are persuaded, shaped, and hopefully assimilated into the final product that can be seen as a network of interested actors. "Actors are the heterogeneous entities that constitute a network", they interact through networks, subsuming "science, technology and the myriad of other categories" (Bijker et al, 1989, p. 11). Where it differs most from Hughes is that has an emphasis on conflict and the idea that "vigilance and surveillance have to be maintained, or else the elements will fall out of line and the network will start to crumble" (Law, 1987, p. 114). Vigilance, surveillance, struggle, hostility, adversarial, collisions, patterns of force, conflict, resistance, bravery – the war metaphors abound in heterogeneous engineering as they do in the closely related Actor Network Theory which I discuss next (Haraway, 1994; 1997, p. 34).

Another method of analysing heterogeneous assemblages such as VICNET is to use Actor Network Theory (Callon, 1986; Callon, 1987; Latour, 1987; Law, 1987; Law, 1994; Singleton & Michael, 1993). In brief, ANT is a theory that seeks to use a neutral vocabulary to treat with impartiality all entities (human and nonhuman actors) involved in a system so as to reveal the powers and associations that bring that system to some sort of closure—referred to as "Black-boxing" (Latour, 1987). Actor networks bring in the political, the power struggles; they tell stories and trace histories in an attempt to bring about an understanding of the material of the entities under discussion (Law, 1994). For actors to become part of the network, they have to be persuaded to become interested in the assemblage; this is what Callon refers to as an *interessement*[3] (Callon, 1986). They (the actors) are difficult to fix in place, they must have their roles and attributes defined for them; this is referred to as *translation* (Bijker et al., 1989, p. 14) The network so constructed has actors which, as in the heterogeneous case, tend to want revert to their previous roles or take on other roles and so the systems breakdown. Although it might seem that because one of the fundamental components of VICNET is a computer network and as such is "hard-wired," it is perhaps salutary to realise that it is an assemblage of artifacts and as such constitutes an actor network[4] —that is, a network of the social, technical, human and nonhuman. Bruno Latour in a recent paper reminds us that "[n]othing is more intensely connected, more distant, more compulsory and more strategically organized than a computer network" (Latour, 1997, p. 1). A technical or even a computer network is not a metaphor for an actor network. Actor networks may be local, may lack compulsory paths and nodes that are strategic centres, they are also not purely social networks which analyse, without touching, the way humans interact with the social and natural worlds. ANT aims at accounting for the very essence of societies and natures (Latour, 1997, p. 1).

So what do I bring from actor network theory? Well perhaps not much and yet a lot. It was reading about ANT that first led me to see that technologies were assemblages of a variety of different actors, including the social, the political, the scientific and so on. They are part of my history in science and technology studies (Wenn, 1995; 1996b). I like the idea of actors having to become interested in the system being constructed, of being enrolled. In what is to follow, we will see some examples of that. The war metaphors of both heterogeneous engineering and ANT identified above do little for me though and during my research I found more talk of cooperation and co-construction than of struggles and resistance. However, the variety of discourses that takes place between the actors, the politics and the network building activities are of value to my analysis even if the approach is not "pure" ANT. One other problem that I have with ANT is that it tends to be too centralising, focusing on one actor which attempts to stabilise the identity and roles of the other actors[5] (See also Singleton & Michael, 1993). It tends towards the heroic (Law, 1994 p. 100; Haraway, 1997, p. 34). It also does not lend itself well to the analysis of groups of sociotechnical systems that develop in a diversity of spaces. Sociotechnical systems that may for whatever reasons gravitate towards or move apart from each other as things evolve. So whilst I bring to this analysis some of the techniques used by Hughes, heterogeneous engineering and ANT, it is for the reasons outlined above that I move away from ANT and employ an alternative treatment.

In developing my treatment of VICNET, I wish to use the concept of topology as Mol and Law have done. They argue that " 'the social' doesn't exist as a single spatial type" (Mol and Law, 1994, p. 643) but can be seen as a range of spaces in which various actions may take place. Objects may cluster together in regions around which boundaries can be drawn. There are networks where the distance between nodes is determined by the relationship between them and the particular form of the node. To some extent the connections between, and thus, the shape of the network between objects or nodes on the network will depend on the enrolments made and interessements or groups of actions that are imposed in attempts to stabilise the network (Callon, 1986, p. 207). Mol and Law also identify social regions that can act as fluids (1994, p. 643). In a fluid space one cannot easily determine entities— "[a] fluid world is a world of mixtures" (Mol and Law, 1994, p. 661). Fluids can flow and intermingle like water droplets on a sheet of plastic, fluid regions will also have different viscosities which will determine how fast they change. Another device that I wish to introduce is the idea of a sheet or surface which can be deformed, something like a rubber sheet that can be stretched or folded in on itself thus making it easier to picture the transformations. As we will see, using this metaphor allows added discursive flexibility in that we can focus on the multitude of other systems that co-constitute VICNET. All of these devices can be seen in action in the evolution of the open system that is VICNET.

## OPEN SYSTEMS

Although they were mainly interested in the modelling and design of distributed, modular computer applications and systems, Hewitt and de Jong's characterization of open systems is useful when we consider the development and use of the Internet (1984). They saw open systems as continually evolving in an incremental manner, containing no global objects holding it all together and consisting of a growing number of independent communicating sites (Hewitt and de Jong, 1984, pp. 149, 157). These are just the properties that the Internet exhibits. We have standards that are incrementally evolving—just consider Hypertext Markup Language (HTML). Web sites, e-mail servers and the like can be developed and managed independently of each other provided they use the appropriate protocols, e.g. TCP/IP, HTTP, MIME etc. There are no global objects on the Internet. It is just a set of communicating subsystems each of which can be considered as being open as will be demonstrated in the next section.

## An Evolving System

Hewitt and de Jong have characterised open systems as continually changing (1984). I noted in a previous section that VICNET can be viewed as policy documents, financial commitments from sponsors, budget allocations, Web page designs, the expressed intentions of the human participants and so on. In this section I have chosen to represent it in terms of the hardware and software in use at the VICNET site located in the State Library of Victoria PABX/computer room.[6] This is not to say these other representations are unimportant, but looking at the changes that have occurred in the hardware and software over time will help to give a feeling for the system's evolution, albeit from a local fairly specific viewpoint.

At the time of the launch, VICNET essentially consisted of the equipment as shown in Table 1, this having been bought from the first grant allocation. Although the original equipment purchases were adequate for the pilot scheme and the first few months of operation, they were fairly rudimentary in terms of what the RMIT and SLV development group planned for VICNET which was to become not only a provider of information but a "gateway to the world's information".[7]

Since that time, a number of factors have led to an increase in equipment as shown in Table 2, and the list is still growing (as is the number of staff employed at the SLV VICNET site) although the latest changes are not shown here. Increases in the number of users brought with it concerns for reliability (users expect the site to be operational 24 hours a day), hence some of the new purchases were made to provide a certain amount of redundancy thus decreasing the time the network would be down due to equipment failure. Other purchases (modems and 64Kbps ISDN lines) were made just to cope with the demand for access from actual and potential subscribers, and also to increase the number of public libraries that had access to VICNET. To improve the management and presentation of information and to aid in the construction of databases, a Microsoft NT-based server with

*Table 1: Computer and Communications Equipment used by VICNET in November 1994. (Kurzeme, 1994)[8]*

| Item | Quantity | Description |
|---|---|---|
| CPU | 1 | Sun Microsystems SPARCserver 20 Model 51 |
| | | 64 Mb memory, 6.3 Gb hard disk, 10 Gb tape drive |
| Operating system | n/a | Operating system Solaris 2.4 |
| Other software | n/a | Other software, C compiler and SunNet manager |
| Httpd software | n/a | CERN httpd |
| Router | 1 | Telebit Netblazer 40 with 3 LAN ports, 32 async ports and 2 sync |
| Modems | 2 | Dataplex racks with 32 28.8 Kbps modem cards |
| Terminal adapter | 1 | JTEC J1200 ISDN |
| Ethernet hub | 1 | Synoptics 2813 |
| AARNet link | 1 | 64 Kbps ISDN B-channel |
| Telecom lines | 20 | |

*Table 2: Computer and Communications Equipment used by VICNET in May 1996. The items highlighted with the light grey are ones that existed previously but their quantity or nature changed while those highlighted with the dark grey are new additions.* [10]

| Item | Quantity | Description |
|------|----------|-------------|
| CPU | many | Sun Microsystems SPARCserver 20 Model 51 |
| | | 64 Mb memory, 6.3 Gb hard disk, 10 Gb tape drive |
| Operating system | n/a | Operating system Solaris 2.4 |
| Other software | n/a | Other software, C compiler and SunNet manager |
| Httpd software | n/a | Netscape Commerce server |
| CPU | 1 | NT Server |
| Operating system | | Windows NT |
| Other software | | Emwac httpd, MS Access |
| Router | many | Telebit Netblazer 40 with 3 LAN ports, 32 async ports and 2 sync |
| Modems | 60 | Dataplex racks with 32 28.8 Kbps modem cards |
| Terminal adapter | 1 | JTEC J1200 ISDN |
| Ethernet hub | 1 | Synoptics 2813 |
| AARNet link | 11 | 64 Kbps ISDN B-channel |
| Telecom lines | many | |

Microsoft Access and the Emwac server software was installed. Concerns about security and management led to a swap from the free CERN WWW (World Wide Web) server software to the Netscape Commerce server. Normally a commercial product, this was available free to VICNET because the SLV team had included Netscape's Browser software on the VICNET distribution discs.[9]

Thus, it is not only the quantity of equipment that is changing, but also the type of software being used. Because of the factors mentioned above, it makes no sense to draw a boundary around the human and nonhuman artifacts involved at some particular point in time and say "this is VICNET" – it (VICNET) is not invariant, the quantity and type of equipment changes frequently as does the number of people and organisations involved in its structure. Regions can coexist and the way they hold together and co-constitute this thing called VICNET varies both spatially and temporally. There is a fluidity to the evolution—as Mol and Law say "[w]e're looking at *variation without boundaries and transformation without discontinuity*. We are looking at flows. The space with which we're dealing is fluid" (Mol and Law, 1994, p. 658).

## INFLUENCES TO-ING AND FLOWING

Unless public libraries continually redefine themselves, and see their broad business as information and recreation, not books, we will end up exactly the same way as the Mechanics Institutes and the subscription lending libraries.

...

Our libraries were seen very much as book lenders, both by our major stakeholders and by our patrons. It seemed important to me that we should redefine ourselves as information providers and navigators. (Mackenzie and Trembath, 1996, p. 147)

One of the first public libraries to participate in the extension of VICNET was the Mornington Peninsula Library Service (MPLS). They were seeking a way of modernizing the library's image and of redefining their place in the 'modern world' and VICNET offered just this opportunity. VICNET, the MPLS and its stakeholders (who consist of the local community, council and others who have an interest in the activities of the MPLS) can be considered as clusters which may or may not interact depending on their interests at the time (Figure 1). The MPLS wants to redefine its image thus ensuring its survival, so they commence a dialogue with representatives from VICNET. From lunchtime discussions with VICNET, the MPLS emerged

*Figure 1: The Mornington Peninsula Library Service (MPLS), VICNET and some other actors can be thought of as droplets enclosing other heterogeneous entities (clusters) positioned on a flexible rubber sheet. Before the meeting between the MPLS and VICNET representatives takes place, they are quite separate.*

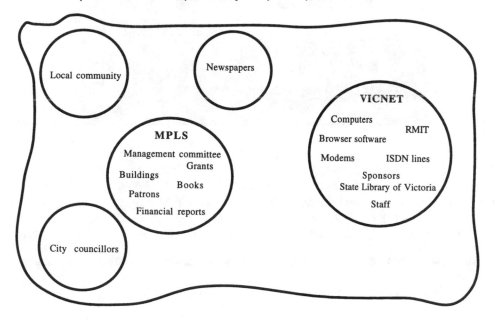

infused with the "contagious enthusiasm" of the VICNET staff and returned to their own region "determined to be part of the action" (Mackenzie and Trembath, 1996, p. 147).

Subsequent to these discussions, Nepean Net was established which has ties back to both the local Mornington Peninsula community and to VICNET (Figure 2). This co-constitution brings with it local (to the peninsula community) advantages:

> The big advantage is the very positive image of the service that is generated, of being seen as innovative. Publicity is easy to get, especially in local papers. It has captured the imagination of our [City] Commissioners, our [the MPLS] management group and others in the organisation as well as the local community. (Mackenzie and Trembath, 1996, p. 147)

*Figure 2: The Nepean Net Home Page at http://www.nepeanet.org.au/ with links to local services and VICNET. It acts both to make the Mornington Peninsula Library visible to the world, as well as providing a navigation aid to the world's knowledge for the local community.*

| contents | peninsula information | peninsula tourism | feedback | credits |

| festivals and events | other peninsula information sites |

The MPLS is in another region, distinct from the original SLV one, with a different set of stakeholders to charm. It is simultaneously local and global: local in that it has local concerns for its image and provision of access to information, but global also as information can be obtained from and sent to the larger world. It simultaneously allows other Victorians (and indeed the world) to see and access the local peninsula community.

That VICNET and the MPLS are heterogeneous systems is unquestionable. One has only to refer to the background discussion of VICNET to see that it is made up of a variety of human and nonhuman artifacts. Libraries as we all know are also heterogeneous assemblages of staff, books, buildings, computers, rules and regulations, borrowers, book browsers, financial reports and funding grants. Imagine that both VICNET and the MPLS are droplets of fluid each made up of heterogeneous entities—each has their own boundary (Figure 1). These boundaries are defined by me, as a reporter, for analytical purposes. They are purely contingent. Others may define them differently, for example the local community would be more likely to see the city councillors as part of that cluster, rather than as a separate entity. To some extent it depends on the local power structures and how one sees the alliances and enrolments taking place.

Now imagine that these VICNET and MPLS droplets are on a surface. The dialogue, the interaction between them, brings them closer together; as this happens the sheet begins to fold in on itself (Figure 3). The droplets are reshaped, roll, and combine with each other to co-constitute a larger entity; the boundary

*Figure 3: The MPLS and VICNET commence a dialogue that in effect brings them closer together and deforms the rubber sheet creating a depression that others may be attracted into.*

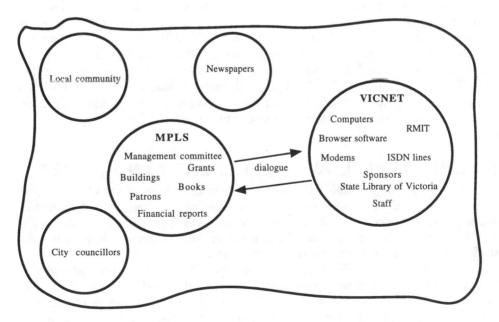

*Figure 4: The separate droplets have combined to co-constitute a larger entity. As they do so, they have deformed the sheet even more and brought the newspapers, local community and city councillors along with them*

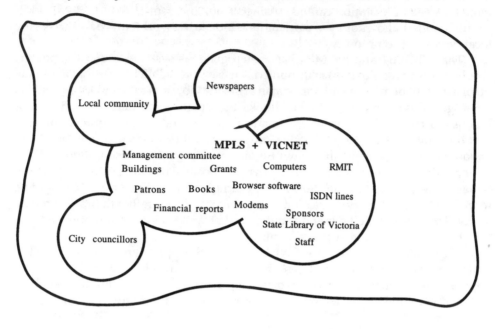

becomes larger but there are still heterogeneous entities within (Figure 4). Just as raindrops can be shaken apart so may the droplets break up—not necessarily returning to their original state. If the raindrops can be seen as heterogeneous regions then consider that social networks, such as the MPLS, appear in regions and regions can flow together to create a larger one and the networks within may also come together. VICNET now has a link to Nepean Net, its state has altered, while the MPLS has a link to VICNET—it has undergone a change of state, it has been transformed and made visible to other regions. Wine lovers can find out about peninsula wines, holiday makers are enticed to explore the peninsula.

## INFORMATION FLOWS – GENEALOGY AND VICNET

In this vignette, we view VICNET from the point of view of one of the content contributors, and as an illustration of how the Internet can be reshaped and subsequently utilised to obtain information. In this case we also see how viewing the droplets as clusters that can be broken up and reformed may assist our understanding of the formation of an open system.

From its inception VICNET has always been seen as a community, where people with similar interests could contact one another and exchange ideas and knowledge. "VICNET aims to create a rich information environment for Victorians" (Hardy, 1994, p. 2). Part of this will be "pages of information about organisations, clubs and societies" (Hardy, 1994, p. 3). One of the first public interest user groups on VICNET was the Genealogy Special Interest Group. In an article for the VICNET Newsletter, Gordon, the coordinator of the Group says of the VICNET service:

> I envisage VICNET, through the Genealogy Special Interest Group, acting as a catalyst to this large group. It would act as a bulletin board enabling people to share information and assist one another. It would pace [sic] regional Victorians on a more equal footing with their city-based cousins. It would allow access to a range of databases of interest to historians. And it could perhaps in time extend the scope and range of material available[11] (Holt, 1994, p. 4).

It is about including Victorians who are remote from the city and hence the genealogical resources of the State Library. VICNET extends boundaries and incorporates others into its sociotechnical milieu, and as it does so, the others may bring with them new information or assistance. VICNET is being co-constituted. In this case through a strategic alliance between two networks. One that has existed for quite some time – a network of genealogists and an emerging communications network.

Via e-mail, I interviewed Gordon some 18 months after the publication of that article. Here is a transcript of part of that interview.[12]

Andrew:    Was this initial enthusiasm warranted?
Gordon:    Yes, very much so. The amount of material on the net about family history is overwhelming!

    ...

    Amateur genealogy on the other hand is positively booming on the net. The volume of traffic is increasing all the time, and I am constantly staggered at the amount of trouble people will go to to answer a query from another person across [sic] the globe. It restores one's faith in human nature.

Andrew:    Do you think that VICNET has helped place regional Victorians on an equal footing with their metro counterparts in respect to the access to genealogical resources?
Gordon:    Most assuredly. Except that in my own case, living mainly at Camperdown, I still don't have a local provider which makes things difficult!

With VICNET comes the possibility of joining country and metropolitan regions together. Information has the potential to flow from region to region. However, at the time of writing, the information couldn't flow from VICNET to the rural city of Camperdown (some 160 km from Melbourne) because a local Internet service provider was not available there. (In fact, Gordon had to come to Melbourne before he could answer my e-mail.) There was in fact some resistance to the growth of our technical network. More evolution in the open system was needed; other parts—computers, cables, modems and interested parties had to be persuaded that this system was one that was worthwhile being part of. In the actor network terminology they had to become interested in the development of the system and enrolled.[13]

Gordon has also used the Internet to find relatives both in Australia and overseas. Taking one instance of how he did this reveals the fluid nature of the information gatherers and sources.

Gordon:  ... I have personally discovered several Australian relatives locally by using the Web, and have spent a happy time meeting them and their family. More excitingly for me, I have finally located information on a small school attended by my late father-in-law in UK. All I knew was that he went to Prices [sic] School, and that its blazer had a lion embroidered in gold. He was born in Manchester and I had assumed the school was in that area. But despite checking numerous directories of schools in Lancashire and England generally, it had me stumped. In desperation about six weeks back, I put a message on the Web asking for help with this problem—Does anyone know where Prices school is or was? I chose one of the numerous genealogically exclusive newsgroups—<soc.genealogy.uk+ireland>

In only two days I got back an encouraging response, and after several messages back and forth, I now have a complete history of this public school, founded in 1721, closed in 1908 located right at the bottom of England near Southampton. And my correspondent is even going to the County Record Office to check the enrolments for the period 1905-1915 to gain details of my father-in-law's attendance. He has already been to his local library, located a history of the school, and scanned it into his computer. He then sent the whole multipage article to me via the net. Without the Web this sort of discovery would have been impossible!

One of Gordon's objectives was to gain access to difficult-to-find information about his relatives. Traditional means of correspondence between the UK and Australia didn't work. How do you write to someone you don't know on the other side of the globe and get them to find information?

Once access to the Internet is gained, it becomes a way of finding relatives and information about them—it works to make the previously invisible visible. VICNET allows Gordon to bring the world seemingly closer, he can send out a message to a bulletin board (BB), asking for help to find a school that he knows his father-in-law attended. Someone from this region replies and the remaining actors in this bulletin board are no longer necessary—the regions of the bulletin board and Gordon no longer interact (Figure 5).

The unknown becomes the known. The space and the network are reconfigured

*Figure 5: Initially Gordon begins a dialogue with the bulletin board system which in this figure has been simplified to just the users and the notices that are posted to it.*

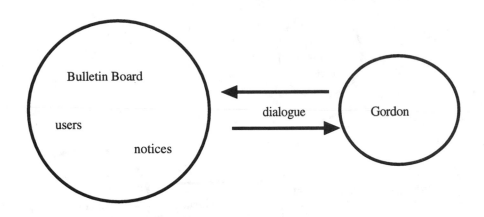

to create a more direct link between the two correspondents. By sending out a message asking for help in finding an invisible school in the UK, not only has the school been rendered visible, but a flow of information between regions was established. The heterogeneous nature of these regions is also revealed to us as interlocutors. Gordon's correspondent enrolled the services of a number of different artifacts; the library, documents of the school's history, and a scanner which transformed the printed text into a electronic one. The resulting stream of binary 1s and 0s was then sent via another heterogeneous hard-wired network to Gordon. England and Australia were brought closer together. However, it would be incorrect to think that the physical distance between the two countries had changed rather it is as if something which could be called the "virtual distance" had been altered.

One way of picturing this is to think of Gordon's Southampton correspondent as being situated in one region on a large rubber sheet, Gordon situated in Camperdown in Victoria, Australia—another heterogeneous region. The socio-technical system that is VICNET, Gordon and his UK correspondent, acts on this sheet to fold it (continuously deform it, to use the topological parlance) so that the regions coalesce allowing the information to flow (Figure 6).

## SLOWING DOWN THE FLOW

As mentioned previously, the VICNET editors expressed a wish to involve as many community organisations from as broad a spectrum as possible. One group to express an interest was the Koori (the indigenous Australian) community. Peter, a Koori studying at Ballarat University, encountered the VICNET home page whilst surfing the web, telephoned VICNET, and was asked to become involved in setting up a homepage for Kooris in Victoria.[14] Ballarat is approximately 110km from Melbourne, and once again we see the topological transformation at work

*Figure 6: The dialogue continues and the focus moves from the BB cluster to that of a single user, and as they interact and move closer together, they bring with them other actors which assist with the information flow.*

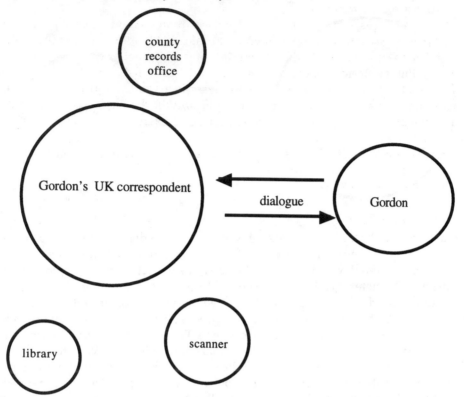

folding the space occupied by VICNET and the Koori community to bring them closer together. Peter created a first page which was subsequently installed on VICNET and was given some software to enable the development of a more comprehensive site because as he says, "I want to redo it as I feel it is of inferior quality, but there are very few people around our area that have much experience with Internet, let alone homepages."[15]

Lack of experience is one thing preventing the creation of a site pleasing to Peter, but there are also other things acting to increase the viscosity of our fluid region and hence slowing the coalescence. Some are technical, others are financial:

... tomorrow we have some advisers arriving which I'm looking forward to; hopefully we can get some good programs to use. But there are frequent computer problems which waste enormous amounts of time; if technology was more reliable I would be more inclined to put more effort into it. We also need more funds to buy extra storage gear, zip drives, etc.

He also adds, when speaking of equipment, that access is also a problem. Peter runs classes for other Kooris which include lessons on how to use the Internet as well as having cultural content. In general these Internet classes work well with elders getting involved ... because five-day courses are done over 15 days, but I have to wait for holidays before [getting] access to desktop computers that have to be dismantled and assembled and a bus used for transportation. But submissions for laptops are turned down.

Many of the participants "are unemployed, depressed, just out of gaol, hate schools," and lack many of the written and oral skills that are needed for many things. Peter sees the multimedia capabilities of the Internet as making "sessions more exciting and lessening the dependency on these skills".

Sometimes though it is just lack of confidence in his ability to use the software, something that many people new to computers and the Internet also suffer from. But it is just these sort of things that cause the transformations to occur in different ways to what may be desired.

Peter is ambivalent when asked whether having Koori information available on VICNET has been worthwhile but,

> I get a few interesting letters, but more exchange is occurring through chat groups and a homepage avoids repeating yourself; they can get location objectives and details from it. One chap from Sweden visited our campus years ago and when he saw the homepage, he just wrote to say hi which is good for maintaining feedback.
>
> ... again it is fantastic for long distances. Indigenous students here swap general messages with native Americans. I constantly ask advice from overseas groups.[16]

Throughout our exchange there is an element of pride sneaking in. Pride in the fact that indigenous peoples can, despite the myriad of cultural differences, create a presence on the Internet and get e-mail from Sweden and the native Americans. One can detect a rising sense of equity and justice tempered by the fact that financial aid is very hard to obtain. Moral and social issues of pride, equity and justice flow through Peter's e-mail. Despite the lack of support from "the ones in power" it is possible for the Koori community to have access to technologies. Using the technology, they can gain a sense of community with other indigenous peoples, seek advice and feedback, and later on, maybe even give advice. The regions of the Koori and Western Technical cultures meet and intermingle allowing the Koori community in Victoria to become more visible.

Peter was very enthusiastic about the VICNET staff who were active in bringing the two communities together. They provided an information day for the Koori community where they became converted to the idea of using VICNET. Peter also sees VICNET as helping all Victorians gain access to indigenous resources. Again there is the feeling that more equality might be provided even though there are things acting to slow the transformation down. The regions of the Kooris and the Victorian community are flowing towards some sort of equilibrium: justice, access, understanding flow across the boundaries.

# VICNET AS AN OPEN SYSTEM/TOPOLOGICAL TRANSFORMATION

If we think of topology as the study of the way things act under continuous deformations, then perhaps we can see VICNET as acting to deform (in the sense of reshaping) the information space. This artefact (VICNET) acts, in the mathematical sense, like a transformation that folds the map of the territory in such a way that the apparent distance between the two diminishes. This is a topological transformation, a study of things that remain invariant under continuous deformations (Kac and Ulam, 1979). The introduction of an artefact acts to reshape our territory, our regions (Mol and Law, 1994). It performs in a similar way to one of Latour's immutable mobiles (Latour, 1986) acting to bring territories closer together. However, one must be careful not to push the metaphor too far. Obviously the physical distance between Australia and the UK does not change, for example, nor does the distance between Melbourne and the Mornington Peninsula alter;what does change is something that we might call the virtual distance. It is possible to think of this "virtual distance" as being like a wormhole in space, providing a "short cut" between the various regions.[17] I would now like to extend this topological investigation even further into the realms of the fluid (Mol and Law, 1994).

Picture a flat surface with a large number of pools of fluid (raindrops for instance) randomly spread across it. These pools are slowly spreading out over the surface. As they spread, they may meet and combine with others, thus increasing the size of the pool hence expanding the boundary. If we were to look in these pools we would see a variety of entities, it can be a region of mixtures—our raindrops may contain dust, or chemicals from the atmosphere or even micro-organisms—but things within the pool exist in relative harmony (Mol and Law, 1994, p. 660). Conditions may change, but all things in the pool are informed of the change, the raindrop may dry up or the chemicals may crystallise out, either way the composition of the pool alters affecting the environment for the other entities.

The way VICNET evolves can be likened to these pools. There are regions, for instance libraries, where many entities coexist. The boundaries of these regions may change in shape or character and interact with other libraries, coalescing as did the boundaries of the Mornington Peninsula Library and the State Library to form one larger pool. These interactions, alliances and enrolments between regions deform our flat surface; it may let's say fold in on itself, then raindrops will run together more quickly.

In the case of the Nepean Net-VICNET co-constitution, several deformations were performed. It brought the Mornington Peninsula Library Service and the local papers, community and city commissioners closer together. The world of the Peninsula was brought closer to users elsewhere in the world.

Imagine that the SLV VICNET node and the MPLS are fluid droplets, each made up of heterogeneous entities, each having their own boundary. These droplets are on a surface and the discourses that take place between them causes it to fold in on itself, or create a depression, the droplets combine to co-constitute themselves into a larger entity, the boundary becoming larger, the depression becoming deeper and thus able to bring more things into the system. In a similar way, we see information flow as the regions of Gordon and a school in the United

Kingdom coalesce; as those of the Ballarat Koori community intersect with VICNET we can add pride, access and understanding tempered with technical and financial problems that increase the viscosity of the fluid regions thus slowing down the coalescence.

One way of thinking about this open system is as a fluid topology where pools of liquid (centres of interest) can come together (form an alliance) or split up due to other pressures for example other regions which seek and offer a stronger alliance to one of the participant regions. Another might be to consider it as a topological transformation of a surface where the web acts to bring things closer together, reducing the virtual distance by creating a wormhole in the information space. There are multiple ways of seeing this—just as VICNET has multiple meanings, no one particular point of view should have privilege over any others. It is helpful to remember, at this point, that this is only one ordering out of many, because as Mol and Mesman say: "... semiotics also allows one to assume that everything which is noise in relation to one order is information in another. It's not chaos, but another kind of tune" (Mol & Mesman, 1996, p. 433). It would be incorrect to see the surface as doing the work; it is the interactions between our sociotechnical networks that deform the sheet and thus shape the resulting system.

## FLOWING TO A CONCLUSION?

So, to paraphrase Mol and Law, how does VICNET flow (Mol & Law, 1994, p. 664)? Both slowly and quickly, one is tempted to answer, there are regions of differing viscosity, some move fast to join up with others, some more slowly, our study helps reveal why. There are repulsions, attractions and frictions between regions each serving to determine the shape of the territory. As regions join the shape and nature of the pool, boundaries change, but some things inside remain the same. The system is undergoing continual evolution, but it is difficult to determine what exists at any given point in time. Open systems such as VICNET may never be completely described, treating them as fluid topologies at least allows us to get a feel for the way they roll towards wherever it is that they are headed.

Now to the watershed. Why is this way of thinking about open systems useful? This question is perhaps best answered by thinking about some of the disadvantages and advantages of the model.

### Disadvantages

Dealing with the disadvantages first will allow me to end the chapter on a positive note.

- Firstly, I think it must be admitted that this method of analysis adds many more layers of complexity to systems analysis and design. System designers are still trying to cope with the complexities of technical design, new languages, new analysis techniques and so on and they are unlikely to want to take the additional complexities of social effects as well. However, see some of the work that is being done in Scandinavia (Bjerknes et al, 1991; Hanseth et al., 1996) and by Avison and Wood-Harper (1990).
- Although it may give systems designers an idea of what has happened, how

can they integrate this into current practice?

- This model may allow us to understand what has happened, but how do we begin to understand what factors may be involved in the development of new systems?[18]

### Advantages

Despite the worries of trying to overcome the disadvantages mentioned above, it seems to me that anyone wishing to study evolving systems may benefit from this model for a number of reasons:

- There is an increasing body of evidence that shows that information systems are heterogeneous, and this method does allow us to deal with this.
- One big advantage of the model is that it allows us to see both the large and small-scale events. It allows us to focus on the many parts of the system and see how they co-construct one another.
- Social effects are not just an added on explanatory afterthought (Law, 1987, p. 117). We see that the social is not lost within the technical or vice versa, but that they form part of a "messy" whole that we must be ready to deal with.
- It allows the actors/environment to interact. That it is a slight displacement of the actors, affects others in the environment which may in effect cause more change. By seeing things as being on a flexible rubber sheet, we may understand how actors may accelerate together more quickly, that is cooperate. On the other hand, introduction of a third system may encourage dissociation of the current system and bend the sheet in other ways, causing new alignments to occur.

Throughout this chapter, I have attempted to show that there are a variety of social and technical, human and nonhuman actors that can come together to form networks—social networks. Networks such as Gordon and his genealogical interests and U.K. contacts, the MPLS and the local Mornington community, the VICNET group and the associated equipment at the SLV, Peter and the Koori community at Ballarat. All have their local issues which we can focus on and we can see them as regions each different from the other, but these regions can and do interact—flow together or apart to help shape the global entity we may call VICNET. We are no longer forced to see things as having to happen through some central agency. The true heterogeneity of the assemblage is revealed on both a macro and micro scale.

# ACKNOWLEDGEMENTS

I would like to thank the anonymous reviewers for comments on an earlier draft of this chapter. Without the helpful advice of a number of people including Helen Verran, Michael Arnold, Marilys Guillemin, Rosemary Robins, Steve Clarke and Joe Pitt, this chapter would not be as cogent as I would like to think it is. Of course thanks must also go to my partner, Felicity Garrigan, who made the task of writing far easier and who put up with my long hours at the computer keyboard.

This work was in part supported by Time Release Grant from my teaching institute, Victoria University of Technology.

## ENDNOTES

[1]Not only is VICNET an information provider, marking up and publishing documents in its own right, it also provides disk space to non-profit organisations for their Web sites, which may be created by the organisation or by the VICNET staff. Thus it can also be seen as an enabler for information provision. It also acts as an information service provider (ISP) providing subscribers with access to the Internet and global information sources. I am indebted to Marilys Guillemin for prompting me to make clear this distinction.

[2]Qualitative research is not only reliant on multiple sources of data but the study attempts to build a holistic picture that will of necessity be complex because it looks at actual processes, not just the product. For a much more detailed discussion of qualitative research, see Creswell (1998).

[3]Callon says "[t]o interest other actors is to build devices which can be placed between them and all other entities who want to define their identities otherwise" (1986, p. 208). There is a sense of competition with the actor who is the most persuasive, able to build a better argument, mousetrap, or whatever, being the one who interests the other actors who have been identified as being important to the development of the system.

[4]Star and Ruhleder in their examination of large-scale information spaces also provide us with a timely reminder that such infrastructures are not just carriers of information alone, but that "computers, people, and tasks together make or break a functioning infrastructure" (1996, page 118). There is no divide between the social and the technical.

[5]In more recent writings Latour has tended to highlight the networked, distributed aspects of the theory (Latour, 1996).

[6]Other aspects such as changes in staff numbers, the alteration in the Web-page formats as the underlying markup language HTML changed allowing more flexibility in terms of layout and navigation, the growth in the number of public libraries connected to VICNET, and so on could also be used to illustrate that VICNET is continually evolving. However, using the alteration in the equipment inventory at the State Library of Victoria site provides something that is perhaps more easily quantifiable and of course the reasons for the changes provide some idea of the growth mechanisms that are driving this incrementally changing system.

[7]The Project: VICNET, http://www.vicnet.net.au/vicnet/abtvic.html, accessed May 4, 1995. This is essentially the proposal document that was put to the State Government in 1993. The phrase gateway to the world's information comes from the State Library of Victoria Strategic Plan (SLV, May 1994).

[8]Even this table is out of date, as I compiled it more equipment and software was being purchased and installed. But of course, there must be some cut-off point or this story would never have been told.

[9]The distribution disks contained the software necessary for VICNET subscribers

to make a remote connection to and use the service. At the time Netscape's browser was by far the most popular.

[10]This table was compiled from information supplied via e-mail from Adrian Bates of VICNET on 20 May 1996 and 3 June 1996. I had met Adrian sometime earlier whilst interviewing another member of the foundation team.

[11]Gordon is of course a pseudonym as are the names of any other people mentioned in the body of the document.

[12]Email, Gordon, 8 June 1996.

[13]In the more formal terminology of ANT there had to be an interessements, a persuading of other parties who could supply the missing pieces and become caught up in the network.

[14]Again notice how the network co-constitutes itself with VICNET's Internet presence encouraging people to contact the editorial organisation so that they can increase the range and usefulness of the content of the site.

[15]Email, Peter 26 May 1996. Peter was even doubtful that I would receive this message because the equipment was playing up.

[16]Peter made the remark that "snail mail" (the ordinary postal service) just does not have the same response rate.

[17]Joe Pitt's note of caution about pushing the metaphor too far were useful in helping me formulate this idea of virtual distance and wormholes. There is a parallel between the idea of the regions deforming the rubber sheet in a well-like depression similar to the gravity well that allows us to picture how the relativistic theory of gravity works, and the wormholes in the information space and those of relativistic space, but again the metaphor should not be pushed to far.

[18]But perhaps as Donna Haraway argues "[t]he point is to get at how worlds are made and unmade in order to participate in the processes" (Haraway, 1994, p. 62). Some sociotechnical networks should be fostered while others should not.

## REFERENCES

Avison D.E. & Wood-Harper A.T. (1990). *Multiview: An Exploration in Information Systems Development*, Melbourne: Blackwell Scientific Publications.

Bijker W.E., Hughes T.P. et al (eds) (1987). *The Social Construction of Technological Systems*, Cambridge, Mass: The MIT Press.

Bijker W.E., Hughes T.P. et al (1989). "Introduction", in *The Social Construction of Technological Systems*, Bijker W.E., Hughes T.P. et al (eds) Cambridge, Mass: The MIT Press, 9–15.

Bjerknes G., Bratteteig T. et al (1991). "Evolution of Finished Computer Systems: the dilemma of enhancement", *Scandinavian Journal of Information Systems*, 3, 25–45.

Callon M. (1986). "Some Elements of a Sociology of Translation: Domestication of the Scallops and the Fishermen of St Brieuc Bay", in *Power, Action and Belief*, Law J. (ed.) London: Routledge and Kegan Paul, 197–234.

Callon M. (1987). "Society in the Making: The Study of Technology as a Tool for Sociological Analysis", in *The Social Construction of Technological Systems*, Bijker W.E., Hughes T.P. et al (eds) Cambridge Mass.: The MIT Press, 83–103.

Hanseth O., Monteiro E. et al (Fall 1996). "Developing Information Infrastructure: the tension between standardization and flexibility", *Science Technology and Human Values*, 21(4), 407–426.

Haraway D. (1994). "A Game of Cat's Cradle: Science Studies, Feminist Theory, Cultural Studies", *Configurations*, 1, 59–71.

Haraway D.J. (1997). *Modest_Witness@Second_Millennium.FemaleMan©_ Meets_OncoMouse™*, New York: Routledge.

Hardy G. (1994). *"VICNET"*, [Online. Internet.] Available: http:// www.vicnet.net.au/vicnet/Vnetprop.html .

Hardy G. (1994). "Publishing on VICNET ...", *VICNET Newsletter*, 1, 2–4.

Hewitt C. & de Jong P. (1984). *Open Systems*, New York: Springer Verlag.

Holt J. (1994). "Genealogy on VICNET", *VICNET Newsletter*, 3, 4.

Hughes T.P. (1987). "The Evolution of Large Technological Systems", in *The Social Construction of Technological Systems*, Bijker W.E., Hughes T.P. et al (ed.) Cambridge, Mass: The MIT Press, 51–82.

Hughes T.P. (1983). *Networks of Power: Electrification in Western Society, 1880-1930*, Baltimore: The John Hopkins University Press.

Kac M. & Ulam S.M. (1979). *Mathematics and Logic*, Harmondsworth: Penguin.

Kurzeme I. (1994). *Administrative Progress Report for the VICNET Technical Advisory Group*, 11 November, Melbourne, Vic.

Kurzeme I. (1994). "VICNET Newsletter", *VICNET Newsletter*, 1.

Latour B. (1986). "Visualization and Cognition: Thinking with Eyes and Hands", in *Knowledge and Society: Studies in Sociology Culture Past and Present*, Anon. (ed.) 1–40.

Latour B. (1987). *Science in Action*, Cambridge, Mass: Harvard University Press.

Latour B. (1997). *"On Actor-Network Theory: A Few Clarifications"*, Centre for Social Theory and Technology, Keele University, [Online. Internet.] Available: http://www.keele.ac.uk/depts/stt/stt/ant/latour.htm, Accessed 15 Sep. 1997.

Law J. (1991). "Power, Discretion and Strategy", in *A Sociology of Monsters*, Law J. (ed.) London: Routledge and Kegan Paul, 165–191.

Law J. (ed.) (1991). *A Sociology of Monsters*, London: Routledge,

Law J. (1994). *Organizing Modernity*, Oxford: Blackwell.

Law J. & Mol A. (1994). *On Hidden Heterogeneities: The Design of an Aircraft*. Unpublished draft manuscript.

Law J. & Mol A. (1994). *What is Social Context? A Note on Boundaries, Fractals and Technologies*, Unpublished draft manuscript.

Law J. (1987). "Technology and Heterogeneous Engineering: The Case of Portuguese Expansion", in *The Social Construction of Technological Systems*, Bijker W.E., Hughes T.P. et al (eds.) Cambridge, Mass.: The MIT Press, 111–134.

Mackenzie C. & Trembath A. (1996). "Weaving Nets to Catch the Wind: the creation of Nepean Net" from: *VALA Biennial Conference Proceedings*, VALA (ed.) Melbourne: VALA, 147–153.

Mol A. & Law J. (1994). "Regions, Networks and Fluids: Anaemia and Social Topology", *Social Studies of Science*, 24, 641–671.

Mol A. & Mesman J. (1996). "Neonatal Food and the Politics of Theory: Some Questions of Method", *Social Studies of Science*, 26, 419–44.

Myers M.D. (1995). "ICIS Panel 1995: Judging Qualitative Research In Information Systems: Criteria For Accepting and Rejecting Manuscripts" from *ICIS 1995*.

Neumann L.J. & Star S.L. (1995). "Untitled Draft", *Draft of Paper given at the Society for the Social Studies of Science (4S) Meetings, Charlottesville, VA. October 18-22*, MS.

OMA (Office of the Minister for the Arts) (1994). *Victorians to Travel the Information Highways of the World: Storey*, Office of the Minister for the Arts: Melbourne.

Pinch T. & Bijker W.E. (1987). "The Social Construction of Facts and Artifacts: Or How the Sociology of Science and the Sociology of Technology Might Benefit Each Other", in *The Social Construction of Technological Systems*, Bijker W.E., Hughes T.P. et al (eds) Cambridge, Mass.: The MIT Press, 17–50.

Singleton V. & Michael M. (1993). "Actor-Networks and Ambivalence: General Practitioners in the UK Cervical Screening Programme", *Social Studies of Science*, 23, 227–64.

SLV (1994). *L21 State Library of Victoria Strategic Plan*, May, SLV: Melbourne.

Star S. (1991). "Power, technology and the phenomenology of conventions: on being allergic to onions", in *A Sociology of Monsters*, Law J. (ed.) London: Routledge, 26–56.

Star S.L. & Griesemer J. (1989). "Institutional Ecology, "Translations" and Boundary Objects: Amateurs and Professionals in Berkeley's Museum of Vertebrate Zoology, 1907-1939", *Social Studies of Science*, 19, 387–420.

Star S.L. & Ruhleder K. (March 1996). "Steps Toward an Ecology of Infrastructure: Design and Access for Large Information Spaces", *Information Systems Research*, 7, 111–134.

Van Maanen J. (1982). "Introduction", in *Varieties of Qualitative Research*, Van Maanen J., Dabbs J.M. et al (ed.) Beverley Hills, CA: Sage Publications Inc, 11–29.

Wenn A. (1995). "Actors, Networks and the Internet: Developing an alternative View of the Information Superhighway." from *University of Melbourne HPS Department Postgraduate Conference*, Melbourne.

Wenn A. (1996a). *(Dis?)organising VICNET: a topological investigation of access*, unpublished MSc. thesis, History and Philosophy of Science, University of Melbourne.

Wenn A. (1996b). "Constructing VICNET - building a model suitable for studying an information technology artefact in the making", *Department of Business Computing Occasional Paper Series*, Victoria University of Technology, Melbourne.

Winner L. (1986). *The Whale and the Reactor: A Search for the Limits in and Age of High Technology*, Chicago: University of Chicago press.

Winner L. (1989). *Autonomous Technology Technics-out-of-Control as a Theme in Political Thought*, Mass: The MIT Press.

## Chapter III

# "Excellent" Systems Analysts: A Grounded Theory Approach to Qualitative Research

M. Gordon Hunter
St. Francis Xavier University, Canada

There is evidence which suggests the software crisis still exists and is negatively impacting both information systems (IS) development and maintenance. Kendall (1992) has reported IS development backlogs averaging 30 work-months. Others (Senn, 1985; Yourdon, 1989) including Kendall (1992) suggest a hidden backlog, users' plans not even submitted as requests because of the identified backlog, may result in IS development delays of up to four to seven years. Further Laudon and Laudon (1998) have determined that 51 percent of software development projects require up to three times more than the initial budget for both cost and time.

The situation regarding IS maintenance is also of concern. Kendall (1992) suggests the IS maintenance software crisis has resulted from problems created in phases prior to programming. This situation is further confounded by the fact that the later in the System Development Life Cycle (SDLC) that an error is discovered, the more it costs to fix (Boehm, 1981).

Understanding the reasons for these circumstances, and identifying ways of reducing them, are clearly in the interests of both IS professionals and business professionals. Boehm (1981) has suggested three components of potential productivity improvement: People, Process, and Technology; and that the first component, People, will have the greatest relative impact. Thus, while it is acknowledged that Process and Technology components are important, this research project has focused on the People component. On one hand, rapid advances in technology have caused changes in the means by which IS are developed and maintained. On the other hand, various skills are used throughout the process of IS development and maintenance. It is not clear which specific skills and personal characteristics of systems analysts contribute to the appropriate IS development and maintenance. What do "excellent" systems analysts do that is different from other systems analysts? The answer may contribute to a better understanding of the functions performed by systems analysts and to the overall effectiveness of the IS development and maintenance function.

The dilemma in evaluating professional work performed by systems analysts in this research project is to determine a consensus of what is considered "excellent". Because of this dilemma, it is necessary to adopt a research method, which is particularly suited to measuring relativity. That is, "excellent" could be regarded as a relative concept when determining and comparing the skills and personal characteristics of systems analysts.

More specifically, two major research objectives were originally identified (see Hunter, 1993 and 1994; and Hunter and Beck, 1996a and 1996b). The first objective was to determine a better understanding of "excellent" systems analysts skills and personal characteristics. This research project investigated what the research participants expected "excellent" systems analysts should be able to do. The project gathered data relating to how research participants interpret what contributes to an interpretation of an "excellent" systems analyst.

The second objective was to determine whether it is possible to differentiate systems analysts based upon skills and personal characteristics. It was anticipated the results would advance the currently accepted body of knowledge regarding systems analysts to a point where, based upon the research participants' interpretations, a relative priority of importance may be attributed to the identified skills and personal characteristics. While it may not be possible to identify an "excellent" systems analyst, it may be possible to identify which skills and personal characteristics contribute towards an interpretation of "excellent".

## NEW APPROACHES TO INFORMATION SYSTEMS RESEARCH

Turning to IS research in general, it has been suggested that newer approaches be adopted. Klein and Lyytinen have suggested that information systems as an academic discipline "...will remain a doubtful science as long as it continues to strive to develop its stock of knowledge primarily through the practice of the so-called scientific method." (Klein and Lyytinen, 1985:133). Hirschheim has contended "...that information systems epistemology draws heavily from the social sciences because information systems are, fundamentally, social rather than technical systems" (Hirschheim, 1992, p. 28). Boland discussed phenomenology as an approach to IS research. He defined phenomenology as "...the intuition of essences" (Boland, 1985, p. 193). Boland suggested phenomenology "...does not assert the existence of absolute knowledge. In the end, a phenomenological study cannot claim to have a proof of its findings, only a reliance on its method and the hope that others will "see" its descriptions as true and accurate" (Boland, 1985, p. 194). Boland concluded with the following comment, "Data becoming information is what information systems are: Data becomes information in the consciousness of a human subject, and that is where we must look if we are to understand

*Figure 1: Information Systems Research Approaches: A Revised Taxonomy*

| Object | Modes of traditional empirical approaches (observations) | | | | | | | Modes of newer approaches (interpretations) | | |
|---|---|---|---|---|---|---|---|---|---|---|
| | Theorem proof | Laboratory experiment | Field experiment | Case study | Survey | Forecasting & futures research | Simulation & game/role playing | Subjective/ argumentative | Descriptive/ interpretive (including reviews) | Action research |
| Society | No | No | Possibly | Possibly | Yes | Yes | Possibly | Yes | Yes | Possibly |
| Organization/ group | No | Possibly (small groups) | Yes | Yes | Yes | Yes | Yes | Yes | Yes | Yes |
| Individual | No | Yes | Yes | Possibly | Possibly | Possibly | Yes | Yes | Yes | Possibly |
| Technology | Yes | Yes | Yes | No | Possibly | Yes | Yes | Possibly | Possibly | No |
| Methodology | Yes | No | Yes | Yes | Yes | No | Yes | Yes | Yes | Yes |
| Theory building | No | No | No | Yes | Yes | Yes | Yes | Yes | Yes | Yes |
| Theory testing | Yes | Yes | Yes | Yes | Possibly | No | Possibly | No | Possibly | Yes |
| Theory extension | Possibly | Possibly | Possibly | Possibly | Possibly | No | No | No | Possibly | Possibly |

information systems. Phenomenology as a social science method holds the best promise for doing so because it is one method designed with that purpose in mind" (Boland, 1985, p. 200).

Galliers and Land have proposed that IS research "...methods must take account of the nature of the subject and the complexity of the real world." (Galliers and Land, 1987, p. 901). Their revised taxonomy of information systems research approaches (Galliers, 1992:159), included here as Figure 1, is divided into "traditional" and "newer" approaches to IS research. They recommend that IS researchers should not blindly adopt the methods of traditional research, but the choice of research approach should relate to the research objectives. It is interesting to note that Galliers and Land associate "observations" with traditional approaches in turn providing a description of the traditional uninvolved research in a research-subject relationship. Alternatively, "interpretations" are associated with the newer approaches and reflect the emphasis of qualitative researchers interacting with research participants. Thus, rather than sampling many sources and drawing statistical inferences, newer approaches tend to investigate fewer sources in more depth. This association with newer approaches suggests the type of research originally described as New Paradigm Research by Reason and Rowan (1981) which is discussed in a subsequent section of this chapter.

While the above discussion indicates that newer approaches to IS research should be adopted, evidence suggests this evolution has not transpired. Orlikowski and Baroudi (1991) examined 155 information systems research articles published between 1983 and 1988 in three major information systems journals (*Communications of ACM, Management Science,* and *MIS Quarterly*) as well as the Proceedings of the International Conference on Information Systems. Figure 2 indicates the results obtained and shows that a full 92.3% of the articles (highlighted with an *) related to the more traditional approaches to IS research. While there has been a call for more research based upon newer approaches, the findings of the research by Orlikowski and Baroudi suggest that published articles still tend to reflect a continued reliance upon the more traditional approaches. The authors concluded, "...much can be gained if a plurality of research perspectives is effectively em-

*Figure 2: Articles Classified by Research Design*

| Research Design | Frequency | Percent |
|---|---|---|
| Survey | 76 | 49.1 * |
| Laboratory Experiment | 42 | 27.1 * |
| Case Study | 21 | 13.5 * |
| Mixed Method | 5 | 3.2 |
| Field Experiment | 4 | 2.6 * |
| Instrument Development | 4 | 2.6 |
| Protocol Analysis | 2 | 1.3 |
| Action Research | 1 | 0.6 |
|  | 155 | 100.0 |

* *Associated with more traditional research approaches*

*Figure 3: Articles Classified by Research Category*

| Research Category | Frequency | Percent | |
|---|---|---|---|
| Case | 131 | 17.61 | * |
| Engineering | 87 | 11.70 | * |
| Experiment | 80 | 10.75 | * |
| Field Test | 28 | 3.76 | * |
| Subjective/ Argumentative | 180 | 24.19 | |
| Survey | 210 | 28.23 | * |
| Theorem Proof | 28 | 3.76 | * |
| | 744 | 100.00 | |

* *Associated with more traditional research approaches*

ployed to investigate information systems phenomena" (Orlikowski and Baroudi, 1991, p.1). Banville and Landry (1992) further support this conclusion by suggesting that IS research can best be conducted by employing pluralistic models rather than taking an inappropriate monastic view of science.

Also, Lending and Wetherbe (1992) investigated the type of research published by MIS journals. Their research included 13 IS journals published from 1984 to 1990, which resulted in the classification of 744 articles. Their research represents an update to a similar investigation conducted by Vogel and Wetherbe (1984). Figure 3 presents data about the proportion of research published by research category. In this case, 75.8% of the articles (highlighted with an *) relate to the more traditional modes of research. The only category identified with the newer approaches is "subjective/argumentative". In the 1984 article, 15% of the articles were assigned to this category, while in the 1992 update article this figure rose to 24.2%. This indicates a higher proportion of published research related to the newer approaches.

Upon closer review of the data, it is noted that in both articles, all occurrences of articles adopting newer approaches related to the "subjective/argumentative" category. Lending and Wetherbe (1992) are not clear in reporting their results whether they discovered only the subjective/argumentative form of newer research approaches or if this is simply a general category for research approaches, which were considered nontraditional. This further level of detail would certainly have provided more insight into the direction of research approaches between the two sample periods relative to Galliers and Land's (1987 and Galliers, 1992) taxonomy on information systems research approaches.

If no publications appeared in the categories where there has been no response, then the question needs to be asked, "Why does this situation exist?" The fact these approaches are *newer* suggests one answer. That is, there is currently little existing infrastructure to support the proposed type of IS research. Indeed, as reported by Lending and Wetherbe (1992), this category is dominated by three universities, which account for over 25% of the identified subjective/argumentative articles.

# THE RESEARCH APPROACH

If a goal of research is to generate theory, then how can the general research statement be supported? On one hand, some researchers would argue that within a particular framework the results of the research will either support or refute a particular component of the framework, thus expanding the general understanding of the framework itself. On the other hand, if a researcher approaches a problem with no preconceptions, then a framework must necessarily emerge from the data. This process of the framework emerging from the data is referred to in the literature as Grounded Theory.

The major proponents of Grounded Theory argue for grounding theory by generating it from the research data. They define Grounded Theory as "...the discovery of theory from data systematically obtained from social research." (Glaser and Strauss, 1967, p. 2). A category, which stands by itself as a conceptual element of the theory to be generated, "emerges" from the data. A property is a conceptual aspect or element of a category. Both categories and properties are concepts indicated by the data and are not the data themselves. A major strategy used in discovering Grounded Theory is Comparative Analysis whereby emerging categories and their properties are compared. As Glaser and Strauss state, "By comparing where the facts are similar or different, we can generate properties of categories that increase the categories' generality and explanatory power" (Glaser and Strauss, 1967, p. 24). The authors further describe Grounded Theory as follows:

"In discovering theory, one generates conceptual categories or their properties from evidence; then the evidence from which the category emerged is used to illustrate the concept. The evidence may not necessarily be accurate beyond a doubt (nor is it even in studies concerned only with accuracy), but the concept is undoubtedly a relevant theoretical abstraction about what is going on in the area studied. Furthermore, the concept itself will not change, while even the most accurate facts change. Concepts only have their meanings respecified at times because other theoretical and research purposes have evolved" (Glaser and Strauss, 1967, p. 23).

More recently, Strauss and Corbin (1990) have presented a Paradigm Model, which may be used to depict the relationships between subcategories and categories, when a researcher is attempting to think systematically about the data. The model is presented in Figure 4. The authors state, "...Unless you make use of this model, your grounded theory analyses will lack density and precision" (Strauss and Corbin, 1990, p. 99). Later in this chapter the results of the current research project will be discussed relative to the Paradigm Model.

An extension of the concepts discussed in the Grounded Theory approach is presented by Reason and Rowan (1981) under the title, "New Paradigm Research". This approach to research is about researchers exploring and attempting to make sense of human action and experience. Reason and Rowan explain their approach, as follows:

"What we are building in new paradigm research is an approach to inquiry which is a systematic, rigorous search for truth, but which does

*Figure 4: The Paradigm Model*

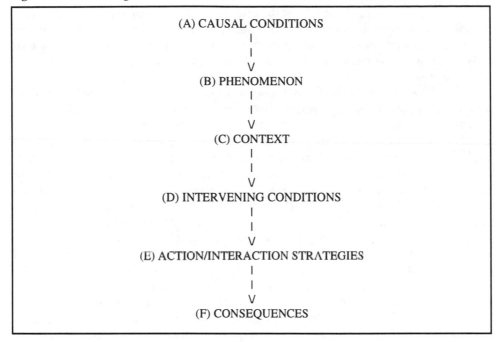

not kill off all it touches: we are looking for a way of inquiry which can be loosely called 'objectively subjective'(see Figure 5). The new paradigm is a synthesis of naive inquiry and orthodox research, a synthesis which is very much opposed to the antithesis it supersedes" (Reason and Rowan, 1981, p. xiii).

*Figure 5: New Paradigm Research*

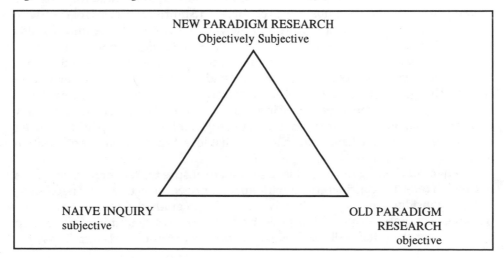

# THE RESEARCH TECHNIQUE

The question to be dealt with at the outset of a research project is one of which technique to adopt. With regard to the specific research objectives and within the purview of a Grounded Theory approach, Kelly's RepGrid technique was employed. The following discussion presents an explanation of why this technique was adopted.

The Theory of Personal Constructs was first proposed by George Kelly (1955 and 1963), a psychologist, based on his work in attempting to help individuals (clients, as he referred to them) analyze their own interpersonal relationships. The theory is based upon the assumption that individuals develop a means (referred to by Kelly as a personal construct system) of interpreting, predicting, and thus, hopefully controlling their personal environment. Thus, individuals attempt to respond to the external world by interpreting situations, based upon their personal construct system, and they then behave accordingly. He regarded individuals as "scientists" and believed that in order for them to gain control of their environment, it was necessary to be able to interpret and predict (i.e., construe). Thus, Kelly proposed, individuals, based upon their past experience, would devise a system of personal constructs which would assist them in dealing with current or anticipated situations. He referred to this system as a *personal construct system*. A technique developed by Kelly, to study personal construct systems is the Role Construct Repertory Test (RepGrid). While the RepGrid technique was originally devised to assist in counseling his clients, this technique has subsequently been applied in a number of other areas. Some articles discuss the use of the RepGrid technique in general or for specific problem construction and market research (e.g., Bannister and Mair, 1968; Corsini and Marsella, 1983; Eden and Jones, 1984; Eden and Wheaton, 1980; Fransella, 1981; and Shaw, 1980). RepGrids have also been used for various aspects of knowledge acquisition in relation to the development of expert systems (Botten, et. al., 1989; Latta and Swigger, 1992; and Phythian and King, 1992).

The use of the RepGrid technique was very appropriate for this research project. Stewart and Stewart suggest, "At its simplest, Grids provide a way of doing research into problems—almost any problems—in a more precise, less biased, way than any other research..." (Stewart and Stewart, 1981: vii). These authors also suggest the RepGrid technique "... enables one to interview someone in detail, extracting a good deal of information ... and to do this in such a way that the input from the observer is reduced to zero" (Stewart and Stewart, 1981:5). Further, Pervin states, "There have been studies of the reliability of the Rep Test and the evidence to date suggests that the responses of individuals to the role title list and constructs used are reasonably stable over time" (Pervin, 1989:271). Thus, RepGrids, as used in this research project, have proven to be a reliable technique to gather qualitative data.

When conducting research it is important to ensure the technique adopted is one which reflects a consideration for the specific project objectives. It is necessary, then, to consider the research objectives in order to guide the consideration of a research technique. One of the project objectives is to determine how group members construe the skills and personal characteristics of "excellent" systems analysts. In light of this objective, it is also considered important that research participants base their comments upon their own experience. The adopted research technique supports the gathering of research participants' interpretations of their experiences. It supports a structured, yet flexible method of conducting the research. The technique does not inhibit exploration of ideas or concepts, which emerge during the project in general and specifically during the data-gathering stage. Also, the adopted technique influences the research participants as little as possible. On one hand the questions asked of participants should allow, as much as possible, for a response based upon how the participant views the subject matter. On the other hand, whatever biases the researcher brings to the project should, as far as possible, be eliminated.

A number of different techniques were considered, and eliminated, for this specific program. The decision regarding which one to adopt is driven by the objectives of the research. While each of the following four alternatives may have decided advantages in another situation, the current discussion relates to the objectives of this research program.

First, the questionnaire technique requires the development of a list of questions in advance of the administration of the questionnaire. However, deciding in advance which questions to ask meant increasing the potential for incorporating unwanted bias on the part of the researcher. Because it was considered important to obtain the research participants' unbiased responses, the use of questionnaires was eliminated. Second, the use of structured interviews was also considered. However, this technique simply represents the personal administration of a questionnaire. Thus, the problems as outlined above in the discussion of questionnaires remain to be resolved. Third, consideration was given to the Critical Incident technique, which requires the participant to describe a specific incident relating to the research topic. This technique seemed appropriate regarding the current research. However, a concern existed regarding the participant's initial reference point. Using this method, the participant would initially focus on the incident which may inhibit the identification of the skill components involved in the incident itself. Finally, a Time Reporting technique could have been used to keep track of, and subsequently analyze the time that research participants spent performing various aspects of their job. While this data provides insight into what the participant does, it does not indicate which activities are more important than others.

The above techniques were eliminated because of some aspect which inhibits the research objectives of the project. The acceptable technique should provide for open-ended responses and be participant-driven. It should emphasize a skills and personal characteristics orientation to the discussion involving groups considered important regarding an interpretation of skills of "excellent" systems analysts. In light of these comments, the RepGrid technique was adopted for this research project.

# DATA COLLECTION

The research interviews were carried out at four fieldwork locations:

**C1** is a large member owned cooperative organization specializing in providing services to farmer-members relative to the production and sale of various grain crops. Production-related services are provided to farmers solely within a western Canadian province. There exist other similar organizations, such as C-3, in other Canadian grain producing provinces.

**C-2** is a large computer services provider which supplies data processing, network management, facilities management, office products, healthcare information technology, and consulting services. C-2 markets these services to financial institutions and health care organizations. C-2 and C-1 are located in the same western Canadian city.

**C-3** is a large member-owned cooperative organization specializing in providing services to farmer-members relative to the production and sale of various grain crops. Production-related services are provided to farmers solely within a western Canadian province adjacent to where C-1 and C-2 are located.

**A-1** is a large airline company with headquarters based in Southeast Asia. The airline provides scheduled passenger and freight services with its fleet of modern jet airplanes throughout the world.

The selection of the fieldwork locations was based upon many factors. Opportunity played a major part, as all four fieldwork locations were included in the research project because of availability. They were close to the researcher's employment at the time the fieldwork interviews were conducted, even though three are in Canada and one is in Singapore. Also, however, their inclusion reflected a desire to have relatively similar locations, such as C-1 and C-3. These two companies are in the same industry. C-2 was included as representing a location in the same geographic region as C-1, but a different industry. A-1 was included to provide further variability of locations. This selection process allowed for good variability of location by geographic region and industry.

All of the locations have a corporate philosophy of internal employment of systems analysts, which resulted in the ability to identify enough internal research participants who had sufficient exposure to systems analysts. The inclusion of the five groups at each location provided variability within a location as well as an attempt at consistency among the similar groups at different locations.

Five major groups, as indicated in Figure 6, were identified which were considered able to provide an assessment about the performance of a systems analyst. Each of these groups interacts with the systems analyst during IS development or maintenance. The varying perspectives brought to the interaction by each group, it was anticipated, would add to the richness of the data. The group determination decision provided the potential for consistency among the locations.

One-to-one confidential interviews were conducted which allowed the researcher to pursue research participant comments to a fair degree of detail. It should be noted this type of interview process tends to lead to a small sample size, because it is a time-consuming technique. At the beginning of the interview the research participant was asked to talk about his/her experience in working with systems analysts. This discussion allowed the research participant to focus his/her

*Figure 6: Systems Analysts Audiences*

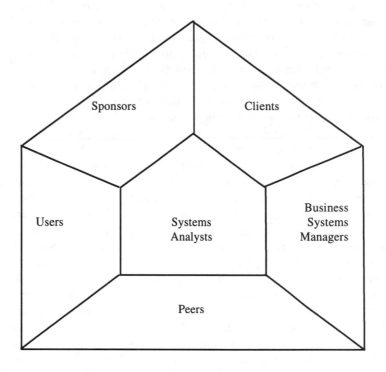

**Peers:**
Those individuals who perform the same or similar function as "Systems Analysts" within the organization.

**Business Systems Managers:**
Those individuals responsible for the administration of the corporate unit to which the functions of "Systems Analysts" are assigned.

**Users:**
Those individuals who interact directly with the information system as developed or maintained by "Systems Analysts".

**Sponsors:**
Those individuals whose corporate budget includes the development or maintenance cost of the information system, or who are responsible administratively for the Users, but do not interact directly with the information system.

**Clients:**
Those individuals who interact directly with the information system, and whose corporate budget includes the development and maintenance cost of the information system, but who are not responsible administratively for Users.

thoughts on the qualities of systems analysts. Then the RepGrid technique was introduced. A completed RepGrid is shown in Figure 7. The technique was reviewed, in general and related to systems analysts. Each research participant was asked to identify up to six systems analysts with whom he/she had interacted in the current or a previous organization. This number (6) would provide sufficient variability in the subsequent triadic elicitation process. It was suggested the identified systems analysts should be individuals about whom the research partici-pant was able to form an opinion regarding the use of skills in a working environment. To this list of identified systems analysts were added "ideal" and "incompetent." The research participant was encouraged to use these titles as representative of his/her concept of an ideal or incompetent individual who was currently working as a systems analyst. These titles would be used during the interview as comparison "anchors" in relation to the six actual systems analysts. If the researcher wants to know what the research participant's views are about effective subjects, Stewart and Stewart suggest, "... obviously you will ask him to construe elements that include effective [subjects], but to know how he differenti-ates between effective and less effective ones you must include some less effective ones in your element list." (Stewart and Stewart, 1981:30). The names of the actual systems analysts plus the two added elements were transferred to individual recipe cards. With one name or title per card, the research participant was presented with three of the eight cards. The three cards are generally known as a "triad" in the literature. So that each of the eight cards has an equal chance of being included in a triad, the three cards to be included are chosen randomly. For each triad, the research participant was asked to identify, *with regards to the skills of an "excellent" systems analyst, how two elements of the triad were alike, yet different from the third.* The research participant was encouraged to physically separate the two cards from the

*Figure 7: RepGrid*

| AUDIENCE: Systems Analysts | | | | | | | PARTICIPANT: Name | |
|---|---|---|---|---|---|---|---|---|
| | ELEMENTS | | | | | | | |
| CONSTRUCTS | 1 | 2 | 3 | 4 | 5 | 6 | 7 | 8 |
| 1. Delegator - Does Work Himself | 7 | 2 | 5 | 4 | 2 | 6 | 1 | 9 |
| 2. Informs Everyone - Keeps to Himself | 8 | 2 | 3 | 3 | 8 | 6 | 1 | 9 |
| 3. Good User Rapport - No User Rapport | 5 | 2 | 4 | 2 | 4 | 2 | 1 | 9 |
| 4. Regular Feedback - Inappropriate Feedback | 6 | 1 | 5 | 3 | 5 | 3 | 1 | 9 |
| 5. Knows Detail - Confused | 2 | 1 | 4 | 3 | 5 | 1 | 1 | 9 |
| 6. Estimates Based on Staff - Estimates based on Himself | 8 | 3 | 4 | 6 | 4 | 6 | 1 | 9 |
| 7. User Involvement - Lack of User Involvement | 6 | 2 | 5 | 5 | 3 | 3 | 1 | 9 |

third and to verbalize the decision process. These descriptive comments were noted regarding the differentiation within each triad.

This method of "triading" promotes a discussion of similarity and contrast, which is how Kelly viewed all constructs. Kelly believed that understanding the nature of a construct requires knowledge of both the similarity and the contrast regarding a triad of elements. The word or phrase used to describe both the similarity and the contrast is determined solely by the research participant. Taken together, the similarity and contrast represent a bi-polar description ("dichotomous construct") relating to one component of the investigation.

Also, interview notes were taken in support of the RepGrid construct. Figure 8 represents the notes, which support one construct from Figure 7. It should be noted that both audio and video recording had been considered but rejected because of the potentially limiting influence on the participant during the interview. So, handwritten interview notes were taken. In order to understand what a research participant means by a particular construct, it is necessary to attempt to understand the content of the construct. Thus, the more data one gathers about a specific construct, the better the chance of understanding what the research participant means.

Continuing with the interview, the research participant was then asked to rate each systems analyst and the two added elements in relation to the elicited

*Figure 8: Interview Notes*

AUDIENCE: Systems Analysts                    PARTICIPANT: Name

GOOD USER RAPPORT
    - good relationship on all subjects
        - work, interests, family
    - user feels more comfortable
    - how is this done?
        - good listener
        - finds out user's interests
            - doesn't forget
        - takes time to answer user's questions
            - speaks in terms users can understand
            - provides an answer that users are happy with
            - learns why and understands

NO USER RAPPORT
    - not a good listener
    - no concern for user
    - aggressive
        - user is intimidated
        - uses big words
    - implies that the system is his
        - "I develop - you use"

construct.  The research participant was encouraged to physically place all eight cards beside each other representing relative variation of the elements with regards to the specific construct.  Stewart and Stewart (1981) suggest this technique helps research participants decide which elements are similar and which are different relative to a specific construct.  The research participant was then asked to assign a number to each card based upon a 9-point rating scale, where 1 represented the positive end of the construct and 9 represented the negative end.  Stewart and Stewart (1981) suggest acceptable scales range from 2-points to 9-points.  A 9-point scale was chosen for this research project for the following reasons.  First, the scale is composed of an odd number, thus allowing a midpoint, which provides research participants with a reference point when rating systems analysts.  Second, a 9-point scale provides sufficient flexibility for rating the eight elements associated with this research project.  That is, with a 9-point scale the research participant could, if desired, rate each systems analyst separately.  While, with any smaller scale the research participant would be forced to give equal rates to some systems analysts.  These numbers were entered into the RepGrid as representative of the participant's differentiation of the systems analysts.  The results of this rating process are shown in Figure 7 as the numbers in the cells of the RepGrid.

At the end of each interview, when the RepGrid was completed, a preliminary confirmation was obtained regarding which actual systems analysts were considered, by the research participant, to be most like the research participant's interpretation of "ideal" and "incompetent".  This process entailed the visual comparison of columns in the completed RepGrid.  This technique is similar to what Stewart and Stewart (1981) refer to as "visual focusing" which attempts to identify those elements or constructs which are the most similar or most different.  In all interviews, the researcher's preliminary RepGrid interpretation and the research participant's interpretation was the same.  This comparison proved to be an appropriate method to confirm, at the end of an interview, that what had been recorded fairly represented what the research participant had stated during the interview.

## DATA ANALYSIS

Overall, the RepGrid technique created a vast amount of qualitative interview notes.  In order to analyze the data, some way of storing and manipulating it was necessary.  The COPE (Cognitive Policy Evaluation) software package (Eden and Ackermann, 1989) was selected because it enables the graphic depiction of hierarchical relationships such as those which exist within the detailed interview notes of this project. COPE implements Kelly's Personal Construct Theory and "...can be used by social scientists in the analysis of qualitative data derived from interviews and documents'. (Cropper et al., 1990:346).

The COPE map of the interview notes presented in Figure 8 is presented in Figure 9. The RepGrid construct has been placed at the top of the map, which in this case is "good use rapport."  The interview notes have then been organized from more general statements to specific comments relative to the construct.  This method creates a tree-like structure with various branches representing different ideas, expressed by the research participant, when discussing the construct. The narrative content of each branch was then used to determine a label for the branch. The labels in Figure 9 relate to *communication* and are representative of the emergence of categories within the general Grounded Theory approach. All of the data from all of the interviews were analyzed in this manner. A count of the occurrence of each label was determined and is discussed in the next section.

Figure 10 presents the data (count of occurrences) relative to C-1. The values are used to represent the measure of relative importance of the emerging categories. Analysis of these data suggests two conclusions. First, universal categories are emerging which represent all of the groups' interpretations of what constitutes an "excellent" systems analyst. That is, certain universal themes have emerged from this fieldwork location, which relate to the different groups' interpretations. Second, the values, which represent relative importance, portray local interpreta-

*Figure 9: COPEMap with Paths*

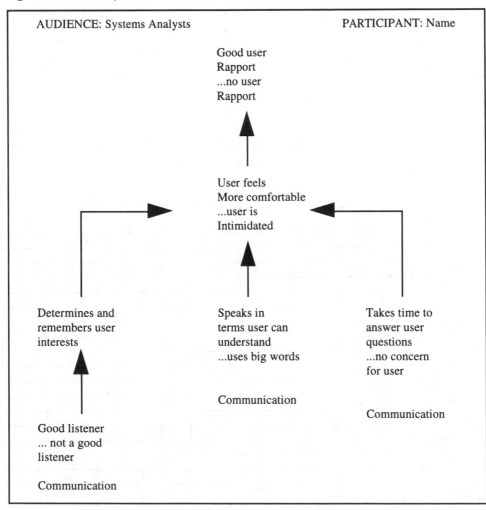

tions. So, while common themes exist, their relative importance varies from one group to another.

These findings are further supported when the subsequent fieldwork locations are considered. Figure 11 presents the data for all four locations, at the

*Figure 10: Location C-1 - Occurrence of Themes by Group*

| Theme | Users | Sponsors | Clients | Systems Analysts | Business Systems Managers | Total |
|---|---|---|---|---|---|---|
| 1. Communication | 32 | 18 | 19 | 16 | 26 | 111 |
| 2. Attitude | 6 | 14 | 1 | 6 | 6 | 33 |
| 3. Investigation | 8 | 8 | 3 | 7 | 3 | 29 |
| 4. Thorough | 12 | 0 | 4 | 6 | 4 | 26 |
| 5. Knowledge | 11 | 1 | 7 | 2 | 1 | 22 |
| 6. Involve User | 10 | 2 | 0 | 3 | 5 | 20 |
| 7. Flexible | 10 | 1 | 0 | 2 | 6 | 19 |
| 8. Experience | 7 | 0 | 3 | 4 | 4 | 18 |
| 9. Plan | 2 | 5 | 2 | 0 | 9 | 18 |
| 10. Delegation | 0 | 0 | 4 | 7 | 5 | 16 |
| 11. Design | 0 | 2 | 3 | 2 | 0 | 7 |
| 12. Team Member | 0 | 1 | 4 | 0 | 1 | 6 |
| Total | 98 | 52 | 50 | 55 | 70 | 325 |
| Participants | 8 | 5 | 4 | 5 | 5 | 27 |

*Figure 11: Occurrence of Themes by Location – Frequency and Ranking*

| THEME | C-1 FREQ. | C-1 RANK | C-2 FREQ. | C-2 RANK | C-3 FREQ. | C-3 RANK | A-1 FREQ. | A-1 RANK |
|---|---|---|---|---|---|---|---|---|
| Attitude | 33 | 2 | 95 | 1 | 112 | 2 | 131 | 1 |
| Communication | 111 | 1 | 73 | 2 | 143 | 1 | 74 | 3 |
| Control | 0 | 14 | 2 | 13 | 0 | 14.5 | 0 | 14 |
| Creative | 0 | 14 | 0 | 15 | 5 | 11.5 | 2 | 12 |
| Delegation | 16 | 10 | 1 | 14 | 13 | 8.5 | 3 | 11 |
| Design | 7 | 11 | 9 | 11 | 5 | 11.5 | 16 | 7.5 |
| Experience | 18 | 8.5 | 23 | 5 | 20 | 6 | 14 | 9 |
| Flexible | 19 | 7 | 11 | 10 | 13 | 8.5 | 19 | 6 |
| Investigation | 29 | 3 | 50 | 4 | 64 | 3 | 23 | 5 |
| Involve User | 20 | 6 | 13 | 7.5 | 13 | 8.5 | 5 | 10 |
| Knowledge | 22 | 5 | 70 | 3 | 62 | 4 | 116 | 2 |
| Learn | 0 | 14 | 12 | 9 | 2 | 13 | 0 | 14 |
| Plan | 18 | 8.5 | 17 | 6 | 13 | 8.5 | 25 | 4 |
| Team Member | 6 | 12 | 3 | 12 | 0 | 14.5 | 0 | 14 |
| Thorough | 26 | 4 | 13 | 7.5 | 25 | 5 | 16 | 7.5 |
| TOTAL | 325 | | 392 | | 490 | | 444 | |
| Participants | 27 | | 26 | | 17 | | 17 | |

*Figure 12: Spearman Rank Correlation*

| Locations | C-1 | C-2 | C-3 |
|-----------|-------|-------|-------|
| C-1 | - | | |
| C-2 | 0.842 | - | |
| C-3 | 0.941 | 0.843 | - |
| A-1 | 0.841 | 0.812 | 0.855 |

*Figure 13: Chi-Square Analysis*

| Locations | C-1 | C-2 | C-3 |
|-----------|--------|-------|-------|
| C-1 | - | | |
| C-2 | 70.68 | - | |
| C-3 | 49.40 | 21.52 | - |
| A-1 | 126.52 | 33.29 | 75.44 |

company level. Also, Figure 11 presents frequency and rank data which was used to conduct two non-parametric analyses.

Spearman rank correlations were calculated for all combinations of locations (see Figure 12). This data shows that there is an association for all combinations based upon rank order. This result further supports the emergence of universals.

However, a Chi-square analysis of frequencies does indicate differences. The calculations shown in Figure 13 show differences in all combinations based upon frequency. Again, this supports the conclusion that locals have emerged from the data reflecting the values of universal themes.

## DISCUSSION

The initial research question related to which skills and personal characteristics of systems analysts were important factors in identifying and differentiating "excellence". This question originally arose because of the researcher's interest in systems analysts and, further, because of prior research, such as that by Boehm (1981) who suggested the personnel component offers the greatest potential for productivity improvement, which in turn may have the greatest impact on the resolution of the software crisis.

RepGrids were used during the interview process because they bring structure to the interview while allowing flexibility and reducing researcher bias. It was considered important in this project to determine the interpretations of the research participants. Thus, it was necessary to adopt a tool, which emphasized gathering data from the participant while allowing the participant to determine the subject matter and content of the data. This aspect is one of the advantages of the RepGrid technique. According to Pervin, "One of the remarkable features of the Rep Test is its tremendous flexibility. By varying the role titles or instructions, one can determine a whole range of constructs and meanings" (Pervin, 1989:246). Further, because a number of participants were interviewed some amount of structure during the interview process would eventually assist the subsequent data analysis. Again, the RepGrid technique adds structure to an interview.

The research participants determined their own list of elements and also were able to decide upon their own constructs, as well as indicate their interpretation of the elicited constructs. Common RepGrids were not used because this would have forced the research participants to respond to previously identified (and therefore potentially biased) elements and constructs. While each RepGrid is therefore unique, common Themes were identified via the subsequent analysis of the detailed interview notes. Thus, it is possible, using the technique described above, to be able to offer the research participant the fullest amount of freedom to comment upon a subject, yet still maintain a structured method to the data-gathering process.

RepGrids may also be used to generate a large amount of rich, in-depth, qualitative and narrative data relating to a research participant's explanation of an elicited construct. The documentation of the research participant's explanations as interview notes forms the basis of the research data for this project. Detailed comments were recorded for each pole of the elicited construct. The researcher determined a system of hierarchies for each construct which depicted the relationships, within the interview notes, between an elicited construct, at the RepGrid level, and a detailed action statement, at the interview note level. The interview notes were obtained via the technique of "laddering" whereby the researcher probes further regarding the research participant's detailed interpretations of a general comment.

Also, the method and the results represent a way of implementing such currently popular productivity improvement frameworks as those proposed by the Software Engineering Institute (SEI), namely the People-Capability Maturity Model (P-CMM). The P-CMM framework outlines the underlying concepts of personnel management of information systems professionals. While the framework describes what aspects should be included in a personnel management program, it does not indicate how to implement the various concepts. The research technique used in the projects reported in this chapter represents one implementation method. The technique supports the concepts outlined in the P-CMM framework and grounds the data obtained from the specific organization. The technique gathers data based on and relevant to each individual corporation. Thus, data are grounded in the experience of those individuals within the corporation, and reflect the organization's current environment. The following excerpt from the P-CMM Draft Version 3.0 supports this approach:

> "Goodness" attributes can only be interpreted in the context of the business environment and specific circumstances of the unit and the organization. Such "goodness" judgements can be made only by the organization as part of its continuous people management cycle. Perfection is never achieved, and continuous improvement never ends." (P-CMM, 1995, p.35-36).

Further, the technique will be sensitive to the P-CMM level of the organization. So, as the organization matures regarding the application of the P-CMM framework, the technique may be repeated, as part of a continuous improvement process, to obtain an up-to-date account of the organization's approach to personnel management.

The results obtained from this current research project may be reflected in the Paradigm Model of Strauss and Corbin (1990). The letters in brackets in the following paragraph refer to the components of the Model as shown in Figure 4.

The software crisis (A) identified at the beginning of the article led the author to investigate interpretations of what constitutes an "excellent" systems analyst (B). What emerged from this investigation was the identification of major themes (C), which, depending upon the organization, have localized levels of relative importance (D). The themes and their identified level of relative importance may be used in the management of systems analysts (E) in order to attempt to attain satisfied users and/or the successful completion of projects (F).

This data leads to the suggestion that before taking any administrative action (hiring, training, etc.), with respect to systems analysts the relative importance of the universal themes should be grounded in the specific organizational situation.

The analysis of research data leads to the generation of the following theory statements:

1. *The interpretation of what constitutes the skills of "excellent" systems analysts can be represented by 15 universal themes.*

The research participants have interpreted "excellent" with regards to a systems analyst based upon these themes, which have emerged from all four locations involved in the fieldwork.

2. *These universal themes represent evidence of an emerging occupation community.*

If the characteristics of an "excellent" systems analyst are perceived in a similar way, then there is evidence of an emerging occupational community. The research results raise the possibility that IS professionals are members of a global occupational community whose qualities transcend both the organization and the society in which they work.

3. *The relative level of importance of these themes will vary by group and company, reflecting a local interpretation.*

While there is evidence of a global IS profession, this research has also found evidence of variation of the relative importance of the universal themes.

4. *The factors of corporate culture will play a greater differentiating role than will societal or national culture.*

The corporate culture, as reflected by such factors as industry sector, organization structure, and employment philosophy, will have more of an impact on the interpretation of what constitutes an "excellent" systems analyst than will the variability resulting from national or societal culture.

## CONCLUSION

This research project was conducted to determine interpretations of "excellent" systems analysts. A qualitative approach was adopted in order to attempt to let the results emerge from the data as espoused by Grounded Theory. One research objective was to determine a better understanding of what "excellent" means relative to systems analysts. Another objective was to investigate any differentiating aspects to the interpretation of "excellent." These objectives have been attained as explained throughout this chapter.

The research is considered significant regarding the general method of conducting an interview to gather research data. The data gathered, described as interview notes above, represent the relatively unbiased comments of the research participants. It is possible then to analyze the data to identify emerging themes and, in turn, to use the data to also define these same emerging themes. This method is supported by the underlying concepts expounded by Grounded Theory (Glaser and Strauss, 1967).

Further, the findings of this research project are significant. As Galliers and Land suggest, "...the measure of the success of research in an applied topic such as information systems is whether our knowledge has been improved to the extent that this improved knowledge can be applied in practice" (Galliers and Land, 1987, p. 901). In this project two of the companies involved were able to apply the research results in the personnel administration of systems analysts. C-1 agreed to use their research results to review a hire decision made just prior to conducting the fieldwork reported on in this chapter. An evaluation hierarchy was constructed based upon the data obtained form C-1. The two final candidates were rated based upon this hierarchy. While this process supported the original decision, C-1 representatives were better able to justify their decision and felt that a more thorough analysis of the candidates had been conducted. C-2 also agreed to apply the results of their research, this time regarding the development of training plans for three systems analysts. A supervisor at C-2 established an evaluation hierarchy and, in conjunction with the systems analysts individually, rated them based upon this hierarchy. C-2 management felt that the process was acceptable to everyone involved because the evaluation hierarchy reflected those items considered important at C-2 at the time of the development of the training plans.

Finally, this chapter has described the appropriate application of qualitative research using a proven technique, RepGrids, to address an important problem in a relatively under-researched area in a unique and novel way.

## REFERENCES

Bannister, D. and J. M. M. Mair (1968). *The Evaluation of Personal Constructs*. New York, Academic Press, Inc.

Banville, Claude and Maurice Landry(1992). "Can the Field of MIS be Disciplined?", Chapter 4 in, Galliers, Robert (Ed.). *Information Systems Research - Issues, Methods and Practical Guidelines*. Henley-on-Thames, England, Alfred

Waller Ltd., 61-88.

Boehm, Barry (1981). *Software Engineering Economics.* Englewood Cliffs, New Jersey, Prentice-Hall.

Boland,Jr., Richard J. (1985). "Phenomenology: A Preferred Approach to Research on Information Systems", Chapter 10 in, Mumford, Enid et al (Eds.). *Research Methods in Information Systems.* Amsterdam, North-Holland, 193-201.

Botten, Nancy, Andrew Kusiak and Tzvi Raz (1989). "Knowledge Bases: Integration, Verification, and Partitioning". *European Journal of Operations Research,* 42(2), 1.

Corsini, Raymond and Anthony J. Marsella (1983). *Personality Theories, Research and Assessment.* Itasca, Illinois, Peacock Publishers, Inc.

Cropper, Steve, Colin Eden and Fran Ackermann (1990). "Keeping Sense of Accounts Using Computer-Based Cognitive Maps," *Social Science Computer Review,* Duke University Press, Fall, 345-366.

Eden, Colin and Fran Ackermann (1989). "Strategic Option Development and Analysis - Using Computers to Help with the Management of Strategic Vision", in Doukidis, G. I., F. Land and G. Miller (Eds.), *Knowledge-Based Management Support Systems.* Ellis Horwood, Chichester, 208-224.

Eden, Colin and S. Jones (1984). "Using Repertory Grids for Problem Construction". *Journal of Operations Research,* 35(9), 779-798.

Eden, Colin, and G. Wheaton (1980). "In Favour of Structure", Centre for the Study of Organisational Change and Development, *University of Bath, Working Paper 80/06.*

Fransella, F. (Ed.) (1981). *Personality - Theory, Measurement and Research.* Methuen and Co., New York.

Galliers, Robert D. (Ed.) (1992). *Information Systems Research - Issues, Methods and Practical Guidelines.* Henley-on-Thames, England, Alfred Waller Ltd.

Galliers, Robert D. and Frank F. Land(1987). "Choosing Appropriate Information Systems Research Methodologies". *Communications of the ACM,* 30(11), 900-902.

Glaser, Barney G. and Anselm L. Strauss (1967). *The Discovery of Grounded Theory: Strategies for Qualitative Research.* New York, Aldine De Gruyter.

Hirschheim, Rudi (1992). "Information Systems Epistemology: An Historical Perspective", Chapter 3 in, Galliers, Robert (Ed.). *Information Systems Research - Issues, Methods and Practical Guidelines.* Henley-on-Thames, England, Alfred Waller Ltd., 61-88.

Hunter, M. Gordon (1993). "A Strategy for Identifying "Excellent" Systems Analysts". *The Journal of Strategic Information Systems,* 2(1), 15-26.

Hunter, M. Gordon (1994). "Excellent" Systems Analysts: Key Audience Perceptions". *Computer Personnel,* ACM Press, April, 15-31.

Hunter, M. Gordon and John E. Beck (1996a). "A Cross-Cultural Comparison of "Excellent" Systems Analysts". *Information Systems Journal,* 6(4).

Hunter, M. Gordon and John E. Beck(1996b). ""Excellent" Systems Analysts: The Singapore Context". *Asia-Pacific Journal of Management,* 13(2)m 25-46.

Kendall, Penny A. (1992). *Introduction to Systems Analysis and Design: A Structured Approach.* 2nd. Ed. Dubuque, IA, Wm. C. Brown Publishers.

Kelly, G. A. (1955). *The Psychology of Personal Constructs.* Norton, New York.

Kelly, G. A. (1963). *A Theory of Personality*. Norton, New York.

Klein, Heinz K. and Kalle Lyytinen(1985). "The Poverty of Scientism in Information Systems", Chapter 8 in Mumford, Enid et al (Eds.). *Research Methods in Information Systems*. Amsterdam, North-Holland, 131-161.

Latta, G. F. and K. Swigger (1992). "Validation of the Repertory Grid for Use in Modelling Knowledge". *Journal of the American Society of Information Science*, 42(2), 115-129.

Laudon, Kenneth C. and Jane Price Laudon (1998). *Management Information Systems - New Approaches to Organization and Technology*. Upper Saddle River, New Jersey, Prentice Hall, Inc.

Lending, Diane and James C. Wetherbe (1992). "Update on MIS Research: A Profile of Leading Journals and U.S. Universities". *DATABASE*, 23(3), 5-11.

Orlikowski, Wanda J. and Jack J. Baroudi (1991). "Studying Information Technology in Organizations: Research Approaches and Assumptions". *Information Systems Research*, 2(1), 1-28.

People - Capability Maturity Model (P-CMM)(1995). *The Software Engineering Institute*, Pittsburgh.

Pervin, Lawrence A. (1989). *Personality - Theory and Research*. 5th Ed. New York, John Wiley and Sons, Inc.

Phythian, Gary John and Malcolm King(1992). "Developing an Expert System for Tender Enquiry Evaluation: A Case Study". *European Journal of Operations Research*, 56(1), 15-29.

Reason, Peter and John Rowan, (Eds.)(1981). *Human Inquiry - A Sourcebook of New Paradigm Research*. Chichester, England, John Wiley and Sons.

Senn, James A. (1985). *Analysis and Design of Information Systems*. New York, McGraw-Hill Ltd..

Shaw, M. L. G. (1980). *On Becoming a Personal Scientist - Interactive Computer Elicitation of Personal Models of the World*. Academic Press, London.

Stewart, Valerie and Andrew Stewart(1981). *Business Applications of Repertory Grid*. McGraw-Hill, Ltd., London.

Strauss, Anselm and Juliet Corbin (1990). *Basics of Qualitative Research - Grounded Theory Procedures and Techniques*. Sage Publications Inc., Newbury Park, California.

Vogel, D. R. and Wetherbe, J. C. (1984). "MIS Research: A Profile of Leading Journals and Universities". *DATABASE*, 16(1), 3-14.

Yourdon, Edward (1989). *Modern Structured Analysis*. New York, Yourdon Press.

## Chapter IV

# Bottom up Management and System Design

W. Hutchinson
Edith Cowan University

Development techniques almost always use top-down approaches to develop software and business systems. Humans need to simplify the external world by using cognitive models to build a boundary around a problem. These necessary, but artificial, boundaries help us cope with the complexity of the problem at hand. However, this deductive process produces dilemmas, as it leads to misconceptions about the real behavior of systems and the people in them. This chapter will look at system design using the system elements (and their interactions) as the starting point of design, that is an inductive approach. Whilst this will not replace the top-down approach, its use will enhance problem solutions. In a contemporary world of loosely coupled organisational elements, it is necessary to view the system from this perspective to fully understand it. This chapter will offer a preliminary methodology to approach system design using 'bottom up' thinking. This view is not the opposite of top-down thinking but a supplement to it. It results in asking questions about the desired system, which are fundamentally different in nature to conventional techniques

## TOP-DOWN THINKING AND ITS LIMITATIONS

To make sense of the world humans create intellectual boundaries around elements to produce concepts. Each boundary is necessarily incomplete to focus on certain elements in the world. The problem solver's worldview and the problem situation form the boundary (Checkland and Scholes, 1991; Wilson, 1990).

It can be said that over the last two decades the energies of systems thinking has concentrated on the formation of the system boundary. Checkland (1981) formulated his Soft Systems Methodology based on the observation that 'hard' system designers had a very narrow focus of what elements entailed the system. It was an attempt to make system designers more 'people friendly' by including as many viewpoints of the problems as was practically possible. This was a great leap forward in making the system design process more inclusive and thus, more effective. At a later stage, Ulrich (1987, 1993) created his Critical Systems Heuristics, which in practical terms made the system developer think about the power implications of the design plus increasing the elements to be considered when designing a system. The previous 'hard' system's concentration on input, process, and output had certainly been expanded.

Midgely et al. (1998) expand the idea of the boundary by introducing the concepts of *primary* and *secondary* boundaries. A narrow boundary outline created by one set of people and a wider boundary definition by another will create a group of *marginalised* system elements. The inclusion of these marginalised elements is likely to be contentious and most prone to 'power play.' His work actually crystallised the work of system thinkers of the previous years. The essence of good design was to ensure that it was the secondary boundary that was established in the problem definition and hence, the solution presented. In a practical project development situation, it is the definition of the scope of the project that is important (Hutchinson, 1998).

It is at this point that the two formal types of problem approaches should be introduced: deduction and induction. Deduction reasons from general rules, or theories to particular cases, whilst induction generalises from observation. The most distinguishing feature between deductive and inductive arguments is that of proof (Hospers, 1976). Deductive arguments can have formal justification, while inductive arguments can be defended in pragmatic terms. This chapter will argue that top-down (deductive) arguments dominate formal management and system design thinking. Yet, they do not take into account what happens in the 'real' world, but reflect the assumptions made to justify their acceptance. However, inductive (bottom-up) approaches look at behavior to make sense of situations. Therefore, formal justification is difficult as no theoretical framework is assumed. It is this latter point which upsets many managers, philosophers, scientists, and system designers. The need for the security blanket of a theoretically provable outcome is desired, even if the outcome is not achievable in practice.

Actually, this chapter is probably more concerned with *abduction*, which is less formal than induction. Abduction searches for a pattern in specific observations, and suggests hypotheses to explain the observations. Induction tests hypotheses with empirical data, and justifies the validity of an assertion by asserting a general principle. A good, practical overview of abduction can be found in Waltz (1998, pp. 57-67, 84-88). It must be said here that the definitions of deduction, induction, and abduction are not consistent in the literature. For example, Friedman (1990, p.4) defines abduction in terms of "the generation of hypotheses to explain *given* data", rather than the more informal view of Waltz. It is for this reason that the more general terms 'top down', and 'bottom up' are used here.

In this chapter, the term 'top down' is used to describe this approach to problem solving, where the problem space is defined first. The worldviews of the participants are used to conceptualize the desired state of the proposed system. Once this is achieved, the system is developed within this boundary. The components or subsystems are derived within the context of the predefined desired state.

So what is wrong with this type of approach? Well, nothing is! Top-down thinking is necessary to make sense of the world and get things done. However, there is one major drawback of drawing a boundary around a 'conceptual definition of a system'. By definition, the boundary is artificial, and so the system only includes a limited number of elements from a limited number of views. Also, there is a problem that people believe the system boundary to be true, and then try to fit other people's behavior into the context of that viewpoint. These concepts then allow managers, and system developers to blame the 'victims' of a system for not behaving as they should, when it is the 'system' which should have been designed to fit them. Hence, system designers expect system elements to conform within the limitation set by the design, rather than allowing for the limitations of the system elements—a subtle but significant difference.

It is a common experience of those actually involved in running systems that managerial statements of how systems are running are totally alien to experience. The differential between theory and practice can be enormous. One can only recall the anecdotal tale of nail production in the old Soviet Union. It was claimed that nail production by weight was increasing exponentially. This was correct, but it was discovered that some factories were producing nails which were four metres in length to keep the figures up. Kam (1988) also explain the limitations of some American intelligence officers in the Cold War period when observations from satellite photographs were interpreted within in certain context. Events, which were mundane, were given meaning to fit in with some preconceived motives. Actual behavior was interpreted in the limited boundaries of expected behavior. Hence, really minor events were perceived to be important, and vice versa. One can only speculate that, at some time, a Russian military truck driver stopping for a cup of coffee sent the Pentagon in a spin.

## THE BOTTOM-UP VIEW

The term 'bottom up' is used to describe an approach where no assumptions are made about the boundary of the problem space. The behavior of component parts is rationally observed to determine the properties they have. Management decisions or system designs are then based on the observed behavior of components. It is accepted there are a number of paradoxes and limitations to this approach. The first is the nature of 'rational observation'. The term 'objective observation' is deliberately not used in recognition of the subjective nature of any observation. The idea of starting with no assumptions about the system is also rather idealistic, and because of the nature of human thought, impossible in practice. However, this chapter is attempting to propose a practical and pragmatic way to deliver good design and management practice. It is the philosophy of the approach that is being described rather than the purity of its practical application.

The organization can be viewed as a conceptual whole, or as a set of semi-autonomous objects (Tsoukas, 1993). Here, it is assumed that the organization has an overt, stated purpose. This view, *which is still using top-down thinking,* sees the organization as consisting of elements (usually individuals or groups) which are all carrying out their own activities. If the purposes of these elements are beneficial to the overall purposes of the whole system, the organization will remain healthy (in its own terms). Within the system, elements have different purposes, which may contradict the main system purpose. Thus, the organization can have a myriad of 'purposes'. If these sub-purposes do not dominate, the organization will still carry out its main purpose. However, a situation could occur where the sub-purposes can dominate. Hence, the actions of the system elements will not serve the overt system purpose. The priorities of system purposes will change in fact, if not officially. This model has been included to give some idea of the chaotic character of organizations. Top-down management and design thinking often assumes all the objectives of the system elements are all in step with the main purpose of the company. Experience tells many of us that this is just not so. People and groups of people have different agendas and motivations; assuming they correlate with the official organisational objectives is extremely naive. As Tsoukas (1993, p.514) says, "While social organizations are inevitably human artifacts, they are not necessarily the product of human design".

When an organization is viewed in bottom-up mode, each component has a set of attributes and potential. How each element behaves will be determined by that element's internal state and the behavior of other elements affecting it. Hence, people, groups, technology, and other resources determine a system's behavior. It is these elements, and how they interact that will determine how the system works. Therefore, examining these will give a realistic image of what is *really* happening, and any achievable potential in the system. A criticism of managers using top-down styles is that they do not know what 'really goes on'. Managers and designers view staff behavior with some preconceived notion of what *should* be happening. This can cause a discrepancy between ideas and practice. It might be valid to view management problems this way to get things achieved, but can cause problems if the ideal and practice are divergent. Bottom-up views look at the actual practice of system elements, and develop ideas from them.

What is this, the real state of affairs in the modern organization? Increasingly, organizations possess flattened management structures. The move toward part-time and nonpermanent work and the practice of outsourcing are increasing. It seems likely that, in this environment, the main aim of people will be self-interest (not that of the organization). Staff mobility will increase (hence, any loyalties will be transitory). Organisational structures become much more loosely coupled. Management will have to accomplish its task with much less authority. Has management practice come to grips with this change?

## A PROPOSED BOTTOM-UP STRATEGY

A bottom-up strategy should allow the user to view the problem from the perspective of the system elements. Boundaries should not be assumed, but built up as the investigation progresses. The observed behaviors of system elements as they interact, in terms of their processes, and information and material flows, should be recorded to demonstrate the potential for different combinations of these elements. Thus, the system or problem investigation allows a solution to *emerge*.

A suggested bottom up strategy is offered below. It was designed as an informal management tool to examine problems situations and design systems for them. It is less specific than the method offered in the next section. It consists of ten stages, they are:

### Stage 1

*Establish initial elements to be investigated.*

This stage is similar to the process of producing a Rich Picture in the Soft Systems Methodology (Checkland and Scholes, 1991; Checkland, 1981; Wilson, 1990). As many views as possible are obtained to find the elements which are to be considered initially. This process also determines the context of those elements. This is the starting point of the problem solving and, as the whole series of stages are iterative, other elements may be added later.

### Stage 2

*Establish internal attributes and states of elements.*

The individual characteristics of each element are determined to provide the limitations of their behavior. If an element can have more than one state, the prevailing state should be recorded.

### Stage 3

*Evaluate needs of the elements.*

The general needs of each element are determined, as well as the different needs for each state. These general needs can vary from temperature to psychological condition. A general need is anything that will affect the state or existence of a system element.

### Stage 4

*Establish effects elements on each other.*

This is similar to the previous stage, except it is the effects of the other overtly stated elements on other elements (in terms of their state, or 'health') that are determined.

### Stage 5

*Determine how elements communicate.*

This stage determines the information needs of each element, and the information supplied by each element. The media for information transmission is determined, as well as the data format needed.

### Stage 6

*By observation, establish emergent properties of combinations of system elements.*

From the information gathered in the previous stages, the behaviors of groupings of elements in different states (and the environment needed) are explored. Any control mechanisms should be noted.

### Stage 7

*Set up feasible element combinations for desired emergent properties discovered.*

At this stage, the desired behaviors are determined, and the elements and their required needs (including control systems) are set up to produce those outputs.

### Stage 8

*Set up contingencies for detrimental emergent properties of potential element combinations.*

Any undesired outputs from the element combinations set up in Stage 8 are noted, and their probability and impact resolved. Contingency plans are drawn up to cope with them. This stage might involve the inclusion of more system elements. Hence, the investigator would to return to Stage 1.

### Stage 9

*Determine if any other elements are implemented in your problem space. If there are, repeat stages with new elements. (These tasks should be considered at all previous stages, and if changes are made, process should return to Stage 1).*

This stage decides if the boundary, which has been created by the previous stages, is suitable for the problem at hand. This is resolved by reflective pragmatism. This stage is important, as there can be a danger of constant iteration through the previous stages until the boundary becomes so wide it is unmanageable in the actual problem context.

### Stage 10

*When the designed system is in place, monitor any emergent properties and repeat when necessary. Iteration is important.*

This stage is performed after the implementation of a system. It reflects the iterative nature of problem solving, the dynamism of the real world, and the incomplete knowledge of all practitioners.

There are a number of assumptions made in the above. The first is that it is possible to isolate system elements and determine their characteristics. Of course, this positivist approach should be tempered with the knowledge that complex interactions may not be predictable. Also, it does not overcome the problem of who determines what are *desirable* emergent properties. Therefore, Stage 7 is problematic, and produces the same problem associated with top down approaches; that is, *who* decides *what* is desirable. (Added to that is who decides *who is to decide, ad infinitum*). This problem will not be covered further in this chapter, except to say that management decisions are made in a context of a power structure. Regardless of the overtly moral and ethical issues, it is this power structure which determines the outcome. The power structure might include pressure groups, physical laws, the media, or financial institutions. Whatever the powerful elements are, the real outcomes are resolved in this context.

The objective of this strategy is to start with the elements and proceed to build the system with no preconceived ideas of how the system elements will react. No emergent properties are assumed, and no boundary drawn. There is a paradox here. It can be argued that in Stage 1 the inclusion or exclusion of elements automatically draws a boundary. However, these elements are intended as a *starting* point, not an end point. In real-world problem solving, a decision has to be

*Figure 1: Outline of a Bottom-Up Strategy*

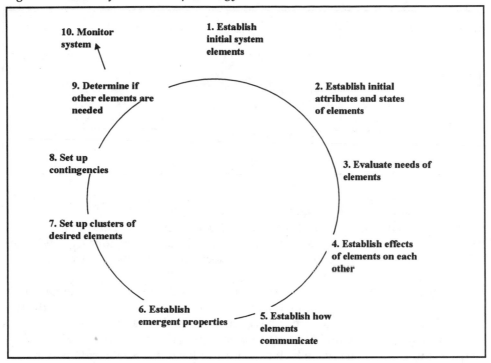

made. The intention here is to use these elements to build a system, and to add more as appropriate. Nevertheless, it has to be admitted that the choice of elements will be profoundly affected by the worldviews of the participants. Therefore, as in many system methodologies, it is extremely important to be as inclusive as possible with the choice of participants (see Hutchinson, 1998).

Stage 9 is an important one and demonstrates the iterative nature of the strategy. Whilst it is placed as the penultimate stage, it can be executed at any point during the process. The strategy is illustrated in Figure 1.

However, as it is based on the same assumptions of the bottom0-up approach, the method is similar to that illustrated above.

The model presented below represents a specific view of a system, which allows a more formal, bottom-up approach to design. It consists only of two basic components: *system elements* and *change agents*. The assumption made is that a system consists of elements interacting with each other. Each element has a limited number of states and parameters.

Figure 2 represents the fundamental element in the system. Element X could be a physical or a conceptual component of a system, for example, a person, piece of equipment, a team, department, morale, or profit. Each system has its own characteristics. It may be relatively dynamic or constant over time. Change agents are those characteristics of system elements that alter other system elements (or themselves).

Each system element has change agents, which effect it ($n_1$). The element itself

*Figure 2: A System Element (X) and its Associated Change Agents (n1 - n3).*

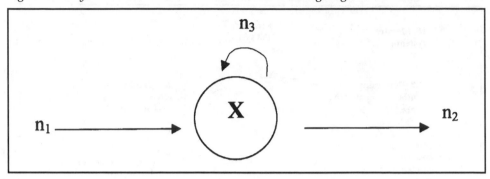

produces changes to other elements ($n_2$), and because over time the element itself will change, it has internal change agents ($n_3$). These change agents themselves can be resources, energy, or conceptual (for example, information, ideas, knowledge). The change agents may be constant in their effects or spasmodic. Their aeffects may be linear or exponential or erratic.

Figure 3 illustrates that change agents 1 and 2 affect system element A in different ways. Change agent 1 has a greater affect than 2. The 'x' factor is there to show that each change agent may have an effect on the other. It can be seen that viewing a system from this perspective is becoming complex as each element may have a multitude of agents, which can affect it. Each of these agents may have a different effect over time or when coupled with other agents.

Figure 4 shows the interaction between different system elements and their change agents. It can be seen that element A is affected by change agents 1 and 2. Change agent 2 is derived from element C, and change agent 1 from 'nowhere'. This latter observation shows that the model is incomplete and that the element producing change 1 should be included. Element A produces a change (3) to the system, which affects both elements B and C. Notice that the lines for the 'output' change agents are only given magnitude when they are input change agents to other system elements. Thus, this change agent has a greater impact on element B than C. All the change inputs to an element should add up to 100%. Hence the sum of all the widths of the input change agents should be the same for all elements. Notice that element B has a change agent (5), which does not seem to affect anything. This implies that an

*Figure 3: Illustration Emphasizing the Relative Impact of Change Agents (1, 2) on A, and Possible Influence of Change Agents on Each Other (x)*

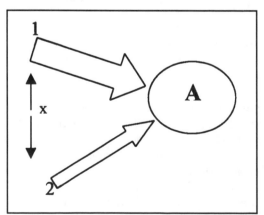

element is missing (or perhaps the change element is erroneous or irrelevant).

Note also that the conventional notion of a system's *environment* (that is, elements that affect the system or are affected by it but are not considered a part of the system) is not relevant here. If an element affects another it should be included. Of course, this is the "Achilles' heel" of the bottom up approach. When do we stop adding elements? The answer is, "when it is thought useful to do so". Of course, by stopping, a boundary is drawn around the solution. The difference between the boundaries drawn by the top-down and bottom-up approaches is *how* the end is achieved. The two boundaries are unlikely to be the same.

The actual theoretical method for using this approach is illustrated in Figures 5a to 5i. It consists of nine stages. The whole process like most system design methods, is highly iterative. To avoid making the process elitist, as many viewpoints as possible should be used. Those advocated by Checkland and Scholes (1991) for obtaining a rich picture can be used (as in the process offered in the previous section).

It must be noted that the method described below is an attempt to formalise a bottom-up design approach. In system design terms, it can be *functionally* useful where the system elements are not highly problematic, and their behaviors are relatively predictable. Object Oriented Systems Design (see Yourdon, 1994) is especially suited to bottom-up approaches such as this. In a problem consisting of people with varying viewpoints and values, it can be useful as a *guide* to the manager to produce solutions. The nine stages are as follows:

### Stage 1

Here the system elements thought to be of concern to the context of the problem are examined (see Figure 5a). This is the most paradoxical part of the method, as choosing the elements appears to have put a boundary around the problem. This should not be the case, as this is the *starting* point of the process. It

*Figure 4: Illustration Showing Interaction of System Elements (A-C) and Associated Change Agents (1-5)*

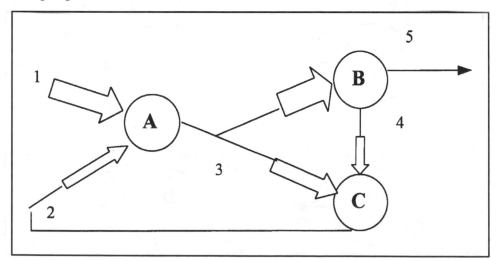

is from this point that the solution is built up. The following stages add to the limited set of elements rather than putting a boundary around them.

### Stage 2

The change agents produced by each of the elements chosen are determined (see figure 5b). For simplicity's sake only one for each element is illustrated.

### Stage 3

The input change agents needed by each system element to produce the output change agents are then determined (see Figure 5c). Hence system element A produces change agent 1, and needs change agents 2 and 3 to produce this.

*Figure 5a: Stage 1 - Identify System Elements*

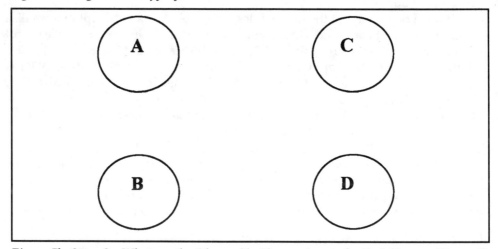

*Figure 5b: Stage 2 - What are the Observable Change Agents for Each System Element?*

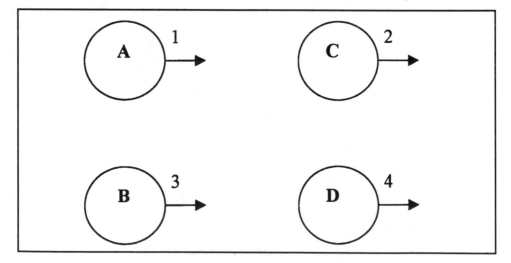

*Figure 5c: Stage 3 - Identify Change Agents Needed to Produce Changes Needed in System Elements to Produce Output Change Elements*

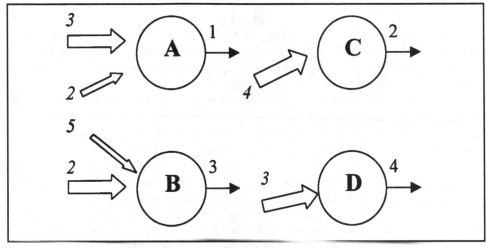

**Stage 4**

The needs for each system element are then matched with the appropriate change agent and its source (see Figure 5d). Thus element C needs change agent 4 and produces change agent 2, which is needed by A and B. Element B needs change

*Figure 5d: Stage 4 - Combine Element and Change Agents.*

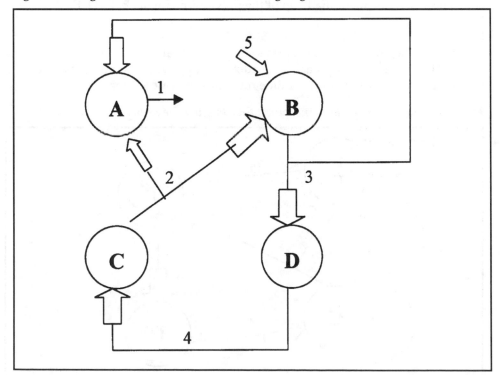

agents 2 and 5 and produces change agent 3. However, there are a number of anomalies here. These are dealt with in the next stage.

### Stage 5

From Figure 5d, it can be seen that element A needs a number of change agents (2 and 3) from C and B. However, the change agent it produces has not affect on any other elements. At this stage it has to be decided whether this situation is caused by a missing element which would need change agent 1, or whether, as element A has no affect on any other element, it should be dropped from the problem space. In this illustrative case, it has been dropped (see figure 5e). Also, it can be seen that element B has the need of a change agent 5, which has no source. This means an iteration back to stage 1, where another element must be added. In this case, it is element E, which itself needs change agent 2 from element C. This relation between C and E was put in to simplify the example, but element E could easily have needed another change agent. Hence there would be another iteration back to Stage 1.

Figure 5e represents an ideal situation where all the interactions are recorded between each element. In the real world, this does not occur. Of course, it can in the idealised top down world, because the rules and constraints are defined. Thus by its own definition it may be complete, even if it is far short of reality.

### Stage 6

Once the elements have been finalised, the emergent properties (if any) should be determined. Figure 5f shows two emergent change agents ($em_1$, $em_2$) emanating from the system element made up of the previous elements B, C, D, E.

### Stage 7

One of the limitations of the previous stages is that they assume everything is static. This time slice approach is needed to cope with the complexity of the problem. However, the effects of time must now be catered for. Changes to each

*Figure 5e: Stage 5 - Eliminate Anomalies, Add Missing Elements.*

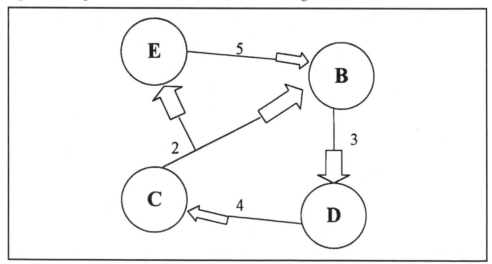

*Figure 5f: Stage 6 – Determine Emergent Properties.*

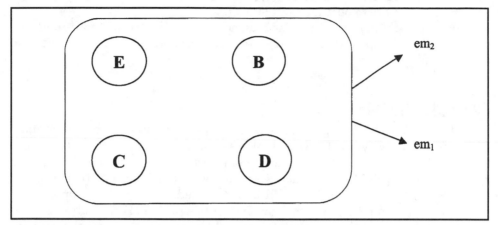

element and combinations of elements over time should be observed or postulated. Changes may occur at different rates for each element or combination of elements. Scenarios for each time slice can then be taken, much like that used in system dynamics software such as STELLA® or iTHINK® (see Wolstenholme, 1990; 1994).

### Stage 8

At this point, the change agents needed to produce the emergent properties of the cluster of original elements should be determined. Figure 5g illustrates this stage.

### Stage 9

This is really a return to Stage 1. Stage 8 determines the change agents needed to produce the emergent properties of the cluster of elements. The source of these

*Figure 5g: Stage 8 - Determine if Input Change Agents Needed to Produce Emergent Properties*

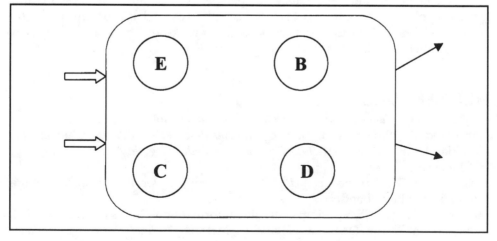

agents now needs to be determined. The process is now iterated as many times as is deemed necessary to obtain a useful result.

Stage 9 is an important one, and demonstrates the iterative nature of the method. Whilst it is placed as the last stage, it can be executed at any point during the process.

## CONCLUSION

The method and strategy offered in this chapter are based on the assumption that using top-down views to design systems limits the quality of the end product. It is necessary to put boundaries around problems to allow solutions to be created: problem solving would be an endless search for perfection if we did not. However, the limitations of these views should be recognized. A bottom-up approach is valuable in examining the system from another perspective. For instance, a manager in top-down mode would ask 'Who could carry out these tasks to achieve outcome X?' In bottom-up mode the question would be 'We have these people, what is their potential, what can they do'? System designers tend to make people and resources fit their concepts, rather than designing a system for the elements in it. This is not to say that bottom-up approaches can replace top-down methods, but they do have the potential to produce much richer problem solutions.

The bottom-up approach is very useful for examining top system designs to measure the integrity of the assumptions made in the design. It is especially useful in examining why systems fail. However, its most important contribution to system design is that it takes account of how elements actually behave with each other (especially people). Top-down processes make certain assumptions, it is these that need to be tested. Management and information systems are often arrogantly forced upon their victims with the assumption that the victims must change to suit the system. The bottom-up approach tend to design a system from the view of how people and other system elements actually behave, thereby making it more user friendly to the system actors (but maybe not system's management). It is often this conflict of managerial wants along with what actually can occur that causes a system to fail (even under the managerial perspective). Creating new systems and managing old ones are complex tasks, where ethics as well as function should be considered. The bottom-up approach is another tool to help in the ongoing search for more effective ways of solving complex problems.

## REFERENCES

Beer, S. (1985). *Diagnosing the System for Organizations*. John Wiley, Chichester.

Checkland, P. (1981). *Systems Thinking, Systems Practice*. John Wiley: Chichester.

Checkland, P.B., Scholes, J. (1991). *Soft Systems Methodology in Action*. John Wiley: Chichester.

Hospers, J. (1973). *An introduction to philosophical analysis – second edition.*: Routledge and Kegan Paul, London.

Hutchinson, W.(1998). 'Scoping: Designing Information Systems to Meet People's Needs'. In Avison, D., Edgar Neville, D., *Matching Technology to Organisational*

*Needs*, p.413-419. McGraw Hill, UK.

Friedman, K.S. (1990). *Predictive Simplicity*. Pergamon Press, Oxford.

Kam, K. (1988). *Surprise Attack*. Harvard University Press, Cambridge.

Midgley G., Munlo I., Brown M. (1998). The Theory and Practice of Boundary Critique: Developing Housing Services for Older People. *Journal of the Operational Research Society*, 49, 467-478.

Tsoukas, H. (1993). 'Organizations as Soap Bubbles: An Evolutionary Perspective on Organization Design'. *Systems Practice*, 6, 5, 501-515.

Ulrich W. (1993). Some difficulties of ecological thinking, considered from a critical systems perspective: a plea for critical holism, *Systems Practice*, 6, 6.

Ulrich W. (1991). Critical Heuristics of Social Systems Design, reprinted in: *Critical Systems Thinking-Directed Readings*, eds. Flood R.L., Jackson M.C. Wiley, Chichester.

Waltz, E.(1998). *Information Warfare: Principles and Operations*. Artech House, Boston.

Wilson, B. *(1990).Systems: Concepts, Methodologies and Applications - 2^{nd} edition.* John Wiley: New York. 1

Wolstenholme E.F. (1994). A systematic approach to model creation, in: *Modeling for Learning Organisations*, eds. Morecroft J D W, Sterman J D. Productivity Press, Portland.

Wolstenholme, E. F.(1990). *Systems Enquiry: A Systems Dynamics Approach*. Wiley, Chichester.

Yourdon, E.(1994). *Object-Oriented Systems Design*. Prentice Hall, Englewood Hills.

## Chapter V

# System and Training Design for End-User Error

Jonathan K. Lazar
Towson University

Anthony F. Norcio
University of Maryland Baltimore County

Errors are a major problem for users. In the distant past, the users of computer technology often were limited to computer professionals with extensive technical training. With the growth of personal computers and the Internet, millions of people without technical backgrounds use computer technology on a daily basis, both at work and for leisure activities.

Because errors can be such a problem for the end user, it is important to examine the causes of error, as well as different approaches for assisting the end user. This chapter presents definitions of error, as well as a taxonomy of user error. There are two general approaches for assisting the end user in responding to errors: system design and training design. Both of these are discussed in-depth in this chapter. The purpose of this chapter is to describe the current situation of end-user error and suggest ways to improve the end -user experience.

## WHAT IS AN ERROR?

Defining an error can be challenging, since several different definitions of errors have been proposed in the literature. These definitions generally fall into two categories (Arnold and Roe, 1987). One set of error definitions is *user-centered*; the other set of definitions is *system-centered* (Arnold and Roe, 1987).

### User-Centered Definitions of Error

Users want to complete their tasks successfully. User-centered definitions consider errors from the point of view of the user. User-centered definitions of error view an error as when a user's desired action is not carried out (Norman, 1983).

Users are concerned with reaching their goals, and from the users' point of view, errors keep them from reaching those goals. Some of the user-centered definitions of error that have been presented in the literature are:
- when a user's intention or goal is not attained (Arnold and Roe, 1987, p. 204)
- the non-attainment of a goal (Frese and Altmann, 1989).

User-centered definitions do not blame users for errors. User-centered definitions of error only state that errors keep users from reaching their goals. Zapf et. al. point out that for an error to be defined as such, a specific program or system must be designed to perform the task that the users want (Zapf et al., 1992). If the user has a specific goal, but the program or system is not designed to perform the tasks to reach such a goal, then this is called a functionality problem (Goodwin, 1987). For instance, if a user attempts to use a statistics program to browse the Web, this would be considered a functionality problem, not an error, because the application (the statistics program) was not designed to meet the user's task goal (browsing the Web). The applications and systems should be designed to perform the tasks to reach the users' goals.

### System-Centered Definitions of Error
System-centered definitions of error view errors from the system's point of view; user goals are not addressed. System-centered definitions of error are more technically oriented. From the system's point of view, if something cannot process successfully, it is due to an error on the user's part. System-centered definitions of error blame the users (Lewis and Norman, 1986). Some of the system-centered definitions of error in the literature include:
- an action that violates a rule (Frese and Altmann, 1989).
- something that the system cannot respond to (Lewis and Norman, 1986, p. 411).
- actions that are inappropriate (Booth, 1991).

### User Perception Of Error
Although system-centered definitions of error blame the user for errors, it is not useful to blame a user (Zapf et al., 1992). In human-computer interaction research, the focus is on assisting and designing for the end users of technology (Dix et al., 1998; Preece et al., 1994; Shneiderman, 1998). We postulate that an error occurs whenever a user *perceives* that an error occurs. If the user perceives that an error occurred, it does not make a difference whether system designers classify it as an error or not. The end user is not concerned with theoretical differences in classifications. Instead, the end user is frustrated because they are not able to reach their task goal. Inexperienced end users frequently tend to blame themselves for making an error (Carroll and Mack, 1984; Lewis and Norman, 1986). Errors intimidate less experienced end users. More experienced end users tend to be confident in their abilities (Carroll, 1990).

# CLASSIFICATION TAXONOMY OF ERRORS

The classification system for user errors that is prominent in the world of system design is provided by Donald Norman. At the highest level, Norman separates errors into two types: mistakes and slips (Norman, 1983). Norman defines a mistake as when users choose the wrong commands to reach their goals (Arnold and Roe, 1987; Norman, 1983). A mistake has also been called a conceptual error (Booth, 1991). A slip, on the other hand, is when a user's intended command is correct, but the user makes an error (such as a spelling error) in entering his/her commands (Norman, 1983). Within slips, there are many different classifications. For instance, Norman defines mode errors, description errors, capture errors, activation errors, and data description errors.

## Mode Errors

Frequently, applications and systems have different modes. A keypress while the system is in one mode will provide a different action than the same keypress when the system is in a different mode. A mode error is when users believe that a system is in one mode, when instead, it is in another mode (Norman, 1988). Users then perform their actions with the mistaken belief that the system is in a certain mode. Because the system is in a different mode, their actions may have results other than what the users intended, and the users do not reach their goals.

## Description Errors

Many times, different actions or procedures are carried out using a similar set of commands. A description error is when users perform a procedure in a correct manner, but perform it on the wrong file, item or object (Norman, 1983; 1988). An example of a description error could be to send a business colleague the wrong file as an e-mail attachment. The user performed the procedure in the correct manner, saving a file in the correct directory, uploading it to their e-mail account, and correctly attaching it to their e-mail message. However, these procedures were performed on the wrong file. Description errors frequently occur when objects, files, or items look similar or are physically close to each other.

## Capture Errors

A capture error is when there is overlap between one set of commands and another, and the user performed the wrong sequence of commands (Norman, 1983). When attempting to perform one set of commands, another set of commands which is similar, takes over (Norman, 1988). There are many commands that are similar. In some of these cases, the commands partially overlap. For instance, a keystroke sequence of control-alt-delete reboots most personal computers. If the key sequence control-alt by itself performed a procedure, it is expected that many times, users would mean to type only control-alt, but instead would type control-alt-delete.

## Activation Errors

An activation error occurs when users fail to complete all of the required procedures to reach their intention (Norman, 1983). This may be due to other events that have occurred while users are performing the appropriate actions. These other events take away the users' attention, causing them to forget the exact procedures to execute and the order in which the procedures should be executed (Norman, 1983). Norman later renamed this specific type of error as a 'loss-of-activation' error (Norman, 1988).

### Data-Driven Errors

A data-driven error is based on the arrival of data to our senses (Norman, 1988). Users may be in the process of entering data, when someone tells them that the current ballgame score is 3 to 1, Orioles winning. The users then may enter the numbers 31 instead of the actual data that should be entered. This differs from an activation error, because it does not completely end the user's procedure. The user can continue with the procedure, however, they will have entered incorrect data at an earlier point.

## FACTOR OF THE NETWORKED ENVIRONMENT

Norman's taxonomy of error was created before the advent of the networked environment. Before the introduction of local area networks and the widespread adoption of the Internet, the paradigm for most users was the stand-alone personal computer. In the stand-alone environment, the user is in control of all of the computer equipment. If there is either a hardware crash, or the user makes an error, the user has full control over the situation. The only technical components involved are the user's hardware and software. Although the end user might not know the best technique for recovery, the fact remains that the end user *could* control the outcome and implement a recovery solution. In the networked environment, there are a number of factors outside the control of the end user. Even if the end user knew what was wrong, he/she might not be in a situation to do anything about it.

From the user point of view, the networked environment is quite different from the non-networked environment of stand-alone PCs. The networked environment does not provide the user with the same level of control. A PC might be connected to a local area network, which is in turn connected through an Internet service provider to the Internet. If the user is attempting to access a Web site, for example, Princeton University, that Web site also has a set of connections to the Internet. All of these hardware and software components (the local area network, the Internet service provider, the Internet, the Princeton University Web site) are outside of the user's control. If any one of these components fail, the user has no control over the situation. This is what differentiates the networked environment from the stand-alone PC environment; *the user has a lower level of control.* Because many components are outside of the end user's control, a new type of error can occur. This type of error is called a *situational error* (Lazar and Norcio, 1999b).

## SITUATIONAL ERROR

If the user attempts to access the Web site of Princeton University, most likely they will type in the correct URL of http://www.princeton.edu. If the user does not type in the URL correctly, they have probably committed one of the errors from Norman's taxonomy, described earlier in this chapter. Assuming that the user has typed in the URL correctly, he/she expects to see the Princeton University Web site come up on the screen. However, there are a number of possible events that might keep the user from seeing the Princeton University Web site. The domain name service might be set up incorrectly. The local network might not be functioning properly. The connection to the Internet service provider might be down. Princeton University might be having some technical problems. Even though the user has typed in the URL correctly, the user may not be able to access the Princeton University Web site. All of these problems are outside of the control of the user; *the user cannot do anything to remedy the situation* (Lazar and Norcio, 1999b). What could be even more confusing to the user is that the user had typed in the correct URL previously, and was able to successfully complete the task goal, and access the Princeton University Web site (Lazar and Norcio, 1999b). If the user has typed in the URL correctly, why is he not able to reach the Web site that he wants? This type of situation calls for a new classification of error. This error is called a *situational error*.

In a situational error, a user's task goal requires the use of a network resource which is not available or is not functioning properly (Lazar and Norcio, 1999b). Even if the users enter all of the commands in the appropriate manner, they are not able to reach their task goal. *A situational error is when a user's task goal requires the use of a network resource, which is not available or is not functioning properly* (Lazar and Norcio, 1999b). A situational error might occur for a number of reasons:

- There might be a problem with the connection from a user's computer to a local area network.
- There might be a problem with the connection between a local network and an Internet Service Provider.
- The domain name service might not be set up correctly, so users on a local network may not be able to access sites on the World Wide Web.
- A network resource may not be properly configured. A remote site may have failed (Johnson, 1998).

Regardless of why a situational error occurs, the fact remains that the user cannot reach the task goal, even though the user may have typed in all commands correctly.

It is important to compare the situational error to the traditional classifications of errors. A situational error cannot be considered a slip. Since the user does not carry out the commands incorrectly, a situational error is not a slip. Furthermore, since the user has chosen the correct commands to reach his goals, a situational error is not a mistake. In mistakes and slips, it is assumed that the user caused an error. However, there is no classification for a situation where a user selected the correct commands, and entered the commands in the correct manner, but was still not able to attain the goal. Other error classification schema have been presented in the literature, but they, too, do not address these situational errors (Zapf et al., 1992).

How is it possible to assist end users in responding to errors (both traditional and situational)? There are generally two approaches to assisting end users with errors. These two approaches are *system design* and *training design* (Lazar and Norcio, 1999b).

## SYSTEM DESIGN FOR END-USER ERROR

Computer systems should be designed in a way that they assist the users in responding to errors. Although it might be virtually impossible to eliminate errors altogether, systems can be designed to minimize many user errors (Lewis and Norman, 1986). In his book, *The Psychology of Everyday Things*, Donald Norman discusses three goals for system design related to error:

- Minimize the causes of error
- Make it possible to reverse actions easily and make it hard to perform actions that cannot be reversed
- Make it easy to discover errors when they occur, and make it easy to correct the errors (Norman, 1988).

## MINIMIZING CAUSES OF ERROR

Many times, systems are not designed to minimize error. There are many different approaches to minimizing error. The type of interface mode can affect the probability for end-user error. For instance, if users have only five or six possible choices to make, a menu might be an appropriate interface choice. By using a menu, the possibilities for user error are limited. If a command language is used, there is an increased chance for the user to make an error (Turban, 1995). With a command language, there are thousands of possible commands for the user to choose from. A command language can be confusing to all but the most experienced user (Turban, 1995).

Regardless of what type of interface mode is chosen, it is important to perform evaluation testing with end users, possibly in the form of prototyping (Booth, 1991; Norman, 1988). By performing user testing, it is possible to learn more about the types of errors that occur (Senders and Moray, 1991). It might be possible to 'engineer-out' some of the errors. By designing a system with consideration of the errors that the user make, it might be possible to limit the number of errors that are made. However, it is not always possible to 'engineer-out' the errors from the system. In cases where it is impossible to eliminate an error-producing behavior, it is important to design the system in a way that errors are easy reversible, without causing large-scale failure (Senders and Moray, 1991).

### Reversible Actions

Since users are very likely to make errors, actions should be easily reversible (Arnold and Roe, 1987; Norman, 1983). This means that there should be an easy way that users can return their system to the last previous good state, before the erroneous action was taken (Arnold and Roe, 1987). Many interfaces provide an 'undo' feature, which can easily reverse the last action performed by the user. Some actions, such as deleting a file, might not be reversible once performed (Norman, 1983). For these irreversible actions, the system should make it harder for users to perform such actions (Norman, 1983). One way of doing this is to require confirmation of the action, or to require users to type in a special command (Norman, 1983). A good example of this is when a user posts a message to a USENET newsgroup using the PINE mail program. If a user indicates that he/she wants to post a message to a newsgroup, PINE first asks them 'Send Message?' If the user responds positively, PINE responds 'Posted message may go to thousands of readers. Really post?'. Once the user has responded yes to 'Really Post?' the message will automatically be sent to thousands of news servers, and it will be very hard to undo this action.

### Error Messages

Before a user can respond to an error, a user must be aware that an error occurred. To maximize the discovery of the error, system status information needs to be available to the user (Patrick, 1987). The sooner a user is aware of an error, the sooner it can be corrected (Lazonder and Meij, 1995). If users are not immediately aware of an error, the error can be compounded over time, into a larger error which is harder to recover from (Carroll and Carrithers, 1984; Carroll and Mack, 1984). This is especially true for end users, who rely on error messages to determine that something could be wrong (DuBoulay and Matthew, 1984). How should an error message attract the attention of the user? Lazonder and Meij emphasize the location of the error message. If an error message is displayed in a dialog box superimposed on the center of the active screen, users will be likely to notice it (Lazonder and Meij, 1995). If an error message is displayed in the lower right-hand corner of the screen, and no other signals (graphics, sounds, etc.) draw the user's attention to the error message, the user might not even notice the error message (Lazonder and Meij, 1995). The user cannot respond to an error when he/she does not even know that one has occurred!

As part of assisting users in recovering from errors, users must be provided with easy-to-understand error messages (Brown, 1983; Shneiderman, 1998). The goal of error messages should be to assist users in recovering from errors (Davis, 1983). If an error message is not clear, users can be confused about what the error is, and therefore, might not be sure how to respond to the error. Shneiderman found that error messages that are easier for the user to understand and interpret can result in users being better able to respond appropriately to errors (Shneiderman, 1982). He suggests that error messages should:

- be specific
- be positive
- tell users what to do to respond to the error (Shneiderman, 1998).

Arnold and Roe go one step further, by encouraging system designers to not just tell the users what to do, but to give users information about the different alternatives that they have to respond to the error (Arnold and Roe, 1987). This can facilitate recovery from the error.

Although guidelines have been presented in the research literature for designing error messages, most of the guidelines are not followed. An example of a confusing error message, as described by DuBoulay and Matthew, is the error message 'fatal error in pass zero' (DuBoulay and Matthew, 1984). In their anecdotal experience with students, novice users have had trouble understanding the meaning of that message (DuBoulay and Matthew, 1984). Current error messages, such as the 'general protection fault' error message, are equally confusing. What does a 'general protection fault' mean to end users? Such a message does not communicate to end users what error actually occurred. Nor does such a message give the end user any information on what the next action should be. From the end-user point of view, a 'general protection fault' message has the same meaning as a message saying 'an error occurred.' Such a message does not provide any useful information to the end user. Error messages for networked applications (such as web browsing) are no better. Users are given error messages that say things such as 'server cannot connect' and '404: file not found.' These error messages do not communicate to the user what occurred, nor does it instruct the user on what alternatives they have to respond to the error.

To assist novice users in responding to errors in the networked environment (situational errors), more information needs to be provided to the user. What is Domain Name Service? What is a "404" error? The novice user may not know what these messages mean. Therefore, it may be necessary to provide the novice user with further information, such as a message saying 'There is an error on the network, but it is not due to your actions.' Another approach, such as 'The network is experiencing problems; please try again later' might be appropriate. This is similar to the phone company message 'All circuits are busy. Please try again later.' These error messages let the novice user know that, although they may not be immediately able to reach their task goal, that:

- This error is not their fault
- They should attempt their goal again later that day
- On their next task attempt, they can use the same strategy.

It is especially important not to give the user the 'feeling' that he has done something wrong, if indeed he has not done anything wrong. If the user feels that he has done something wrong, he may attempt a different set of actions to reach the task goal, when his original set of actions was appropriate. This can only increase the problem.

# TRAINING DESIGN

Systems should be designed to meet the needs of the end user. However, a well-designed system, without adequate training, is not sufficient. Training the end user is an important factor in the successful use of an information system (Martin et al., 1994; Whitten and Bentley, 1997). However, all training is not alike. Different training methods may present the same material using different approaches. Specifically, different training methods approach errors in a different manner.

### Traditional (Procedural) Training

Traditional training methods, also called *procedural training*, typically involve giving users a list of specific steps to follow in order to learn a task (Carroll, 1984; Santhanam and Sein, 1994; Wendel and Frese, 1987). Users are expected to follow the steps exactly (Carroll, 1984). In traditional training methodologies, users are not given any information about the structure of the system (Santhanam and Sein, 1994).

Traditional or procedural methodologies for training novice users in using computer applications tend to focus on avoiding errors (Carroll, 1990; Frese and Altmann, 1989). The assumption of these training methodologies is that users never make errors when performing tasks (Carroll, 1990). This does not realistically model the end user, since it is virtually impossible to avoid errors when learning new tasks (Arnold and Roe, 1987; Carroll, 1990; Greif and Keller, 1990; Lazonder and Meij, 1995). In fact, novice users may make errors as soon as they begin their task (Carroll and Mack, 1984). It is more realistic to assume that since all of the features of a computer system cannot be taught in training sessions, errors will occur in a workplace situation (Frese and Altmann, 1989).

Regardless of why the errors occur, the fact is that errors do occur frequently with novice users. Typically, novice users make insignificant errors, but in traditional procedural training, they are not instructed on how to recover from these errors (Carroll, 1984; Carroll, 1990; Carroll and Mack, 1984; Lazonder and Meij, 1995). Carroll and Carrithers found that a few insignificant errors may combine to form more significant errors, which frustrate users, who are not able to recover from the error sequence (Carroll and Carrithers, 1984). Due to the errors, users may not be able to reach their task goals and simply may give up. Because novice users frequently make errors, it is important to train them in appropriate responses to errors. The literature has described three different approaches to training novice users in responding to errors: error management, exploration, and conceptual models (Lazar and Norcio, 1999a).

### Error Management

When learning a new task on a computer, it is inevitable that at some point, users make mistakes. When novice users make errors, they become frustrated, and many times, they give up (Frese and Altmann, 1989; Frese et al., 1991). Error management highlights the positive aspects of errors (Frese and Altmann, 1989). For instance, novice users are provided with statements such as 'Make Errors! You can learn from your errors!' and 'I have made an error. Great!' (Frese et al., 1991; Greif and Keller, 1990). The cornerstone of error management is to train users that errors are not bad. Users are taught that errors are good, because errors are opportunities for learning (Frese and Altmann, 1989).

Another aspect of error management is making users aware of potential problem areas in a system, where errors are more likely to occur (Frese and Altmann, 1989; Frese et al., 1991). Users can receive information on what types of errors are likely to occur. Users may then pay extra attention to these areas, which might increase the likelihood that users can avoid making errors in those areas. On the other hand, if users do make errors in these areas, they are paying special attention, so they are more likely to notice the occurrence of an error. By warning users of these potential error areas, users are both less likely to make an error, and more likely to be able to respond if they do make an error. This is similar to road signs that warn drivers of road conditions ahead, such as: "bridge freezes before road surface"; "road slippery when wet"; or "sharp curves ahead".

There are other positive aspects of making errors. Errors might keep incorrect sequences from becoming automated (Frese and Altmann, 1989). By making errors, users should be able to correct their actions before a procedure becomes habitual. Users might also learn new procedures as a result of making an error (Frese et al., 1991). Also, in the real-world work environment, errors occur on a frequent basis (Frese et al., 1991). In the work environment, there is not always someone (a trainer) there to assist the user. Users should be prepared for how to handle errors when errors occur on the job.

These error management strategies assist the users in viewing errors as a learning experience and becoming less frustrated by errors (Frese and Altmann, 1989). Greif and Keller agree with this assessment, saying that '...it is important to redefine errors as learning situations for which emotional and cognitive coping strategies have to be developed' (Greif and Keller, 1990, p. 242).

## Exploration

Exploration has been defined as encountering objects and situations with a certain degree of uncertainty (Greif and Keller, 1990). Exploratory training has also been described as an inductive approach to learning tasks (Davis and Bostrom, 1993). In exploration, users are encouraged to explore their task environment (Dormann and Frese, 1994). Instead of giving users a step-by-step list of how to perform a task, a more general overview of the environment is provided (Dormann and Frese, 1994). Users are instructed in techniques for navigating through their task environment.

In traditional training, to instruct the user in moving from a home directory to the 'www' subdirectory, the user would be told to type <cd www>. In exploratory training, the user would receive a description of the <cd> command and how to implement it. The user would not, however, be told exactly what to type. The users are encouraged to attempt the correct command based on their knowledge of the command.

Carroll believes that exploration is a more appropriate methodology for training novice users, because they are not overloaded with too much information (Carroll, 1984). Furthermore, exploration more closely models how novice users naturally tend to approach new tasks (Wendel and Frese, 1987). Greif and Keller state that when interacting with a computer, users usually do not plan their actions in advance. Instead, users follow something akin to trial-and-error (Greif and Keller, 1990). Therefore, Wendel and Frese suggest modeling the training on the users' behavior, and encouraging users to explore (Wendel and Frese, 1987). Payne and Howes also note that exploration might be considered 'more fun' and less like work than procedural methods, for novice users (Howes and Payne, 1990; Payne and Howes, 1992).

With the knowledge of the structure of their task environment, users are better able to respond to errors. There are also other advantages to exploration. Through exploration, users possibly can find a better way to perform the task (Frese and

Altmann, 1989; Senders and Moray, 1991). Exploration can benefit users because it has '...the additional effect of eliciting positive emotional feelings and self-evaluations of competence and efficacy' (Greif and Keller, 1990, p.236). Users may feel more confident when they explore, allowing them to respond to errors with more confidence.

## Conceptual Models

Another method that has been presented to assist novice users in responding to errors is conceptual models (Santhanam and Sein, 1994). A conceptual model is an 'accurate, consistent and complete representation of the target system' (Staggers and Norcio, 1993, p. 588). These models are useful when teaching human users about computer systems (Norman, 1987; Staggers and Norcio, 1993). A conceptual model of a computer system could consist of a basic description of the components of a computer system, along with how those components work together (Santhanam and Sein, 1994). The human users, when given a conceptual model, compare it to what is happening in their world (Staggers and Norcio, 1993).

There are two types of conceptual models: *analog* and *abstract* models (Santhanam and Sein, 1994). An analog conceptual model compares the target system (the system that the user is learning about) to another type of system (Santhanam and Sein, 1994). For instance, a computer network could be compared to a system with two cans and a string. An abstract conceptual model describes a system using charts, diagrams, and mathematical expressions (Santhanam and Sein, 1994). Sein et. al. found that abstract conceptual models were more effective than analog conceptual models in training users (Sein, Bostrom and Olfman, 1987). In a study of subjects learning to use an electronic mail package, subjects who received conceptual models had a higher level of performance than subjects who received procedural training, although the difference was not statistically significant (Santhanam and Sein, 1994). In the commentary on their experiment, Santhanam and Sein note that conceptual models might be helpful in explaining errors to users (Santhanam and Sein, 1994).

## Error Training

A combination of techniques, called 'Error Training,' has been presented in the literature (Dormann and Frese, 1994; Frese et al., 1991; Nordstrom, Wendland and Williams, 1998). Although Frese et al., Dormann and Frese, and Nordstrom, Wendland, and Williams present error training as one training method, it is actually a combination of two different training approaches — *error management* and *exploration*. There are currently three published studies on the effects of error training. These studies are the Frese et al. (1991) study, the Dormann and Frese (1994) study, and the Nordstrom, Wendland, and Williams (1998) study. The 1991 and 1998 studies focused on the task environment of word processing, and the 1994 study focused on the task environment of statistical software. In all three of these studies, subjects who received error training had higher levels of performance than those who received traditional training. In addition, satisfaction levels were measured in the 1991 and 1998 studies, and in both studies, subjects who received error training were more satisfied with their experiences than subjects who received traditional training.

Error training is the combination of two other training methods—error management and exploration. Although the experimental effects of error management alone are unknown, there are studies published on exploration, and researchers found that users preferred using the exploratory approach (Carroll and Mack, 1984; Carroll and Mazur, 1986). It is important to note that there has also been related work done on user manuals using the exploratory approach (Carroll, 1984; Carroll, 1990; Wendel and Frese, 1987).

### Training Methods in the Networked Environment

Since errors occur more frequently in the networked environment, it is important to learn more about how successful the different training methods are in network-based applications (such as Web browsing, groupware, and e-mail). We recently completed an experiment on training methods for Web browsing. This experiment involved over 250 subjects. Although we are still in the process of completing the data analysis and writing up the results, we can present a preliminary finding here. In the experiment, we found that exploration was the most appropriate training method for training end users in Web browsing. Subjects who received exploratory training had the highest level of performance on a set of tasks.

The research on training methods for networked software applications needs to be increased. For example, it would be useful to learn which training methods are most appropriate for other task applications in the networked environment, such as e-mail and groupware. It is possible that in the future, all applications will be 'networked applications.' With each new release of word processing, spreadsheet, and database applications, these applications are becoming more intertwined with the Internet. In the future, it may be that software applications that are stand-alone are a rarity. Indeed, in the future, all software applications might be networked applications.

# LACK OF ATTENTION TO SYSTEM DESIGN AND TRAINING DESIGN

Frequently, concerns related to system design and training design for end-user error are not addressed. Many times, systems are designed with the necessary functionality, but system designers ignore the needs of the end user (Goodwin, 1987). However, usability should be a central consideration in system design (Preece, 1990). In some cases, the interface design is a last-minute consideration—an afterthought. This is a mistake, since to the user, the interface *is* the system. If a system is poorly designed for the end user, appropriate and sufficient training might help make up for the system.

Unfortunately, training is frequently lacking. In many situations, training is a 'less-visible' expense (United States General Accounting Office, 1998). When training budgets are cut, the effects are not immediately as obvious. It is obvious that you cannot provide an e-mail system without hardware, software, and network wiring. However, the absence of end-user training will not be as immediately obvious. Even when training is provided, many times, it does not address user error (Lazar and Norcio, 1999a). Training, and specifically, training that meets the needs of the end user, is necessary to ensure the successful use of technology by the end user.

Paying attention to errors may cost more in the system development life cycle, as well as increase the costs of end-user training. However, if attention is not paid to errors in the system and training design, the end users will wind up being less productive. Errors decrease productivity because users spend a large amount of time trying to recover from them (Carroll and Carrithers, 1984). The end users will wind up being less productive and less satisfied. It is also possible that the end users will overtax the resources of the information technology support staff (usually at a 'help desk') that is assigned to assist the end users. End-user error must be addressed, as it is an important factor in the successful use of an information system.

## CONCLUSION

End-user error is a persistent problem that requires attention. It is important to understand what types of errors can occur. With this understanding, systems can be designed to assist the end user with error. But designing the system is only the beginning. Training can help end users understand why errors occur, and help them learn to respond to errors effectively. With the increasing use of the Internet, new types of errors which are beyond the control of the user can occur. Users need to be made aware of these situational errors, and error messages need to be better designed to assist the user with situational errors.

## REFERENCES

Arnold, B., and Roe, R. (1987). User errors in human-computer interaction. In M. Frese, E. Ulich, and W. Dzida (Eds.), *Human computer interaction in the workplace* (203-220). Amsterdam: Elsevier Science Publishers.

Booth, P. (1991). Errors and theory in human-computer interaction. *Acta Psychologica*, 78(1/3), 69-96.

Brown, P. (1983). Error messages: The neglected area of the man/machine interface. *Communications of the ACM*, 26(4), 246-249.

Carroll, J. (1984). *Minimalist design for active users.* Proceedings of the Human-Computer Interaction- INTERACT '84, 39-44.

Carroll, J. (1990). *The nurnberg funnel: Designing minimalist instruction for practical computer skill*. Cambridge, Massachusetts: MIT Press.

Carroll, J., and Carrithers, C. (1984). Training wheels in a user interface. *Communications of the ACM*, 27(8), 800-806.

Carroll, J., and Mack, R. (1984). Learning to use a word processor: By doing, by thinking, and by knowing. In J. Thomas, and M. Schneider (Eds.), *Human Factors in Computer Systems* (13-51). Norwood, N.J.: Ablex Publishing.

Carroll, J., and Mazur, S. (1986). LisaLearning. *IEEE Computer*, 19(11), 35-49.

Davis, R. (1983). User error or computer error? Observations on a statistics package. *International Journal of Man-Machine Studies*, 19(4), 359-376.

Davis, S., and Bostrom, R. (1993). Training end users: An experimental investigation of the roles of the computer interface and training methods. *MIS Quarterly, 17*(1), 61-85.

Dix, A., Finlay, J., Abowd, G., and Beale, R. (1998). *Human-Computer Interaction.* (2nd ed.). London: Prentice Hall England.

Dormann, T., and Frese, M. (1994). Error training: Replication and the function of exploratory behavior. *International Journal of Human-Computer Interaction, 6*(4), 365-372.

DuBoulay, B., and Matthew, I. (1984). Fatal error in pass zero: How not to confuse novices. *Behaviour and Information Technology, 3*(2), 109-118.

Frese, M., and Altmann, A. (1989). The treatment of errors in learning and training. In L. Bainbridge, and S. Quintanilla (Eds.), *Developing skills with information technology* (65-86). Chichester, England: John Wiley & Sons.

Frese, M., Brodbeck, F., Heinbokel, T., Mooser, C., Schleiffenbaum, E., and Thiemann, P. (1991). Errors in training computer skills: On the positive function of errors. *Human-Computer Interaction, 6*(1), 77-93.

Goodwin, N. (1987). Functionality and usability. *Communications of the ACM, 30*(3), 229-233.

Greif, S., and Keller, H. (1990). Innovation and the design of work and learning environments: The concept of exploration in human-computer interaction. In M. West, and J. Farr (Eds.), *Innovation and creativity at work: Psychological and organizational strategies* (231-249). Chichester, England: John Wiley & Sons.

Howes, A., and Payne, S. (1990). *Supporting exploratory learning.* Proceedings of the Human-Computer Interaction - INTERACT '90, 881-885.

Johnson, C. (1998). Electronic gridlock, information saturation, and the unpredictability of information retrieval over the world wide web. In P. Palanque, and F. Paterno (Eds.), *Formal Methods in Human-Computer Interaction* (261-282). London: Springer.

Lazar, J., and Norcio, A. (1999a). *A Framework for Training Novice Users in Appropriate Responses to Errors.* Proceedings of the International Association for Computer Information Systems 1999 Conference,128-134.

Lazar, J., and Norcio, A. (1999b). *To Err Or Not To Err, That Is The Question: Novice User Perception of Errors While Surfing The Web.* Proceedings of the Information Resource Management Association 1999 International Conference, 321-325.

Lazonder, A., and Meij, H. (1995). Error-information in tutorial documentation: Supporting users' errors to facilitate initial skill learning. *International Journal of Human-Computer Studies, 42*(2), 185-206.

Lewis, C., and Norman, D. (1986). Designing for error. In D. Norman, and S. Draper (Eds.), *User-centered system design* (411-432). Hillsdale, NJ: Lawrence Erlbaum Associates.

Martin, E., DeHayes, D., Hoffer, J., and Perkins, W. (1994). *Managing information technology: What managers need to know.* New York: Macmillan Publishing Company.

Nordstrom, C., Wendland, D., and Williams, K. (1998). To err is human: An examination of the effectiveness of error management training. *Journal of Business and Psychology, 12*(3), 269-282.

Norman, D. (1983). Design rules based on analyses of human error. *Communications of the ACM, 26*(4), 254-258.

Norman, D. (1987). Some observations on mental models. In R. Baecker, and W. Buxton (Eds.), *Readings in human-computer interaction: A multidisciplinary approach* (241-244). San Mateo, California: Morgan Kaufmann Publishers.

Norman, D. (1988). *The psychology of everyday things*: Harper Collins Publishers.

Patrick, J. (1987). Information at the human-machine interface. In J. Rasmussen,K. Duncan, and J. Leplat (Eds.), *New technology and human error* (341-345). Chichester, England: John Wiley & Sons.

Payne, S., and Howes, A. (1992). A task-action trace for explanatory learners. *Behaviour and Information Technology, 11*(2), 63-70.

Preece, J. (1990). *A Guide to Usability*. Milton Keynes, England: The Open University.

Preece, J., Rogers, Y., Sharp, H., Benyon, D., Holland, S., and Carey, T. (1994). *Human-Computer Interaction*. Wokingham, England: Addison Wesley Publishing.

Santhanam, R., and Sein, M. (1994). Improving end-user proficiency: Effects of conceptual training and nature of interaction. *Information Systems Research, 5*(4), 378-399.

Sein, M., Bostrom, R., and Olfman, L. (1987). *Conceptual models in training novice users.* Proceedings of the Human-Computer Interaction- INTERACT '87, 861-867.

Senders, J., and Moray, N. (1991). *Human Error: Cause, Prediction, and Reduction.* Hillsdale, N. J.: Lawrence Erlbaum Associates.

Shneiderman, B. (1982). System message design: Guidelines and experimental results. In A. Badre, and B. Shneiderman (Eds.), *Directions in Human/Computer Interaction* (55-78). Norwood, N.J.: Ablex Publishing.

Shneiderman, B. (1998). *Designing the User Interface: Strategies for Effective Human-Computer Interaction.* (3rd ed.). Reading, Masssachusetts: Addison-Wesley.

Staggers, N., and Norcio, A. (1993). Mental models: Concepts for human-computer interaction research. *International Journal of Man-Machine Studies, 38*(4), 587-605.

Turban, E. (1995). *Decision Support and Expert Systems: Management Support Systems.* Englewood Cliffs, NJ: Prentice-Hall.

United States General Accounting Office. (1998). *School technology: Five school districts' experiences in funding technology programs* (GAO/HEHS-98-35). Washington, D.C.: United States General Accounting Office.

Wendel, R., and Frese, M. (1987). *Developing exploratory strategies in training: The general approach and a specific example for manual use.* Proceedings of the Human-Computer Interaction- INTERACT '87, 943-948.

Whitten, I., and Bentley, L. (1997). *Systems Analysis and Design Methods.* Boston: Irwin McGraw-Hill.

Zapf, D., Brodbeck, F., Frese, M., Peters, H., and Prumper, J. (1992). Errors in working with office computers: A first validation of a taxonomy for observed errors in a field setting. *International Journal of Human-Computer Interaction, 4*(4), 311-339.

# Chapter VI

# Evaluating the Effectiveness of Web Sites

Ruth V. Small
Syracuse University

Marilyn P. Arnone
Creative Media Solutions, Inc.

As millions of people "search-and-surf " the Internet, seeking needed products and services or just exploring to see "what's out there," businesses are concerned that their Web sites will: (1) attract both searchers and surfers, (2) interest them long enough to thoroughly explore the site, (3) motivate them to purchase their product or service, and (4) encourage them to return to the site and/or recommend the site to others. As the number of commercial Web sites continues to grow at an explosive rate, this competitive market requires effective interface design guidelines and evaluation criteria.

Although there are a number of resources that provide guidance on the structure and content of Web interfaces, they typically focus on content. Some focus heavily on content and validity issues (Does it have the right information?), while others focus on functionality issues (Does it work the way it is supposed to?). Few have a theoretical foundation, offer diagnostic methods for assessing and interpreting results, and provide detailed feedback for improvement. Furthermore, few, if any, emphasize the *motivational* aspects of Web sites, i.e., those features that stimulate curiosity and engage the user's interest, while providing relevant content and an easy-to-use interface. These features help to motivate customers to visit, explore, and return to a Web site.

As businesses spend more and more money and effort designing commercial Web sites, the issue of motivational quality becomes critical. While the number of companies offering Web evaluation services continues to grow, most of those services involve an expert or experts assessing the quality of the Web site and offering ways to improve it, largely from a marketing perspective. A need for tools that allow businesses to assess motivational quality *from the user's perspective* becomes paramount. In response to this need, the Web site Motivational Analysis

Checklist for Business (a.k.a. WebMAC Business)© was developed to help diag-
nose, analyze, and assess the motivational quality of Web sites.

This chapter specifies essential criteria that can be used by: (1) Web designers
as guidelines for creating motivating Web sites and (2) businesses interested in
evaluating their existing Web sites. It also provides detailed descriptions of
WebMAC Business and related instruments.

# ESSENTIAL CRITERIA FOR EFFECTIVE WEB RESOURCES

Because of their dynamic, interactive nature, networked electronic information resources like Web sites require different criteria for evaluation than other
types of media, such as print or video. There are two general categories of criteria
that are essential for Web sites. They are *critical content* and *motivational quality*. Let's
begin by taking a look at those features that address critical content.

## Critical Content

Critical content criteria may be thought of as the "bottom-line" elements of
Web site evaluation; i.e., the overall content must be both *valid* and *appropriate* for
the intended audience (Small & Arnone, 1999). Validity refers to the credibility of
the information, the site authors, the site sponsors, the accuracy of the content, etc.
Appropriateness addresses issues such as whether the content is on the specifically
desired topic, the level of background knowledge required, etc. If either of these
characteristics is absent, the user will likely not spend much time at the Web site.
Therefore, content is the first concern that must be addressed in evaluating a Web
site.

In addition, there are a number of content features that characterize the
relevance of a Web site, i.e., information and interface characteristics of the site.
Schamber (1993), synthesizing and building on the work of Taylor (1986) and others
in the information science literature, describes several content-related features that
affect the relevance of documents within a system, many of which are also likely to
have a direct or indirect impact on the motivational quality of a Web site. Some of
these content-related features are:

- logical organization of information;
- accuracy of information contained within the Web site
- ease of intellectual access to information within the Web site;
- clarity of directions on how to use the Web site;
- interesting and useful information;
- current, up-to-date information contained within the Web site
- credibility of information contained within the Web site and related links
- appropriate type, amount and difficulty level of information.
- an interface that provides both help and orientation;

Although these are important criteria for assessing a Web site, focusing on the
site's content fulfills only part of what is necessary for effective Web sites. Now let's
take a look at the other half of the essential criteria equation—motivational quality.

## Motivational Quality

Motivation in a Web environment answers the "why" questions of Web behavior—why a user chooses a specific site to explore, why the user chooses to spend time at a site, and why a user revisits a particular site. A Web site's motivational quality, therefore, becomes an essential factor because it influences whether a user will be attracted to and engaged in a site.

Motivational quality includes those Web features that make a site attractive and interesting. Some features that contribute to making a site attractive and interesting are:

- aesthetically pleasing background and colors
- eye-catching title and/or visual on the homepage.
- variety of formats (e.g., text, visuals, audio)

Motivational quality also incorporates functionality features, i.e., those features that affect access and performance. In a Web environment, functionality describes the technical aspects that cause various functions within the Web site to work the way they should, facilitating navigability, such as:

- a menu or site map
- a help function
- active links

Functionality has a direct impact on customer motivation because when one or more of these features malfunctions, the customer is likely to become frustrated and leave the site, possibly never to return. This explains why some current Web evaluation instruments appear to emphasize functionality of a Web site (e.g., Caywood, 1997).

Taylor (1986), in his Value-Added Model for information systems, describes several functionality-related issues that we believe directly affect a user's motivation to visit and spend time at a Web site. They include:

- ease of physical access to the Web site;
- linkage (e.g., to other relevant Web sites);
- browsing capability (e.g., ability to explore information within a Web site);
- consistent, standardized format (e.g., navigation buttons maintain consistent shape and location);
- response speed (e.g., use of quickly loadable graphics);
- selectivity (e.g., user control of where to go and what information to access);
- variety of access points to information (ability to access information in more than one way and from various points in the system).

# THE WEB SITE MOTIVATIONAL ANALYSIS CHECKLIST

The original *Website Motivational Analysis Checklist©*, better known as *WebMAC*, was initially developed for the business context in 1997 (Small, 1997). The instrument was soon adapted for use in education for teachers: (1) to evaluate the Web sites they use in their instruction and (2) to teach children to evaluate the Web sites they used in homework and research. There are currently several *WebMAC* instruments designed for use in different contexts for different purposes by different populations.

The *WebMAC* instruments differ from other instruments.

1. They are intended to identify areas for improvement of an existing Web site and/or to provide guidance for the development of a new Web site.
2. They focus on motivational quality but also include functionality- and content-related items framed in terms of their effect on motivation.
3. While most other instruments are expert-centered, they are user-centered, i.e. intended to provide feedback from actual potential users of the Web site.
4. They were founded on a well-known motivation theory applied to the Web environment.
5. They focus on motivational issues from an information perspective.
6. They use a research approach and have been tested and validated.
7. They incorporate a variety of methods for analysis and interpretive feedback.
8. They allow feedback for improvement from multiple viewpoints (Nielsen, 1994).

## WEBMAC'S THEORETICAL FRAMEWORK

Expectancy-value (E-V) theory (also referred to as expectancy-valence theory or expectation theory) helps define individual motivation (Vroom, 1964); i.e., E-V theory attempts to explain why a person chooses to expend effort on certain tasks or activities rather than others, and proposes that motivation occurs only when a person both values and is successful at a given task or activity. As Brophy explains, "People do not willingly invest effort in tasks that they do not enjoy and that do not lead to valued outcomes even if they know that they can perform the tasks successfully. Nor do they willingly invest effort in even highly valued tasks if they believe that they cannot succeed on those tasks no matter how hard they try (1998, p. 15).

Until recently, the application of E-V theory has been largely confined to the workplace environment, i.e., focusing on ways to increase the level, amount, and quality of production, using output as a measure of motivation (e.g. Ferris, 1977). E-V theory has also been applied to the classroom to explain student motivation (e.g. Keller, 1983). More recently, researchers have applied this theory to a variety of electronic environments, focusing on ways to promote the motivation to use a particular information system, using engagement and satisfaction as a measure of motivation. For example, a study by Burton, Chen, Grover, and Stewart (1992-93) strongly supports E-V's appropriateness for assessing the motivation to use an expert system. Snead and Harrell (1995) and DeSanctis (1981) found the theory appropriate for evaluating the motivation to use a decision support system.

Expectancy-value theory may also be useful for understanding motivation in a Web environment, i.e., why a person visits a Web site, explores the Web site, and returns to that Web site (Small & Arnone, 1999). Expressed in E-V theory terms, the site must have value and promote positive expectancies for successful use. E-V theory, therefore, forms the theoretical foundation for assessing motivational quality with the *WebMAC* instruments.

## WEBMAC BUSINESS

The *Website Motivational Analysis Checklist for Business (WebMAC Business)* is designed for commercial Web site owners to obtain feedback on the effectiveness of their sites. An evaluation instrument, administration directions, scoring guidelines, and analysis charts have been developed to provide the most complete picture of the site assessment.

Before using the instrument, the evaluator is encouraged to spend some time exploring the targeted Web site in order to have some familiarity with its content and structure before completing *WebMAC Business*'s 32-item Likert-type scale. On the *WebMAC Business* Scoring Sheet, the evaluator records his/her agreement ratings for each item on a four-point scale from 0 (strongly disagree) to 3 (strongly agree). The instrument also allows the scorer to use the designation N/A (not applicable) when a feature is not present at the Web site. Later, the user will be asked to assign a specific score to each "N/A" item after determining whether the site would have benefited from the missing feature, didn't require it, or was better off without it. Sixteen items are related to each of the E-V components: *Value* and *Expectation for Success*.

## WHAT ABOUT CRITICAL CONTENT AND FUNCTIONALITY?

The *WebMAC* instruments incorporate items that address both critical content and functionality issues, but they, too, are framed in terms of motivational quality. Some examples of specific content-related items from *WebMAC Business* are:

- The information contained in this Web site is current and up-to-date.
- All of the information at this Web site is presented using clear and consistent language and style.

In motivational terms, the first item relates to the *Value* dimension. Discovering the site had outdated information would be demotivating for the user who is consequently unlikely to spend much time at or return to that site. The second item might affect the *Expectation for Success* dimension. Lack of clarity and consistency causes confusion and frustration, demotivating factors that affect the site's use.

The *WebMAC* instruments also address functionality as it affects the user's motivation. Some examples of functionality-related items from *WebMAC Business* are:

- At all times, I can control what information at this Web site I wish to see.
- I can control how fast I move through this Web site at all times.

Relating these items to our theoretical foundation, user control over what information is accessed allows the user to access only that information which is useful and important to him or her. This relates to the *Value* dimension in E-V terms. Controlling the pace of moving around the site increases the user's *Expectation for Success*.

# THE FOUR ATTRIBUTES OF MOTIVATIONAL QUALITY

There are several factors that contribute to the value and expectation aspects of a Web site, which we have synthesized into four attributes (see Figure 1). Sites must provide value to a Web site by being stimulating as well as meaningful to the user. Web sites that are organized and easy-to-use promote an expectation for success. The degree to which these attributes are present in a Web site comprises its motivational quality. Let's take a look at each of the attributes as it applies to motivational quality in a Web environment.

### The Stimulating (S) Attribute

The (S) attribute emphasizes Web site features that stimulate curiosity and engage the customer's interest in the site. *Stimulating* features include mechanisms that will immediately attract the customer's attention at the homepage and engage the customer as he/she proceeds through the Web site. Some of *WebMAC's* stimulating items include:
- This Web site had unique features that made it more interesting.
- I found surprising things at this Web site.

### The Meaningful (M) Attribute

The (M) attribute emphasizes those Web site features that add value to the information presented, provide a meaningful context, and improve the usefulness of the site to the customer. Some meaningful items are:
- The purpose of this Web site was always clear to me.
- All visual information (e.g. videos, photographs) included in this Web site is relevant to the topic covered.

### The Organized (O) Attribute

The (O) attribute emphasizes features that provide a logical overall structure and sequence. OE features include ease-of-use and build customers' confidence in

*Figure 1: Attributes That Contribute to Value and Expectation for Success in a Web Environment.*

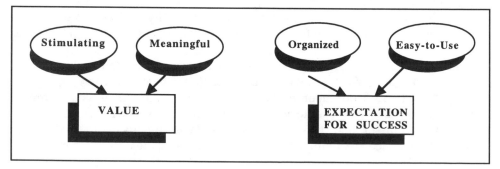

their ability to successfully access needed information or browse through the site easily and quickly. Examples of *WebMAC*'s organized items include:

- This Web site is logically organized.
- No matter where I am in this Web site I can return to the home page or exit.

### The Easy-to-Use (E) Attribute

The (E) attribute emphasizes those features that affect customers' navigation of the site. A site that is easy-to-use is more likely to stimulate longer visits and return visits. Some examples of items that are easy-to-use are:

- Navigating this Web site does not require any special skills or experience.
- At all times, I can control what information at this Web site I wish to see.

After rating all of the *WebMAC Business* items, the evaluator transfers each score into one of four columns (one for each of the *WebMAC* attributes). Each column is then totalled, and total scores for each attribute are recorded on the *WebMAC* Scoring Sheet, allowing the evaluator to compare numerical scores on each of the four attributes. A score of less than 20 indicates a need to improve the motivational quality of that attribute. The evaluator may wish to plot total scores for the four attributes on the *WebMAC Business* line graph (not shown) for a quick visual assessment of specific strengths and weaknesses of the site.

The *WebMAC* Scoring Grid allows the evaluator to combine the (S) and (M) scores into one Value (V) score and the (O) and (E) scores into one Expectation for Success (EX) score. These two scores and their midpoint are then plotted on a grid (see Figure 2). The midpoint falls into one of four quadrants. Each quadrant corresponds to an overall assessment for the Web site. High scores on both (V) and (EX) earn an "Awesome Web Site" rating.

If the overall score or any of the sub-scores is lower than the site owner wants, there is an opportunity to use scoring information to make specific changes and modifications on the site. An item analysis procedure may be used to pinpoint any trouble spots and identify features that may have to be added or enhanced.

## TESTING AND VALIDATION

Testing and validation of the *WebMAC* instrument was conducted over a two-year period (1997-1998). *WebMAC* has been tested with both young children, undergraduate students and adults. A group of 23 graduate students was asked to independently evaluate an assigned commercial Web site using the original 60-item *WebMAC* that included an open-ended question that solicited suggestions for improvement. Items were randomly ordered to prevent clustering and categorization. Analysis focused on the distribution of scores for each question, represented by histograms. Items with a wide spread of scores (standard deviation of 1.00+) were either revised or eliminated. The results were used to test reliability and to identify ways to improve the instrument.

A second test was performed to gather information concerning the understandability and redundancy of the instrument. Researchers individually observed eight graduate students as they evaluated one of two pre-selected Web sites (one

Figure 2

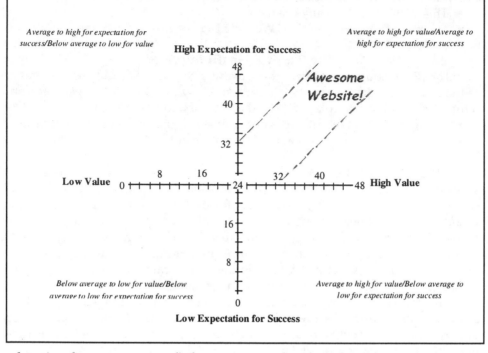

educational, one commercial) that were considered moderately motivating. Students were asked to use the instrument to evaluate several Web sites and provide the authors with feedback on each item and on the usefulness of the instrument. This test identified redundant and ambiguous questions, and provided feedback as to the organization and length of the instrument.

Pilot testing resulted in several changes to the original instrument. The yes-no scale was changed to a Likert-type scale to more precisely reflect the evaluator's rating. An item analysis revealed problematic items; items that were considered vague or poorly worded were modified and irrelevant or redundant items were eliminated entirely. Additional testing of the instrument was conducted with 26 graduate and undergraduate students during the spring and summer of 1998 using a Web site related to a children's television show.

During the initial testing and validation of *WebMAC*, some interesting findings deserve mention. In general, research participants spent only 5-10 minutes exploring the Web site before using the instrument, even though they were told they could spend longer (up to 20 minutes) reviewing the site. In addition, as they began to complete *WebMAC*, participants tended to stay on the homepage to evaluate as many items as possible, only navigating other pages when they could not find a particular feature on the homepage. Participants with more experience exploring and using the Web tended to spend more time overall than novices completing the evaluation. All of these findings suggest that Web site visitors make a determination as to its quality and usefulness very quickly and usually focus on the homepage to give them a quick assessment of the quality of the site. Thus, careful consideration of the design and functionality of the homepage becomes essential.

Additional testing for validity and reliability of the instrument was conducted in the spring of 1999 with approximately 220 college students at a major northeastern university to determine the strength of the theoretical foundation, to determine if the length of the instrument should be decreased and to identify which items might be discarded. Subjects were required to visit the CNN Web site (a rich and multifaceted site) and evaluate it using the instrument. Factor analysis identified those items that clustered most strongly and related items. As a result, the final version of *WebMAC Business* contains 32 items, 16 *Value* (S & M) items and 16 *Expectation for Success* (O & E) items.

## OTHER WEBMAC INSTRUMENTS

*WebMAC Business* is one of seven instruments developed using the *WebMAC* theoretical and conceptual framework. Four instruments were designed for children, including *WebMAC Investigator* and *WebMAC Junior* for very young children, and *WebMAC Middle* and *WebMAC Senior* for children of middle and high school age. *WebMAC Professional* was designed for professional educators to use to determine the motivational quality of Web sites they may be considering for use in their instruction, for research purposes, or as a set of guidelines for Web site design. A companion instrument, the Content Validity Scale, was also developed for educators to determine whether a Web site's critical content is both valid and appropriate for use in a teaching and learning context. *WebMAC Broadcast/Cable* allows producers of television series to assess their Web sites related to their programs.

The *WebMAC* instruments have been used for various purposes by organizations around the world. Examples of applications of the *WebMAC* instruments:
- evaluation of a federally-funded agricultural project Web site
- evaluation of an award-winning nationally televised children's program's Web site
- evaluation of U.S. Department of Education Web sites
- evaluation of science-related Web sites for a museum project
- workshops for college faculty
- courses for graduate students
- assessment of Web-based distance learning courses in Brazil

Although any of the *WebMAC* instruments may be used by an individual or a group, the authors are continuing to provide value-added services to businesses wishing to have objective evaluations of their Web sites. Development is in progress for an automated system for collecting evaluative data on educational and children's Web sites for businesses (the children's television industry, companies who produce educational materials, etc.) who target that audience. Data are collected from content experts, Web designers and target users. This system provides detailed feedback to clients on the overall assessment of their Web site and specific ways to improve it.

## CONCLUSIONS

Businesses that depend on their Web sites to generate business and market products or services must be concerned with the motivational quality of those Web sites. This article describes the theoretical foundation, organization, and testing of an easy-to-use, 32-item diagnostic instrument for evaluating Web sites. *The Website Motivational Analysis Checklist (WebMAC)* focuses on the motivational quality of Web sites, i.e., those features that cause the visitor to come to the site, explore the site, revisit the site, and recommend the site to others. Motivational features are defined in relation to expectation-value theory and four general attributes: stimulating, meaningful, organized, and easy-to-use.

Businesses expect their Web site to attract both first customers and return customers. A high motivational quality rating of that Web site becomes an essential goal for achieving that purpose. *WebMAC* provides quick and easy recognition of areas that are strong in motivational quality and areas in need of improvement. Beyond its usefulness as an evaluation tool, *WebMAC* provides a set of guidelines for Web designers to create exciting and useful Web sites.

## REFERENCES

Brophy, J. (1998). *Motivating Students to Learn*. Boston, MA: McGraw Hill.

Burton, F.G., Chen, Y., Grover, V. and Stewart, K.A. (1992-3, Winter). An application of expectation theory for assessing user motivation to utilize an expert system. *Journal of Management Information systems, 9* (3), 183-198.

Ferris, K.R. (1977, July). A test of the expectation theory of motivation in an accounting environment. *The Accounting Review, 52* (3), 605-615.

Keller, J.M. (1983). Motivational design of instruction. In C.M. Reigeluth (Ed.). *Instructional Design Theories and Models: An Overview of Their Current Status.* Hillsdale, NJ: Erlbaum, 383-434.

Nielsen, J. (1994). Heuristic evaluation. In J. Nielsen and R.L. Mack (Eds.). *Usability Inspection Methods.* New York: John Wiley & Sons.

Schamber, L. (1994). Relevance and information behavior. In M.E. Williams (Ed.). *Annual Review of Information Science and Technology*, Medford, NJ: Learned Information, Inc.

Small, R.V. (1997, Fall*). Assessing the Motivational Quality of World Wide Web Sites.* Syracuse, NY: ERIC Clearinghouse on Information & Technology, ED Document #407930.

Small, R.V. and Arnone, M.P. (1999). "Assessing the Motivational Quality of Web Sites." In Mehdi Khosrowpour (Ed.). *Managing Information Technology Resources in Organizations in the Next Millenium." Proceedings of the 1999 Information Resources Management Association International Conference*, Hershey, PA, May 16-19, 1999, 1000-1003.

Small, R.V. and Arnone, M.P. (1998*) Website Motivational Analysis Checklist for Business (WebMAC Business).* The Motivation Mining Company: Fayetteville, NY.

Snead, K.C., Jr. and Harrell, A.M. (1995). An application of expectation theory to explain a manager's intention to use a decision support system. *Decision Sciences,* 25 (4), 499-513.

Taylor, R.S. (1986). *Value-Added Processes in Information Systems.* Norwood, NJ: Ablex.

Vroom, V. H. (1964). *Work and Motivation.* New York: Wiley.

## Chapter VII

# Vulnerability and the Aware IS Practitioner: A Reflective Discourse on Unfinished Business

Simon Bell
Open University, UK

Information technology (IT) projects regularly fail. IT projects fail rapidly, spectacularly and with monotonous regularity. IT and related information systems (IS) projects seem more prone than other technology-based interventions to prove to be enormously risky ventures for companies and government agencies to invest in. If this phenomenon is pronounced in so-called industrialised economies - the issues and problems around failure multiply when such projects are undertaken in transitional and developing economies.

In all this failure the role of the IS practitioner appears invidious. On the one hand there are rapidly developing technologies and opportunities for change while on the other there are organisations often unable to express what change they desire or to articulate the difference between what they would like and what they feel able to cope with. It is little wonder that the IS practitioner—given the responsibility to manage the change process by analysis and design and other mediating strategies, can end up as the victim of technology failure, organisational inability to make up its mind and half-developed applications.

In all this muddle the role of the action researcher (AR)—deeply involved with the processes and relationships within the research context is oddly empowered to deal with change while appearing even more vulnerable than his or her more managerialist or technologist colleagues.

This chapter, by means of a reflective discourse representing my own learning, attempts to develop the theme of the vulnerability and power of the action research IS practitioner. Using current case study material drawn from working in transitional economies, the chapter indicates lessons learned in the value of the AR approach to analysis and design and the real benefits and powers which can arise from vulnerability such as autonomy and viability.

A key lesson in my own learning will probably appear to be very simple to the reader. The lesson is that articles and chapters and books which academics write are always the summation of all that has gone before, plus the development from this basis and the inclusion of something new (we hope). We carry our intellectual baggage with us into new situations and so, to some extent what we write later in our careers always builds upon and extends (and sometimes, in courageous cases refutes) earlier arguments. This essay is no exception to the rule. In what follows I develop ideas which germinated years ago in my academic and practitioner initiation into information systems and have been reflected upon in years of applying systems analysis to information systems contexts. This has involved learning from where I have been and the mistakes and insights I have made or have been gifted by the teams and stakeholders I have been privileged to work with. Further, I draw out what I feel are some fairly humanising elements latent within my experience of what works and what does not work in IS development.

The following chapter develops along the lines set out in the box below—and these themes are then used in the chapter as the section headings to the reflective discourse which I am constantly having with myself. Initially I began by writing this essay as a conventional academic chapter but I was troubled by the format— the content did not seem to fit. I wanted the essay's format to be a suitable receptacle for what is after all a developing and as yet unfinished discussion resulting from reflection on practice (an activity which has developed for me from a range of sources but the main influences to date are as follows: de Chardin, 1961; Russell, 1986; Briggs, Myers, Kirby et al., 1994; Horney, 1994; Dryden, 1996; Flood, Weil et al., 1997; Wilby, 1997; Esperjo and Stewart, 1998; *Systems Thinker Newsletter*, 1998; Moon, 1999). The discourse structure I provide is given in total in the box below. It is intended that the essay's main discourse can be read as a few sentences—a kind of abstract. These lines are then used as section heads and developed and expanded

---

- It is generally asserted that IT is progressive and dynamic yet
- IS projects are failure prone -although definitions of failure are not uniform.
- and global variation is also evident.
- IS Practitioners
- are vulnerable within this risky world and
- to reduce this vulnerability we have methodology as a means to manage our IS projects but many conventional methodologies do not seem to be a guarantee against problems however
- it seems that useful methodology needs to braid theory and good action research practice within the framework of an inclusive approach to undertaking the IS project but
- this requires the practitioner of methodology to be actively engaged in learning and developing upon practice but
- this is not enough either - methodology needs to be implemented in such a way as to engage the users of IS but
- this means that learning, and tools for developing the means of intervention must be central elements of IS methodology.
- Or is this a partial view in need of further braiding?

---

in more conventional section contents. The device is not intended to be unconventional—I have seen it in use in the development of course material by colleagues and it seems to work in terms of engaging the reader. Rather I used it as a means to help me make sense of my reflection—holding the contents of the essay to the main themes which I wanted to talk about.

## IT IS GENERALLY ASSERTED THAT IT IS PROGRESSIVE AND DYNAMIC, YET ...

### IS projects are failure prone, although definitions of failure are not uniform

Following years of under-reporting IS project failure is now well documented (Lyytinen and Hirschheim, 1987; Lytle, 1991; Sauer, 1993; Drummond, 1996; Collins and Bicknell, 1997; White, 1997; Collins, 1998; *Computer Weekly*, 1998; Drummond, 1998; Poston, 1999). Collins and Bicknell (1997, page 21) indicate that 60% or more of IS projects are failures. Others indicate that the level of failure can be set at 80% (Korac-Boisvert and Kouzmin, 1995).

Some have tried to ascertain the reasons for such failure. In the journalistic domain Collins and Bicknell (1997) have indicated the deadly sins of IS projects which include over-ambition, the uncritical use of consultants and pride. In the academic domain Sauer (1993) has developed a model to explain the nature of some such failures (see Figures 1 and 2).

Figure 1 indicates the cycle for project success—that is, IS encouraging and supporting members of the organisation who become stakeholders and who then provide resources for the IS project endeavour.

Figure 2 shows a potential downside —where IS disappoints stakeholders

*Figure 1: Activity Diagram of the IS Project Scenario - Building from Sauer, 1993*

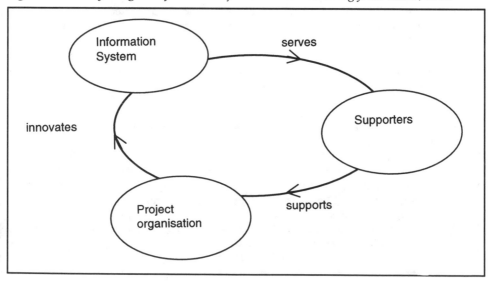

*Figure 2: Activity Diagram of the Failed IS Project Scenario (Building from Sauer, 1993).*

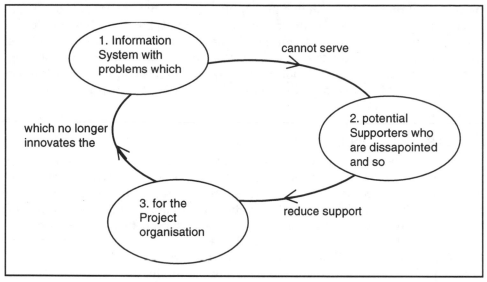

thus encouraging them to become antagonists to any new proposed IS and thus diminishing the capacity of IS projects to develop new and interesting products. A downward spiral of IS failure is the outcome.

Sauer's work indicates the potential for one of two models. But when does a positive project become a negative one? When does the positive tendency start to break down and what are the root causes? How does an IS project team know when failure will happen?

Sauer's model provides an argument to explain why some IS fail—it encourages the belief that these projects are prone to political tampering and that they fail largely due to human reactions to disappointment rather than technical issues (although such issues would be part of the overall causality behind failure). Although this argument does not hold in every case it is a useful outcome of empirical research and to some extent supports the anecdotal findings of Collins and Bignell. IS projects are risky and failure prone.

### And global variation is also evident ...

If IS projects in industrialised countries are generally a risky issue then IS projects in a global context are an immense potential problem resulting in comparatively devastating consequences due to the lack of infrastructural support around them. The literature on IS failure in developing countries (DCs) and transitional economies (TEs) also makes grim reading (e.g. see Correa, 1990; Lytle, 1991; Bell 1996; Odedra-Straub, 1996; Bell, 1998; Grundley and Heeks, 1998; Kouzmin, Korac-Kakabadse et al., 1999), and an apocryphal literature is already developing on the potential problems which the so-called year 2000 bug will cause in these contexts.

Much of the literature dealing with this area is descriptive of the ranges of failures—mirroring those described in industrialised countries but with even harsher consequences. They are also prescriptive with good advice and sound management practices for running IS projects. The fact that similar IS projects fail spectacularly in the industrialised countries where most of these authors reside has not discouraged them from offering reams of advise to practitioners in DCs. This introduces the central concern of this chapter, the victim of the de-humanising excesses of IS failure (e.g., demotion, unemployment for the employee or dismissal for the consultant, contempt, ridicule)—the IS practitioner in this risky world.

## IS PRACTITIONERS

Much of the IS-related work which I have been involved with has related to self-reflection on IS development, I have noted this process elsewhere (Bell, 1994; 1996; 1997). More recently I have come to see the position of the IS practitioner as being more than usually vulnerable to criticism and attack from a wide range of potential sources. IS practitioners are vulnerable within this risky world and projects are risky, they usually fail, and so they are expected to fail. So, practitioners are vulnerable to the slings and arrows of misfortune. In an earlier paper I commented on this (Bell, 1997) and developed a model of the format which I believed this vulnerability took. I argued that in the case of the IS practitioner three separate and linked risk-filled contexts can be assumed to be evident—the physical environment in which the IS occurs, the social context for the IS and the personal context of the practitioner her or himself (the problems are serious for a male expatriate practitioner working in developing countries such as myself—my observation is that they are compounded if the practitioner is female and or of indigenous origin). See Figure 3 and Table 1.

My concern has been to review the perceived reality experienced by IS practitioners in industrialised and developing countries and—building upon the problems of failure and the personal "bruising" which so often accompanies this—

*Figure 3: Overlapping Realities*

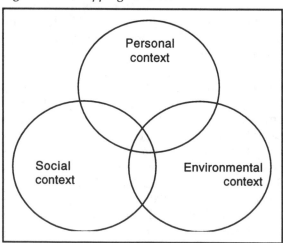

I have drawn out some of the evident problems which are experienced and resulting prizes which could be achieved if the problem is seen as an opportunity. Problems relating to personal, social and environmental context arise for all practitioners, but my experience indicates that they seem most prone to arise when there is little learning from reflection upon the contexts — when vulnerability is denied, ignored or belittled. Anecdotal examples abound — the "gung-ho" practitioner working on IS in Nigeria who — despite repeated warnings — continued to develop a system which served the interests of the donor but not the beneficiary and ended up literally smashed. The colleague who experienced severe depression and other related illness following working on several useless projects in Asia. Not to mention the queues of IS practitioners laid off from IS disasters in financial institutions, hospitals and other businesses all over the world. Vulnerability management is not as yet high up the ladder of required skills expected of IS practitioners — but it seems to be a skill required across the profession. The prizes from managing vulnerability appear most likely to arise when vulnerability is recognised, even expected and seen as being a useful and good condition — when the IS practitioner recognises the human nature of the situation in which he or she is working.

It was with these ideas about failure and vulnerability that I return to review the nature of the methodology which IS practitioners apply. For, it is the expectation of many engaged in teaching and learning IS methodology that it in some way provides insurance against failure, security against disaster and a safety blanket for the vulnerable.

**To reduce this vulnerability, we have methodology as a means to manage our IS projects, but many conventional methodologies do not seem to be a guarantee against problems however …**

In 1996 I completed a book detailing my experience of using the Multiview methodology (Avison and Wood-Harper, 1990) in several developing countries (Bell, 1996). I had selected Multiview partly on the subjective grounds that is was first introduced to me by Trevor Wood-Harper who remains a friend and inspiration and partly because it appealed to my sense of wholeness. Surely we should, as analysts (as human beings!), be able to think from multiple perspectives (involving ontological shifts) and from a variety of different epistemological bases? The result of this experience was to reflect that methodology—as it is usually applied as a form of extended method - is not enough to feel secure that the IS being developed will

*Table 1: Problems and Prizes of Vulnerability (Building from Bell, 1997)*

| Problem of non-self-reflective vulnerability | Prize of self-reflection with vulnerability |
|---|---|
| Unrealistic quality standards | Managing realistic expectation |
| Paranoia | Tolerance |
| Doubt | Humility |
| Self-preservation | Self-giving |
| Incessant self-expression | Listening |
| Undue self-assertion | Self-containment |
| Out of my depth | But I can learn |
| Out of my context | But I can experience |
| Keep it out! | But I am already part of 'it' and 'it' is part of me |

be useful and relevant to local needs. My experience was that methodology did not learn adequately—it was not hard-wired into the often unyieldingly, often egocentric, vulnerability-denying (related to mindsets in the left column of Table 1) structures of method expressed as "methodology." As a final development to the 1996 book I integrated Multiview into a Kolb learning cycle. I felt sure that for methodology to truly represent the braiding of theory and practice, it was essential that the methodology itself be a learning device, a means to develop understanding not just of how to do a project systematically (there are so many examples of this and many have not worked—for example the use of SSADM in the London Taurus project (Kouzmin, Korac-Kakabadse et al., 1999)). Rather methodology needs reflection, learning and braiding of practice into theory built-in. This itself requires the users of methodology to be humble (surely?), to admit mistakes and to grow with new learning (a mindset related to the right-hand column in Table 1). It seemed to me at the time that the Kolb learning cycle might provide just such an opportunity. Figure 4 provides a representation of the learning cycle.

In the 1996 book I began to map analysis and design onto the Kolb cycle. In Figure 5 this is further developed with the Rapid Information Systems development format of Multiview (Bell and Wood-Harper, 1998) expressed in the cycle. Where:

- Reflection upon the context for IS within an organisational context is supported by the Soft Systems methodology (SSM) in any of its multiple forms

*Figure 4: An Activity Sequence Diagram of Kolb's Learning Cycle (Building from Kolb, 1984)*

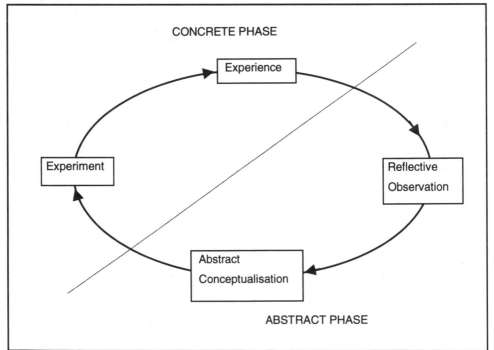

(Chambers, 1981; Checkland, 1981; Checkland and Scholes, 1990; Checkland and Holwell, 1998).

- Abstraction, conceptualising or connecting (depending upon the form of the Kolb cycle being employed) is developed in the information modelling (IM) and socio Technical Systems (STS) element of Multiview. At this stage the IS idea as developed participatively in SSM is mapped onto both the data base of the organisation and the social and technical capacities of that organisation.
- Experimentation or modelling is expressed in the development of the Human Computer Interface / interaction and prototyping (HCI) stage of Multiview as well as the development of the various technical aspects (TA) e.g. management, maintenance and monitoring the system.
- Finally, experiencing the system is expressed in the hardware and software purchases (H/W and S/W), the development of an implementation strategy (Imp.) and the unpacking of a training programme (Tr.).

Ideally, the development and implementation of the IS should then be reassessed and audited by on-going reflection on the nature of emerging problems and issues making use of SSM. The Kolb cycle in Figure 5 depicts the integration of Multiview into the learning cycle.

The explicit equipping of the Multiview approach with a learning device seemed to me at the time to provide a capacity within the IS development process

*Figure 5: Multiview as a Learning Cycle*

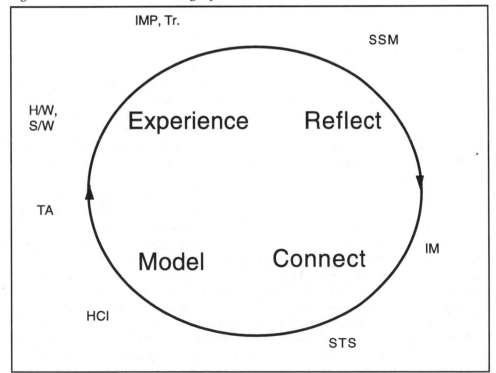

to learn and explicitly accommodate cycles of development. This is what my practice in developing countries had called out for and this was the extent of the development of the methodology as I saw it. This was also all a big move away from the top-down and rigid documentalism of many of the multi-volume, systematic, 'step-by-step', 'how to do it' methodologies currently in vogue in computerised and paper-based form. I applied this form of approach in action research in the UK, West Africa and Asia realising that this braiding of learning with methodology such as Multiview implies that the IS practitioner has to be centrally and actively involved with all the contexts in which the IS is going to be engaged. These would include data, maintenance and information product generation on the technical side, user communities, politics and stakeholders on the social side and procedures, protocols and internal organisational systems on the organisation side. This implies an analyst heavily involved in multiple realities.

More recently I have continued to investigate using Multiview in this manner (1998-99 project work in China) but still—in the mind and eye of project donors and local colleagues working on the information systems the "Lotus Notes" applications, firewalls, file storage and web access seem to come upper-most and the needs of the organisation, the problems which an IS brings to an organisation and the interaction of stakeholders seems to hold a very poor second and sometimes insubstantial place in the analysis process.

### It seems that useful methodology needs to braid theory and good action research practice within the framework of an inclusive approach to undertaking the IS project, but...

To summarise the discussion so far: IS exist in a risky world environment and the nature of IS development means that practitioners are vulnerable to a range of potential problems. One means to deal with risk is to apply methodology but methodology without learning is a blunt and unresponsive instrument it seems. So the outcome of the discussion was the development of the Multiview methodology in a learning cycle. But this still does not seem to me to sufficiently deal with the risk factors which Sauer noted and which are set out here. To avoid failure requires the development and maintenance of support in the social context of the IS project. This means that the format of the IS intervention within the organisation would ideally be attuned to the needs of those in the organisation who can help to guarantee its viability over time.

Action research requires intervention to involve and revolve around the experiences and learning of the community (Bottrall, 1982) but the format for intervention can be altered so that what appears on paper to be participatory and inclusive becomes exclusive and top-down in practice. This is not a new observation. McGregor (1960) noted the tendency towards control-based or facilitation-based interventions—he labelled them as Theory X and Theory Y types of intervention. Figures 6, 7 and 8 depict Theory X and Y and add a potential Theory W.

Figure 6 shows a traditional control approach to intervention. In this approach all elements of the context are kept at 'distance,' possibly in order to maximise an impression of scientific style 'objectivity' (no matter how out of place this is in social environments). The main outcome appears to be the ability of the actors within the IS project to divorce themselves from the context and to intervene without worry-

*Figure 6: An Activity Sequence Diagram of the Theory X Approach to Intervention - Scientific Enquiry (Building from McGregor)*

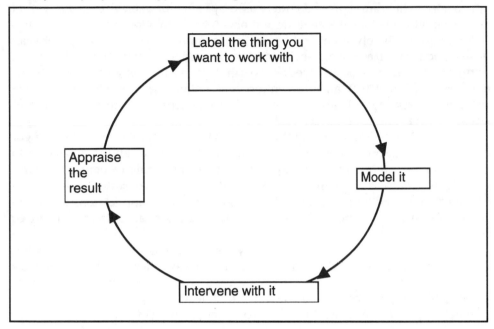

*Figure 7: An Activity Sequence Diagram of the Theory Y Approach to Intervention - Allowing for Autonomous Development (Building from McGregor)*

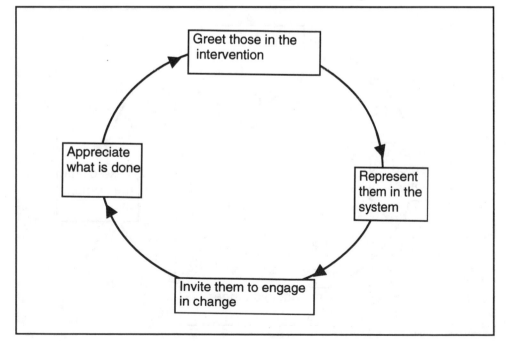

ing to much how intervention is experienced by others in the context. It is my experience that this is the procedural outcome of many of the highly structured approaches which are at present widely used by IS practitioners—it encourages an approach which is pseudo-scientific and objectively problem solving.

In Figure 7 involvement and facilitation is implicit and necessary. There can be less room for objective distancing and there is a necessity for inclusion and an invitation for others to be involved. Acts of greeting and inviting are inclusive and encourage a belief that an intervention can sustain multiple comments from multiple perspectives. It also assumes that the practitioner can cope with and engage with multiple perspectives.

Figure 8 represents abuse. In this situation the form of intervention no longer has even the dignity of being objective; rather, it is an intrusion and an invasion into the lives of those others in the context. (How many of us could recognise this form of IS development in our own experience? Sudden changes of software, inexplicably poorly planned training, and help desks when new IT applications are put in place, unrequested changes to practices which are essential to daily working or living?)

Theory W, X and Y are not real—they are metaphors for our experience but they are important types which might indicate the way in which our own practice is received. The theories provide different ways in which intervention can occur for projects of all types. They also relate to the Kolb learning cycle. Table 2 shows the potential relationship of the three theories to the learning cycle.

*Figure 8: An Activity Sequence Diagram of the Theory W Approach to Intervention - A Tyranny*

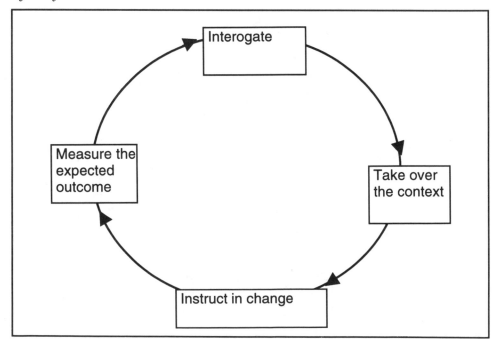

*Table 2: Theories W, X and Y and the Learning Cycle*

| Theory W (abuse) | Theory X (First order cybernetics) A systematic approach | Theory Y Second order cybernetics) A systemic approach | Kolb (open to First and Second order or even abuse forms of application it seems) |
|---|---|---|---|
| Interrogate those involved in the context | Label the thing you want to work with | Greet those in the intervention | Reflect |
| Take over the context | Model the context in an objective fashion | Represent them in the system | Connect |
| Instruct those in the context in the pre-determined change | Intervene with the context | Invite them to engage in change | Experiment |
| Measure the result | Appraise the result | Appreciate what is done | Experience |

This model arose from discussions and learning with colleagues with the Open University Course Team developing the new third-level Systems Course— 'Managing Complexity: A Systems Approach- T306' (most specifically Bob Zimmer). From a review of the three theories, it becomes apparent that a learning cycle approach does *not* necessitate a systemic action research intervention. Rather, the approach could appear to be learning and yet actually be experienced by those involved in the context of the IS development as a tyranny. When this reflection arose for me I was both shocked by it and yet also experienced an "Ahaaa" moment —"So that's why things go wrong!"

### This requires the practitioner of methodology to be actively engaged in learning and developing upon practice, but …

My experience indicates that it is not enough to use methodology to reduce risk and vulnerability in the development of IS. Nor is the application of a learning cycle approach to a multi-perspective approach such as Multiview a means to guarantee a truly systemic and participatory approach to IS planning and development. I realise that my learning as expressed through my writing, is not as yet adequate to the task of developing IS which engage and involve communities.

### This is not enough either—methodology needs to be implemented in such a way as to engage the users of IS, but …

Multiview as expressed may be engaged in a manner according to Theories W, X or Y. Figure 9 demonstrates this.

Intuitively we recognise that Theory Y is the humanised model for IS development, but the problem is that Theory W and X can equally well appear during the IS development process if there is a lack of reflection on the process involved and a related lack of understanding or craft skill on the part of the practitioner(s) as to how to fix the problem. This reflection provides a range of further questions:

- Is there a way to guarantee that IS are developed humanely?
- How can analysts develop humanised and humanising approaches to IS development?
- What are the costs and benefits of investment in humanised approaches to IS development?
- Will humanised approaches reduce the risk of failure? If this is so

**This means that learning and tools for developing the means of intervention must be central elements of IS methodology.**

I do not have the space here to undertake a detailed review of my use of Multiview over the years in the light of the theories analysis set out above. Some personally worrying conclusions I can produce are as follows:

- On reflection, it now appears to me that often my practice has encouraged others working within IS to adopt Theory X perspectives to IS projects when I intended Theory Y, but did not have the craft skills to enable it.
- Often my approach has been voiced as Theory Y, but has been experienced by others as Theory X because I did not provide adequate means for the facilitated form of intervention to be experienced and so (as Sauer indicates) my project disappointed and lost support—eventually to run out of funding and enthusiasm.
- Often donors and financiers of IS have requested Theory Y interventions (but

*Figure 9: Multiview, Learning Cycle and Theories*

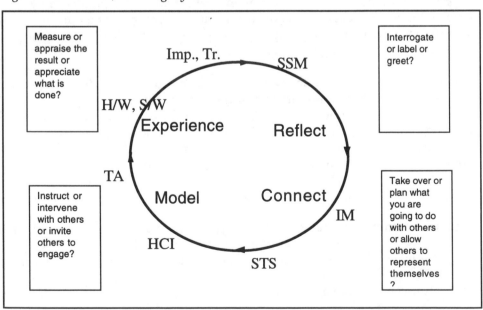

not in this language) of me but have actually seemed to have wanted Theory X.

In conclusion, and working forward from Sauer's position of failure through lack of organisational support, the potential to develop supporters for IS in organisations would seem to be improved if methodology is applied in an open and participatory manner, recognising the benefits of vulnerability in practice, where stakeholders are engaged and invited into the process of IS development without slipping into approaches where they are subsequently controlled or even coerced into systems which are not of their choosing or of central importance to the wider benefit of the organisation at large. The Sauer model for failure was largely based upon the ability of IS projects to deliver benefits and maintain support. The experience of the practitioner engaged in such projects is often bruising. By the development of methodology application approaches—based upon action research and engaged in a manner consistent with participatory methods—it would seem logical that the stakeholders would be more likely to stay with the project and therefore, the project would be more likely to develop applications which the stakeholder would need and approve of. In short, the resulting project would seem then to be both viable, and the management of the project would also have the potential for being autonomous within the organisation as they would operate within an organisational setting of mutual support and trust. But, does this imply that the organisation which contains and supports the IS project would itself have to be viable and autonomous? If this were so, then the focus for the analysis of failing IS would have to be the organisation itself.

**Or is this a particle view in need of further braiding?**

# REFERENCES

Avison, D. E. and A. T. Wood-Harper (1990). *Multiview: an exploration in information systems development*. Maidenhead, McGraw-Hill.

Bell, S. (1994). "Methods and Mindsets: towards an understanding of the tyranny of methodology." *Journal of Public Administration and Development*, 14(4), 323-338.

Bell, S. (1996). *Learning with Information Systems: learning cycles in information systems development*. London, Routledge.

Bell, S. (1996). "Reflections on Learning in Information Systems Practice." *The Systemist* 17(2), 54-63.

Bell, S. (1997). "IT Training, Personality Type and Winnie-the-Pooh." *The Systemist* 19(3): 133-146.

Bell, S. (1997). *Self-Reflection and Vulnerability in Action Research: bringing forth new worlds in our learning*. Forum 2: Action research and Critical Systems Thinking, Hull, Centre for Systems Studies, University of Hull.

Bell, S. (1998). "Information Systems projects in Africa: reflections on learning." *African Development Review* 10(1), 173-189.

Bell, S. and A. T. Wood-Harper (1998). *Rapid Information Systems Development: systems analysis and systems design in an imperfect world: Second Edition*. London,

McGraw Hill.

Bottrall, A. (1982). *The Action Research Approach to Problem Solving, with illustrations from irrigation management*, Overseas Development Institute.

Briggs Myers, I., L. Kirby, et al., Eds. (1994). *Introduction to Type: Fifth edition*. Oxford, Oxford Psychologists Press.

Chambers, R. (1981). "Rapid rural appraisal: rationale and repertoire." *Public Administration and Development* Vol. 1, 95-106.

Checkland, P. and S. Holwell (1998). *Information, Systems and Information Systems: Making sense of the field*. Chichester, Wiley.

Checkland, P. B. (1981). *Systems thinking, Systems Practice*. Chichester, Wiley.

Checkland, P. B. and J. Scholes (1990). *Soft Systems Methodology in Action*. Chichester, Wiley.

Collins, T. (1998). BBC acts on IT Chaos. *Computer Weekly*. London: 1.

Collins, T. and D. Bicknell (1997). *Crash: ten easy ways to avoid a computer disaster*. London, Simon and Schuster.

*Computer Weekly* (1998). Swanwick Battles Against IT Logjam. *Computer Weekly*. London: 18.

Correa, C. M. (1990). Informatics in Latin America: Promises and Reality. *Information Technology in Developing Countries*. S. C. Bhatnagar and N. Bjørn - Andersen. New York, Elsevier Science Publishers.

de Chardin, T. (1961). *The Phenomenon of Man*. New York, Harper Torch Book.

Drummond, H. (1996). *Escalation in Decision Making: The tragedy of Taurus*. Oxford, Oxford University Press.

Drummond, H. (1998). "'It Looked Marvellous in the Prospectus': Taurus, Information and Decision Making." *Journal of General Management* 23(3): 73-87.

Dryden, W., Ed. (1996). *Handbook of Individual Therapy*. London, Sage.

Esperjo, R. and N. Stewart (1998). "Systemic Reflections on Environmental Sustainability." *Systems Research* 15, 1-14.

Flood, B., S. Weil, et al. (1997). *Critical Reflexivity: a multi-dimensional conversation*. Forum 2: Action research and Critical Systems Thinking, Hull, Centre for Systems Studies, University of Hull.

Grundley, M. and R. Heeks (1998). *Romania's Hardware and Software Industry: Building IT policy and capabilities in a transitional economy*. Manchester, IDPM.

Horney, K. (1994). *Self-Analysis*. London, Norton.

Kolb, D. (1984). *Experiential Learning: experience as the source of learning and development*. London, Prentice-Hall.

Korac-Boisvert, N. and A. Kouzmin (1995). "Transcending Soft-Core IT Disasters in Public Sector Organizations." *Information Infrastructure and Policy* 4: 131-161.

Kouzmin, A., N. Korac-Kakabadse, et al. (1999). *Information Technology and Development: Creating "IT-Harems", Fostering New Colonialism or Solving "Wicked" Policy Problems?* Public Administration and Development Jubilee Conference: The Last Fifty Years and the Next Fifty Years: A Century of Public Administration and Development, Oxford. St. Anne's College.

Lytle, R. (1991). The PPS Information System Development Disaster in the early 1980s. *Great Information Systems Disasters*. F. Horton and D. Lewis. London, Aslib.

Lyytinen, K. and R. Hirschheim (1987). "Information Systems Failures: a survey and classification of the Empirical Literature." *Oxford Surveys in Information Systems* 4, 257-309.

McGregor, D. (1960). *The Human Side of Enterprise*. Moston, McGraw-Hill.

Moon, J. (1999). *Reflection in Learning and Professional Development*. London, Kogan Page Ltd.

Odedra-Straub, M., Ed. (1996). *Global Information Technology and Socio Economic Development*. Nashua, Ivy League Publishing.

Poston, T. (1999). Millions lost over Melissa e-mails. *Computer Weekly*. London: 2.

Russell, D. (1986). How we see the world determines what we do in the world: preparing the ground for action research. Hawkesbury, University of Western Sydney.

Sauer, C. (1993). *Why Information Systems Fail: a case study approach*. London, Alfred Waller.

Systems Thinker Newsletter (1998). *The New Workplace*. Waltham, USA, Pegasus.

White, L. (1997). Going Nowhere Slowly. Computer Weekly Web Site, Computer Weekly, 2.

Wilby, J. (1997). *Forum One: Transcripts and Reflections*. Hull, Centre for Systems Studies.

# Part 2

# Socio-Technical
# and
# Critical Systems

**Chapter VIII**

# Enabling Technology for Collaborative Working: A Socio-Technical Experience

Dianne Willis
Doncaster College

Elayne Coakes
University of Westminster

## INTRODUCTION

This chapter looks at the use of enabling technology, in particular the Internet, to share experiences of socio-technical thinking and practice. From an idea of gathering an international perspective on socio-technical practices was born a collaborative venture between three members of the Sociotechnical group of the British Computer Society (BCS). The aim of the venture was to gather together a series of modern socio-technical experiences in book format. As none of the three participants lived close to the other in geographical terms and the basis of the book was to be international experiences, some method of communication was needed that took no account of international timelines and geographical boundaries. Major options considered for the project were the telephone, fax or electronic mail (e-mail). Each communication method has its advantages and disadvantages, but for a truly international perspective, e-mail was considered to be the best option. Whittle (1997) argues that the rapid communication, convenience and economy of e-mail promotes efficiency. The eventual choice of e-mail was influenced by the fact that it takes no account of time differences and people can deal with e-mail as and when they have time. According to Harris (1996), communicating by e-mail is very inexpensive compared to telephone communication, as messages and even files can be exchanged around the world for the cost of a local phone call. This aspect was also highlighted when contributors were asked to send disc and hard copy which proved very expensive, though was undoubtedly more reliable as problems with compatibility of systems disappeared.

At this point, some further consideration of e-mail and the use of the Internet would be beneficial.

## ELECTRONIC MAIL

Hirschheim (1985) described the main characteristics of electronic mail as being:

1. To support the communications of people in the same building and on distant continents
2. To support real-time communications, when the parties are present at their terminals at the same time (this did indeed happen on one memorable occasion when on sending a communication to a contributor in the USA, an instant response was received, as he was on-line at the time—this led to a discussion of the weather on the different continents), and non-real time communications with the recipient reading mail when convenient (the more normal occurrence).
3. To allow all messages to be sent when desired, stored where necessary, routed to the most appropriate destination and then easily retrieved.
4. To provide the users with facilities to prepare, edit, read, store, receive and retrieve messages easily.
5. To cater or to a variety of message types such as formal letter, informal memos and brief notes. (most e-mail systems in use today do not cater for formal letters and memos).

It can be seen that these characteristics are of importance when engaging on a project such as international collaboration for publishing as an audit trail of activities needs to be kept. The major issues arise when, in particular, editors in such a venture use e-mail systems with different capabilities (such as the ability to deal with attachments), and in addition do not store correspondence in the same manner. Harris (ibid) points out that messages longer than 30 pages should be compressed before being sent to avoid the problem of unreadable messages for the recipient.

In the context of the publishing activity, the various e-mail systems used by the editors and contributors can be considered parts of the information system that constituted the whole. In Checkland and Holwell's terms (1998) this whole would be as below:

*Figure 1: The Linked Systems of an Information System.*

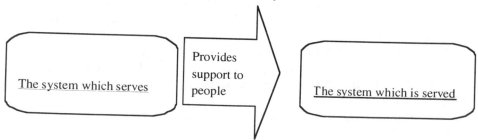

The system which serves provides the processing of selected data (capta) relevant to people undertaking purposeful action, and the system which is served allows for purposeful action whose doers have information needs.

Data here is meant to be the facts about the world which we inhabit that are, in principle, checkable and can have evidence produced to support them. They are the starting point in our mental processing. Capta are the result of selecting some for attention or categorising some together to form a new collection of facts. Once data has been turned into capta, we enrich it and give it meaningful attributes, thus it becomes information. Information can then be collected into larger structures that have links and are called knowledge. However, we only accumulate information and knowledge from our data and capta through context and shared understandings, and it is here that we find that using e-mail over international distances and in a variety of cultures raises interesting issues. Meaning, as Checkland and Holwell (ibid) themselves say, can be attributed in a context which may be any combination of cognitive, spatial and temporal contexts. In the cognitive context we would include culturalissues, both organisational and national.

This perhaps can lead to a discussion about the use of language, which has particular cultural connotations, in computer-mediated activities. All communication between the editors and the book contributors was computer mediated. Communication between the editors was both computer mediated and in person. In fact, the editors found the need to meet on a regular basis to discuss issues in order to avoid the cognitive 'split' caused by using computer-mediated communication.

Herbert H Clark (1996, p.3) says 'Language use is really a form of joint action. A joint action is one that is carried out by an ensemble of people acting in coordination with each other. ... Language use is thus more than the sum of a speaker speaking and a listener listening... It is the joint action that emerges when speakers and listeners, writers and readers – perform their individual actions in coordination, as ensembles. ...Language use embodies both individual and social processes.'

He goes on to say that the settings where conversations take place are either spoken or written. The written settings most like conversation are those where people write to others they are acquainted with. Yet, as discussed below, e-mail communications more closely resemble speech patterns than they do patterns of written words.

Many written messages are not written to people known. As was the case with the book contributors. Language relies on common ground — a joint understanding of the foundations around which the language and the conversation is based — an understudying of the situation, the meanings of words, the social and cultural background and knowledge of the participants.

Pratt (1982) comments that after a person has received and understood the content of a message, in ordinary speech we say that he has become informed about the matter at hand. This is a surprisingly precise and accurate statement. He has been 'in-formed' (Latin in=in; within; formere=to shape or form). He has been inwardly shaped or formed; his image has been affected. Information is the alteration of the image which occurs when it receives the message.

Information is thus an event — an event which occurs at some unique point in time and space, to some particular individual. More precisely, 'information' is the name of a class of events, like the word 'explosion'. Every explosion is unique, no two are identical.

Introna (1997) argues that information must change the recipient, it must lead to a level of interpretation and understanding.

The hermeneutic circle expresses the principle that one must understand the parts from the whole and the whole from the parts. We project significance onto the text, based on the form of life within which we interpret; we then allow the text to inform the tradition, which is the living context from which we seek to understand.

The hermeneutic circle starts in a heuristic manner, the interpreter uses for-understanding and prejudices to establish the ACTUAL meaning of the text. This meaning is then related to the current situation, tradition or form of life. This provides a new understanding of the context which is projected back onto the text and permits further meanings to be projected back to the context. The hermeneutic circle is the dialectic process of understanding.

But Derrida (1982) argues with this as he says that humans exist only within a linguistic play. All attempts to ground language and interpretation are futile, since there is no one term which has any intrinsic meaning. All terms acquire meaning only by their differentiation from all the other terms in the language.

Meaning and communication through both the written and spoken word are thus fraught with potentialities for misinterpretation, misinformation, and misunderstanding, as perhaps this chapter only serves to confirm! Context informs our understanding and interpretation of what we read and hear. It therefore behooves us to take care in what we say or write and how we say or write it. E-mail is particularly fraught with potentialities for miscommunication as most people use it in a slap-dash and often haphazard way. Spell-checking is not always performed; proofreading is less critical; text is not 'polished'; part-sentences are utilised, etc. It

*Figure 2: The Hermeneutic Circle (interpreted from Introna, 1997)*

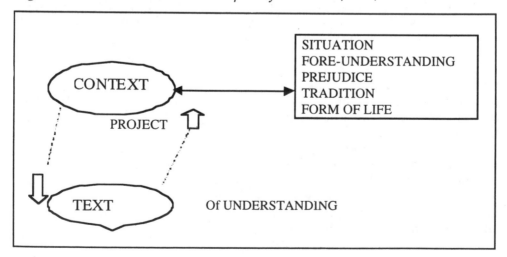

is often treated as an extension of speech and thus less 'formal' than paper-based memos, etc. Responses to communications are 'dashed off' without due care, or at least the care required of a written, paper-based reply. Examples of this can be found in our editorial correspondence—e-mails entitled "oops", or "sorry" or "miscommunication."

As many of the book contributors were not native English speakers (and Americanisms can be counted here!), idiosyncratic speech forms, encapsulated into written form, proved particularly troublesome for some.

## THE INTERNET

It is argued that the Internet offers a new global infrastructure that is changing the way that people interact (Comer, 1996). Ease of communication is said to be the major advantage that has been brought about by the increased use of Internet technology. Is it the case that the Internet represents a single, large wide area network (WAN)? It can be said to be in that it consists of thousands of interlinked computers. If it is truly a WAN, then people anywhere in the world can connect and communicate with relative ease. This then represents a new paradigm of communication, not merely in terms of speed, but rather in scope for a truly international communication experience. Comer (ibid) also argues that a high standard of reliability is needed if communication is going to be successful on an international basis and this is dealt with by the use of transmission control protocol (TCP). TCP automatically checks incoming data for lost or incorrectly ordered datagrams, handles problems and puts things back in order. This proved during the course of the project to be a relatively optimistic version of what actually happened. In several cases, material arrived in garbled formats which proved unreadable and compatibility problems between Macintosh and Windows-based operating systems also proved to be hurdles in the communication process. A more worrying problem was material that didn't arrive at all! This happened in both phases of the communication process, when the editors were sending messages to the prospective contributors and when the contributors were trying to contact the editors. Theoretically, if messages are unable to be delivered, messages are sent back to the sender to say that this has happened. In many cases this did not happen, what is meant to be a reliable process broke down, but more meaningfully, broke down without indication that it had done so. In other forms of communication, if you have the correct number and send a fax, you can be sure when it has been transmitted, it has arrived; with the telephone, you know whether or not you are able to get through; with e-mail, it became obvious that the process was not as secure as the other transmission methods. Norman (1988) discusses the principle of closure—agents performing an action require evidence, sufficient for current purposes, that they have succeeded in performing it and clearly e-mail fails to provide this sufficient closure.

In fact Hunter (1996) also discusses these issues in relation to uncertainty in information systems. He says we believe or use information with certainty when it is accurate. Uncertainty exists in information when it is incomplete, incorrect or approximate and he gives four types of uncertain information:

*Figure 3: A Classification of Certainty (taken from Hunter, 1996)*

|  | All expected information is present | Some expected information is absent |
|---|---|---|
| All incorrect information is absent | Accurate ⟶ | Incomplete |
| Some incorrect information is present | Incompatible ⟶ | Approximate |

- Probabilistic
- Fuzzy (vague)
- Inconsistent (contrary)
- Default (what is used in the absence of better alternative).

E-mail clearly leaves itself open to this concern over uncertainty and on many occasions there were e-mails between editors (and contributors) regarding 'lost' or presumed 'lost' communications, in some cases resulting in default information being used to replace uncertain (fuzzy or inconsistent) information.

A further point for consideration is that the major language in use on the Internet is English and this does have implications for those people not wishing or unable to communicate in that language. (Also see discussions above on meaning and language use). This was an issue that needed to be considered in terms of the project. If people were unable to communicate in English to a high standard, would we be able to gather and include their message and experiences in the final book which was to be the end product of the collaborative venture?

## COMMUNICATING THE MESSAGE

This brings us to the next major point – targeting the message. Obviously, if the book was to succeed in being a set of true international experiences, we needed to reach as wide an audience as possible. Having chosen a communication method which was capable of reaching an international audience – how do we target that message? The method selected was that of a Call for Papers (CFP) through an international mail-list targeting more than 20 countries and over 2,000 potential respondents, a well-tried and tested method for collecting academic responses. Concern was expressed by the editors that it may not be the most appropriate method for targeting practitioners as opposed to academics, but in the absence of any other reliable form of contact, it was accepted that it was probably the method most like to achieve results. In actual fact, there were more than 40 responses to the CFP, from some 10 countries. Additional CFPs were distributed, again by e-mail, to local branches of professional organisations such as the Hong Kong, Korean and Australian Computer Societies, the Association for Computing Machinery in the U.S., and on the web pages of a practitioner Internet newspaper, as well as being published on the Web pages of the British Computer Society. Unfortunately, practitioner responses (as opposed to academic) through these sources were minimal and, in the end, no completed submissions were made from these sources. Responses from African and Asian countries were also not forthcoming. It can only be speculated that this is due in part to the poorer communication infrastructure in that part of the world, but may also have some bearing on the use of English in the CFP. These hypotheses cannot be tested at this time, merely noted as possible factors.

Much work has been done on the analysis of Web-based communication (Jackson, 1997) which indicates that most examples of computer mediated communication (CMC) such as electronic mail extend the interactional mode of communication as all participants have equal access to the communication space. Network analysis can be used for mapping relationships and representing the nature of communication structure. Valuable lessons may be learned about the project by utilising this technique as shown below.

## MAPPING RELATIONSHIPS

A useful network analysis method of looking at relationships is that of the sociogram. Originally developed by Mareno (1960), a sociogram is a diagrammatical illustration of the pattern of interpersonal relationships between a given group of people. It can also be used to display the structure of a group and to record the frequency and/or duration of contacts. Rogers and Kincaid (1981) state that the drawing of a sociogram is 'a highly arbitrary and time-consuming task'. This may be the case in complex relationships, but in terms of the analysis of group communications within the project, looking at the sequence of events and analysing the way in which communication patterns changed over the life of the project is informative and therefore worthwhile.

*Figure 4: Sociogram of Communications Between Editors*

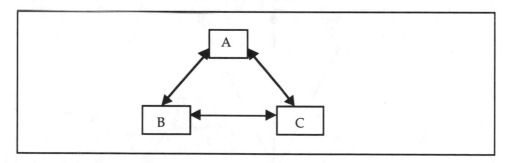

The arrows on the sociogram indicate the directions of communication flow, the heaviness of the arrow denoting the frequency and validity of the communication. Broken arrows, or arrows pointing in one direction only indicate problems or breakdown in the communication process.

*Figure 5: Sociogram of Communications Between Editors and Contributors*

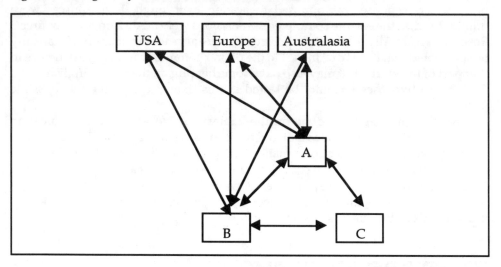

The initial communication patterns demonstrated a two-way flow between all three editors. Communications between the editors and contributors are defined by the technology with the editor whose system is inferior having real problems at the later stages of the process, as all communications eventually have to be filtered by the other editors.

*Figure 6: Sociogram of Communications at Submission Stage of Project*

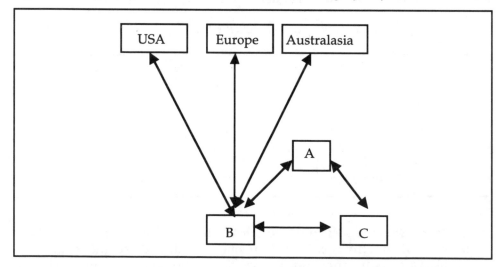

At this stage, all communications are sent to one editor to simplify the process.

*Figure 7: Sociogram of Communications at Editing Stage*

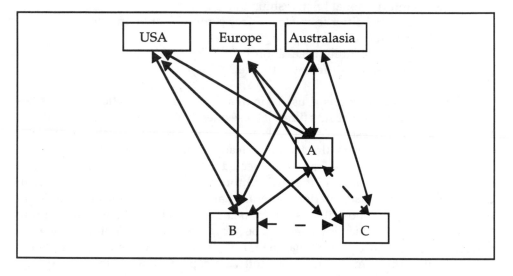

Garton, Haythornthwaite and Wellman (1997) state that when a computer network connects people or organisations, it is a social network. This means that from the point of view of the collaborative venture, a social relationship was built up between, firstly, the three collaborating editors and secondly, the contributors to the book and the editors. One important aspect of successful CMC focuses on the attitudes and behaviour of network members. Analysis of the project shows that these relationships changed over time. Initial analysis of the relationship between the three editors was based around close contact and frequent e-mail communication to supplement occasional meetings as a group. This pattern deteriorated over time as one of the three editors started not to use the e-mail systems and frequently important communications went unread and unanswered. In this case, the communication method had to be abandoned as it did not lead to a successful outcome. In terms of relationships with contributors to the book, relationships were ongoing on a frequent basis until such time as final revised chapters were submitted. This is a good example of the way in which CMC brings together people and groups who have interests in common.

At this stage, problems in the communication process lead to the abandonment of e-mail as the major communication method, the advantages no longer outweigh the disadvantages as the third editor has ceased to respond.

In assessing the role of e-mail in the communication process, Garton et al. (1997) pose the following questions:

1. Who talks to whom?
2. About what?
3. How do ties and relationships

*Figure 8: Sociogram of Final Editors Communication*

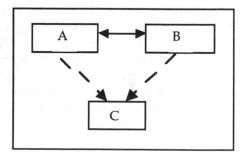

change over time?

4. How do interpersonal relationships change over time?

5. How does CMC differ from face-to-face communication in terms of
   - Who uses them?
   - What people communicate about?

6. Do CMC's describe different networks?

This series of questions is useful in analysing communication patterns between the participants. The first three of these questions are of particular relevance to this project. The question of who talks to whom was largely dictated by the CFP when communication was directed to the lead editor and then by the request for revisions when communications were directed to a different editor. Breakdown of the communication process of the three editors may well be traced to this point in that the third editor had inferior computer hardware and an incompatibility in terms of version with most of the software being utilised by the contributors. From this point on, communication lines had been drawn and it was not until the final stage of the acceptance process that the third editor became a major player in the system. Initial problems arising from software capability were still in play and continued to cause problems.

What people communicated about was in reality limited to the subject of the book. However, relationships were built up over time, in particular in cases where queries and problems involved the frequent exchange of e-mail messages. In one particular instance, an American contributor was unable to send her file in a readable file format and resorted to using the fax — which happened to be out of commission at the time so building the situation up to a very stressful level. Fortunately, changing to a different Internet Service Provider (ISP) solved the problem. This frequent exchange of communication and the need for joint problem solving led to the building up of relationships to the extent that the editor and contributor feel they are friends.

## POSITIVE ISSUES

In terms of the success of the project, issues for consideration are those of speed of communication, efficiency of e-mail as a medium, the ability to span the whole globe, the ability to obtain a cultural profile of the subject area, and the manner in which socio-technical issues have been raised in profile by the publication of a book specific to the area.

One of the more successful aspects was that of being able to gain a view from a series of different cultures where sociotechnical design does not have such strong roots. It was interesting to note that socio-technical practice goes on in many countries and normally leads to benefits for those organisations which take the principles on board. However, it was also interesting to note that in many different countries, socio-technical ideas are being followed despite being called by other versions of the same name, such as ST, STS, Socio-Technical.

# NEGATIVE ISSUES

Despite the success of the project, it was not all plain sailing. There were a variety of issues to be addressed along the way. Already mentioned were the difficulties in targeting the message. Because of a lack of response from Asian and African communities, the book has not achieved its total goal of being truly international. There may be many examples of socio-technical practice in these countries which are not included and which may be of real interest in the study of the field.

A further issue of concern is the lack of professional/practitioner contributions. It was originally hoped that those involved in the day to day issues of socio-technical approaches would contribute valuable experiences to the book. As previously mentioned, this did not happen and may relate to difficulties in targeting the message, or possibly time constraints on the potential contributors.

An issue which became more of a problem as time wore on was that of preferred communication methods. Some people prefer not to use e-mail as a communication method and when this happens, it means the whole process can be put under strain. This is even more of a problem when it is one person from a group of three. Speed and efficiency are badly affected.

A further issue which was to a certain extent time-bounded was that at the time material was being submitted, there was a virus in circulation which attached itself to Word documents being sent over the Internet. Although this did not affect many of the contributors, it was an issue concerning the safety of the Internet as a transmission mode. One contributor preferred to use 'snail mail' (over-land post) rather than risk possible problems caused by electronic transmission. Fortunately for the speed and coordination of the overall project, this was not an attitude shared by many contributors.

# LESSONS AND SIGNPOSTING FOR FUTURE COLLABORATIVE PROJECTS

Lessons to be learned from the project were:
- There are many potential contributors, but targeting is difficult.
- Global communication is possible, but rarely achieved.
- There are dangers inherent in using the Internet as a means of communication.
- Messages can be garbled or lost by using the Internet as the sole means of communication.
- There are still compatibility problems between networks in various countries.
- Communication patterns can be dictated or changed by using electronic media.
- Communication patterns change over time.
- Some people do not readily use e-mail as a communication method.
- Language and meaning are context dependent and thus are not readily compatible with the use of e-mail in international ventures and may cause unexpected hazards.

## Signposts for the Future

- All participants in the project must be equally committed and take care to avoid degradation of the communication process.
- With the advent of cheaper and technically less complicated video links, communication between like minded groups will be able to take place in a much more realistic setting.
- Face-to-face communication is less reliant on language interpretation within context, it is easier and quicker to explain miscommunications, and usually uncertainty can be more easily resolved.
- Collaborative project work on an international basis is taxing but ultimately rewarding and international views should always be sought to validate ideas.
- Groups sharing common interests can form virtual communities and provide a forum for discussion of new ideas.
- Global communications will transform national thinking into global thinking.
- Global relationships will become a common feature of life in the near future.

# REFERENCES

Checkland, P and Holwell, S. (1998). *Information, Systems and Information Systems'* Chichester:Wiley.

Clark, H. (1996). *Using Language* Cambridge: Cambridge Uni. Press.

Comer, D.E. (1997). *The Internet: A global Information Infrastructure*, 2nd Edition, Prentice Hall.

Derrida, J. (1982). *'Differance', Margins of Philosophy* Chicago:University of Chicago Press.

Garton,L., Haythornthwaite, C., and Wellman, B. (1997). Studying on-line social networks, *Journal of Computer Mediated Communication*, 3 (1).

Harris, C. (1996). *An Internet Education*, Thomson.

Hirschheim, RA. (1985). *Office Automation: Concepts, Technologies and Issues* Wokingham: Addison-Wesley.

Hunter, A. (1996). *Uncertainty in information systems* Maidenhead: McGraw-Hill.

Introna, L.D. (1997). *Management, Information and Power* Basingstoke: Macmillan.

Jackson, M.(1997). Assessing the structure of communication on the World Wide Web, *Journal of Computer Mediated Communication*, 3 (1).

Moreno, J.L.(1953). *Who shall Survive?* Beacon House.

Norman, D. (1988). *The design of everyday things* New York:Doubleday.

Pratt, A.D.(1982). *The Information of Image* New Jersey:Ablex Pub Corp, 35.

Rogers, E.M. and Kincaid, D.L. (1981). *Communication Networks: Towards a new paradigm for Research*, The Free Press, 92.

Whittle, D.B.(1996). *Cyberspace, the Human Dimension*, Freeman.

# Chapter IX

# Information Systems as Wicked Problems

Gill Mallalieu
University of Sunderland

Steve Clarke
The University of Luton

The idea of the 'wicked problem' (Churchman, 1967), which advocates a pragmatic oscillation between problem and solution, rather than an attempt to reduce the problem to a series of steps to be followed sequentially, has been particularly helpful to us in conceptualising the relationships between people, organisations and information technology (IT).

This conceptualisation was tested in the RAMESES project (Risk Assessment Model: Evaluation Strategy for Existing Systems), using grounded theory (Strauss and Corbin, 1997) as the basis for the methodology. The overall objective of RAMESES is 'to provide a strategic model for the risk assessment of legacy software systems within SMEs (small-to-medium enterprises) considering business process change.' Thus the relationship between the organisation, the way its staff carried out its processes, and their legacy IT systems was at the centre of our concerns.

This chapter describes how the broad conceptualisation of the problem led to a detailed method to address it and the results available to date.

## THE PROBLEM OF ORGANISATIONS

### Wicked Problems

Four key characteristics (Budgen, 1993) of wicked problems can be identified as particularly relevant to information systems (IS):

- **There is no definitive formulation of a wicked problem.** A wicked problem cannot be reduced to a series of steps that need to be followed in order to reach a solution, since any series of steps so designed will address only part of the problem. By following a series of steps, one may not even arrive at a partial solution, the process may actually make the problem worse.

- **Wicked problems have no stopping rule.** Wicked problems are dynamic. One may derive a solution, which appears to solve the problem at one point in time, but that solution will in itself affect the problem. People will react to the solution that they are given and the problem will evolve in new and unexpected ways. Often, the scenario, which is nominally designated as the solution, is only acknowledged as such because time and/or money have run out on the problem.
- **Solutions to wicked problems are not true or false, but good or bad.** Because the way to tackle the problem is not reducible to a series of steps, the solution will never be a neat fit. The notion of a *good* or *bad* solution is subjective, and can only be evaluated in the light of what one wished to achieve, not in any absolute sense.
- **Every wicked problem can be considered to be a symptom of another problem.** Because of the interconnectedness of things, investigation into a wicked problem might reveal deeper underlying causes, or simply other factors at the same level, which are embedded in different issues. What is a 'good solution' to the problem must be judged entirely on the basis of what was expected and achieved, not on the basis of completeness or finality.

### 'Solving' Wicked Problems

Seeing problems as 'wicked' calls into question the relevance of the waterfall model of software design (Conklin & Weil, 1998; Budgen, 1993). The fact that the waterfall model implies a simple progression from one stage to the next in the process of designing software is unrealistic in the case of wicked problems: it is highly unlikely that a wicked problem could be grasped or understood from the start in order to allow a simple progression to the design of a solution. Concessions to the complexity of real life and to what Budgen (1993) calls 'the wickedness of problems' are the multiple feedback loops that move back up the waterfall. They introduce the notion of going back and reformulating the problem.

In the traditional waterfall model, this manner of oscillating between analysis and design might be considered at best pragmatic, and at worst disorganised, whereas the opposite is true of wicked problems, for which any method that insisted analysis be complete before work may start on the design of a solution would be doomed. In the words of Conklin & Weil (1998): "You don't understand the problem until you have developed a solution."

### Why Organisations are Wicked

Organisations are 'wicked' in a number of different ways. Positivist science tends to look at an area of study, identify variables, isolate them and study each in isolation, and then model the way in which these act together. In this way, hypotheses are accumulated and are articulated as a theory. In the study of organisations, it is possible to identify the variables that bear upon a particular situation, and often to have some feel for their relative importance, but to isolate them is not meaningful. To decontextualise a process or an operator in order to study them is to take away their meaning or *raison d'être*. Positivist scientists feel that an experiment should be 'controlled,' i.e., all extraneous factors should be removed in order to better observe the working of the variable under study. By contrast, many interpretivists believe that there is no such thing as an extraneous factor. If you try to remove some of the factors that operate on a situation, then you are removing context and meaning. It can be seen then that any problem with a social element will ramify greatly (Shurville et al., 1997) thus making it wicked. Just as the interconnection of variables is endless, so are the implications of any change or posited solution.

The relationship between an organisation's legacy system and its business processes has been studied within the RAMESES project, to identify whether the fit was good or where areas of risk existed. It is possible to isolate this relationship in the following way. One could model the way in which the process works according to the appropriate manager, and then using the same technique, show the way in which the software related to that business process works, and then compare the two mappings. This would allow an analysis of fit or lack of it, however many important factors have been excluded. Both managers and the staff who operate the computer system may have different expectations of it from those that it was designed to deliver. A study of the business process and the computer system as they operate will reveal a different pattern from the ideal ones modelled above. Such a study will reveal short cuts, extra activities, and clever solutions to problems, even abuses. Both the way in which the business process is carried out, and the way in which the computer system is being used will be affected by company culture, by the degree of unionisation and demarcation, by the education and flexibility of the staff, and by whether the company is buoyant and profitable or defensive and unprofitable. The geographical locus on a site or between sites will have an effect. The wider context of the organisation may have a huge influence, for instance where a particular computer system may have a role in the supply chain. A particularly important supplier or customer may have dictated its use with no reference to the organisation's business processes. Above all, the *history* of both the computer system and also the business process will have an effect: e.g. resentments may still endure following poor practice in technology transfer or in change management.

Beyond this lies a mirroring layer of complexity. This is the layer of the researchers' own attitudes, shaped by their background, their history of experiences and their personality. In some ways this is not open to study by the researcher since they are inside the situation and cannot see the whole of it. Positivist scientists favour objectivity—the putting aside of the researcher's own views and values in order to establish objective truths. Interpretative social scientists feel this is impossible (Winch, 1958), as being inside the situation, the researcher cannot even identify all those factors that need to be filtered out. In fact, the most fundamental and influential factors may be those that the researcher is least able to see because he is so much a part of them. Interpretative social scientists recommend reflexivity instead. They acknowledge that a researcher's findings will be influenced by his own values and outlook, and instead promote the idea that the researcher should explore and acknowledge them. The self-knowledge will still be imperfect because the researcher is too close to the subject, but at least contemplation is encouraged with the notion of reflexivity.

What has been portrayed so far is a very indeterminate situation. It bears little resemblance to the neat isolation of variables and the extraction of objective truths favoured by positivist natural scientists. However, there are two important anchors in this complexity. One is that there is always some information about an organisation which is empirical: this is often the kind of information which is present on the annual report about number of employees, annual turnover and profit, and also demographic information about the qualifications, age and sex of staff. This kind of information is a good basis for benchmarking and comparison among companies. The other anchor is the kind of information that one needs to know about the company, i.e., what is the researcher's intention in studying the company. If the researcher knows what kind of problem they are interested in, or alternatively, what kind of solution they can offer then they are better able to see which variables are in the foreground and which fall into the background behind them. In this, as in the other features, organisations present situations that conform to the definition of a wicked problem.

## THE RAMESES PROJECT

RAMESES (Risk Assessment Model: Evaluation Strategy for Existing Systems) is a project funded by the UK Engineering and Physical Sciences Research Council (EPSRC). Four organisations in the north of England have been studied as part of this project, the objective of which is to define and categorise the factors that affect the fit between business processes and legacy systems, and develop an evolving risk-assessment method to aid small businesses in understanding the range of risks facing them when they consider change of business process or IT.

The cases studied are seen to be 'wicked' because changes in their legacy systems or business processes may have ramifications in some of the following social and technical areas:

- employee satisfaction
- staff training
- degree of integration of the computer-based systems
- degree of integration of legacy systems in business processes
- personnel profiles
- technology transfer issues
- skills base of the technical staff
- configuration management procedures
- standards operated
- quality systems used
- service issues
- communication between technical and end-user personnel
- data independence
- labour relations

The RAMESES project seeks to provide a tool which allows a manager or consultant within an SME (small to medium sized enterprise) to assess the risk involved in changing either a business process or a legacy IT system. This relationship between business process change and legacy systems is conceptualised in terms of risk: a broad gap in the relationship between a business process and its supporting legacy software systems is seen to represent a large risk, and therefore an opportunity for change.

# THE METHODOLOGICAL APPROACH TO THE RAMESES WICKED PROBLEM

### Grounded Theory

The research method chosen for the RAMESES project was grounded theory (Glaser and Strauss, 1967), which allows for the emergence of theory from an empirical investigation. This exploratory and inductive approach was seen to be highly relevant in the resolution of complex or 'wicked' situations where it is difficult to isolate or measure the cause and effect relationships between variables. Grounded theory allows the use of many different techniques for the collection of data, provided they are based upon observation rather than action and experimentation. This approach matches the research problem of investigation in that it is situated within an environment (small organisations) which, to a large extent, has not been examined by the information systems field. In using grounded theory we can explore the concept of business process and IT change without imposing the generalisations gleaned from research focused on large-scale corporations. This research methodology also allows for the exploration of a complex and multifaceted environment, this being an important aspect of any 'real world' scenario. In summary, the choice of grounded theory for this work was based on the research method being:

- inductive
- qualitative
- flexible in terms of research techniques that can be used
- suitable for the time frame of the project
- investigative not prescriptive

### The Context of the Case Study Organisations

The RAMESES fieldwork was conducted in the northeast of England at three manufacturing organisations and one organisation in the retail and distribution sector. Each of the manufacturing companies is termed a 'job shop' in that its manufacturing activity revolves around made-to-order, low-volume, high-value products. Companies in this sector tend to encounter problems as soon as they attempt to procure, and use, standard off-the-shelf packages that are aimed at the manufacturing industry. The main reason being that in such packages manufacturing is viewed as a batch environment, producing high-volume, low-cost products. The detailed IT audit that was carried out in each company established that the structure of their socio-technical legacy system consisted of a number of loosely coupled components. These components ranged from off-the-shelf packages to bespoke systems. Typical examples of these components are a manufacturing requirements planning (MRPII) system, accounts software and office support software that is used to create company-specific applications.

Company A is a manufacturing company with around 50 employees, working in the area of commercial drive products. Company B is a manufacturing company with around 70 employees, working in the area of prefabricated components. Company C is a retail distribution company with around 80 employees. Company D is a manufacturing company with around 100 employees, supplying components and services to the global defence industry. The senior management at each of these organisations had recognised that their legacy system was not effectively supporting their business requirements. This analysis was precipitated in each case, not by a review of their software, for quality or suitability, but by a management initiated business change. The reasons for these planned changes were varied. Company A was being brought into a larger consortium and, to effectively work within this larger grouping, they needed to assess the interfaces that would exist between themselves and other consortium members. Company B had relocated to new premises following a merger with a sister company and needed to ensure compatibility in work processes and IT support in the new environment. Company C had undertaken formal business process reengineering of the organisation along the lines recommended by Hammer and Champy (1993). Company D was subject to less radical changes, but the directors were planning ahead for a change in management structure.

None of these organisations had set out with the purpose of reviewing their IT systems. However, as they began their business process changes it became obvious to them that what they wished to do was, in certain instances, impeded by their use of software. For instance, Company C had experienced business process reengineering exercises, which had been carried out by internal teams supported by consultants. In the first instance, the company had realigned its activities and personnel to match the identified core business processes. When our fieldwork began, they had identified a mismatch between their unaltered software systems and their, now, processually defined structure.

# THE RESEARCH METHOD USED IN THE RAMESES PROJECT

### The Rationale for the Method

The RAMESES project is aimed at producing a tool which allows risk assessment within SMEs of changes to business processes or to IT systems. This solution therefore requires that the problem be analysed in such a way as to shed light on the organisation, its IT and the way in which people use it. This approach is aligned with a socio-technical systems (Mumford & Beckman, 1994) approach, which seeks to integrate the social, the technical, and the organisational aspects of an open system.

In this scenario an environment is investigated from these three perspectives: the social, the technical and the system, we have aligned this to broadly read that:

- the *social* perspective is equivalent to people factors,

- the *technical* issues relate to the information system,
- the *system* relates to issues of the organisation as a whole

The focus for the research is the relationship between the legacy system and the business process: a large gap in this relationship is seen to be indicative of high risk and may be evidenced by a lack of data integrity, work having to be redone, processing bottlenecks or muddled responsibilities. Therefore, it was necessary to choose viewpoints on the RAMESES wicked problem which would detect a gap, and as a result the following viewpoints for study were chosen:

- The functional view expands the top-level knowledge of the organisation.
- The process view describes a business process from the receipt of an enquiry to a paid invoice,
- The cellular view is a bottom-up approach, which seeks to explain how the process actually happens.

Figure 1 models this, relating the organisational viewpoints to the perspectives accorded by the socio-technical systems approach (Mumford & Beekman, 1994).

### Research Techniques

The research techniques used in this project were observation, informal and

*Figure 1: Model Showing Linkages Between Perspectives*

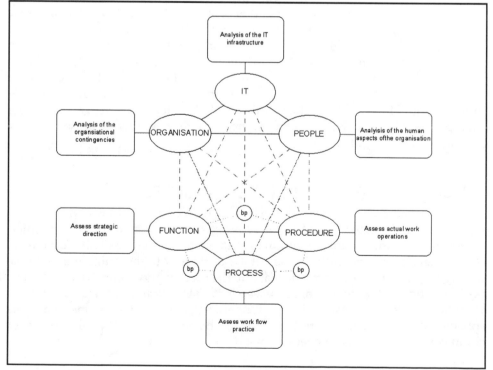

formal interviewing, documentation review, system and process audits. These add validity to the outcomes of the investigation by triangulating data sources, investigators, and methods (Denzin and Lincoln, 1994). Within the first phase of the research, semi-structured interview and process mapping were used. The outcome from this level of investigation was a 'rich' understanding of the interactions between the business process that we were investigating, the people responsible for the implementation of those processes, and the relationship of the process and people in regard to any information system which exists in support of that process.

### Interviewing

Interviews were taped and the data collated through the construction of maps of the functional area under the manager's command. Full transcripts were made of the interviews, which were then subject to analysis, from which themes were identified as being pertinent when they reoccurred in the data. Transcripts were analysed for emergent issues and previous academic work on the subject was sought. This iteration between data and theory is a feature of research conducted within a grounded theory framework and reinforces the rigour that such interpretative studies require. From the emergent themes two key sets of information becomes emergent, first being information which is specifically related to the company under investigation. These sets of themes identify the areas of concern or interest that are context dependent. The second set of themes are those which are of a more generic nature and progress the advancement of the RAMESES method.

### Mapping the Scene

The interviews were reinforced by the construction of maps, which laid out the role of managerial functions; this enabled a more thorough understanding of the data being collated. By mapping the area being studied, the interviewee could improve upon the understanding of the interviewer and further clarify points of confusion. The more complicated the function the more relevant the role of the mapping became. The hand-drawn maps have been duplicated within this chapter in their original format to avoid a further level of interpretation. The maps (for example see Figure 2) were drawn during the interview then analysed using a SSADM tool (see Figure 3).

## EXAMPLES FROM THE CASE STUDIES

The initial data-collection process consisted of 35 interviews with various managerial and support staff from the four case study organisations. The interviews ranged from around 20 minutes to one hour depending upon the complexity of the interviewees' position. In the initial meetings with the companies' general managers, we gained information about the size of the company, its area of business and its expectations of the research. We also offered information on what we would hope to achieve and the amount of time that we would spend on data collection. Arrangements were also made for the next meetings, at which time we could commence with the collection of data.

*Figure 2: Quality Map from Technical Director*

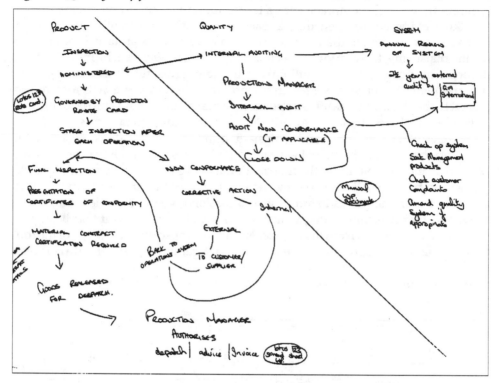

## The Formal Interviewing Process

The first of the formal interviews was with each company's technical director. The first technical director interviewed was involved in a key position in many of the company's functional areas, which made it difficult in some ways to disentangle his roles. He had written the quality manuals of the company for the British quality standard, ISO 9000 accreditation, and was also the key quality controller. During the interview we drew a large map of the function that was being described (this is shown in Figure 2), marking the location of IT support at this functional level.

### The Rich Maps

After the combination of a functional interview (to gather information about the technical director's role) and the technical interview (to establish the support offered to that role by the company's IT system) the information was transferred from the large hand drawn maps to a modelling tool. The translation process itself was a very interesting one, for the researchers had to be aware and alert to the temptation to restructure and influence the data that had been gathered from the interviewees. Our aim was not to transcribe the view as expressed by the technical director but to put it into a format that was more amenable to analysis at a later date. The rich maps that were drawn of the processes were translated into digital format using an SSADM tool. Using the tool allowed us to construct diagrams in a standard format from the information given regardless of the form of the initial rich maps. Figure 3 shows and example of such a transcription for the technical director.

Rich maps constructed during each formal interview with the top-level management of the company were transcribed into the standard format. This meant that using the individual section maps (which were each, initially, very different in character), an overall picture of the organisation was developed. A colour-coded approach has been used so that, although there was a standard format to the organisational/IT support maps, the sections could still be identified. This colour coding enhanced the clarity of the picture developed and as a result the initial stage of data collection and analysis identified two major areas of concern for the company. Although the tool gave us a good representation it was not flexible enough to incorporate all of the information that we needed to present, and the methodology of SSADM was somewhat at variance with our overall aims. Using the tool, the tendency was to force the information given in interview into structured and hierarchical formats, which was not necessarily how it had been presented. It took restraint from the researchers not to impose the limitations of the tool upon the data that had been collected. The data we gathered represented a complex

*Figure 3: Transcribed Rich Map of the Technical Director's Quality Processes.*

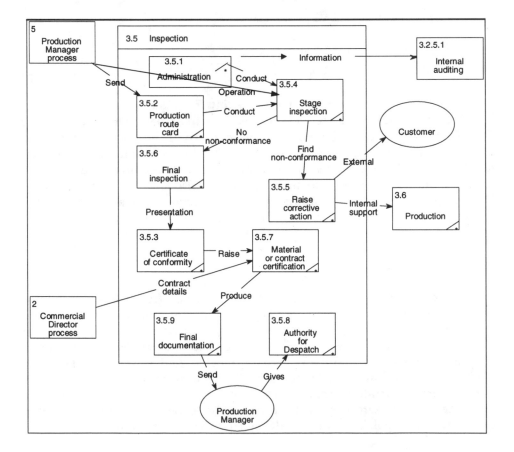

and varied environment seen through the eyes of its owners, and whilst we could perhaps see structure which lay beneath the data, the integrity of the viewpoint which we were analysing required that our understanding was secondary to the interviewees. The maps of each director's functional areas were compiled to create an organisational mapping. This mapping gives an overview of the company, its key figures, main processes and highlights some areas of concern.

## Identification
## of Areas of Concern

The first concern identified was that the technical director carries too many sets of responsibilities, which is a risk to the company if any events occur that mean his knowledge is no longer available to them. The second concern is that there is an overall lack of recognition from the directors of the role of efficiency: this is evidenced by the lack of acknowledgement of the role that job costing played within the organisation's procedures. The general manager had already highlighted these issues as being of strategic importance and saw the organisational map as a support for his objectives.

The second phase of the investigation revolved around a specific business process within Case Study A, following the process from enquiry in to payment for a completed order. Understanding the business process involved a 'walk through' of the business process: the managing director and researcher followed the trail of an

*Figure 4: Diagram of RAMESES Method.*

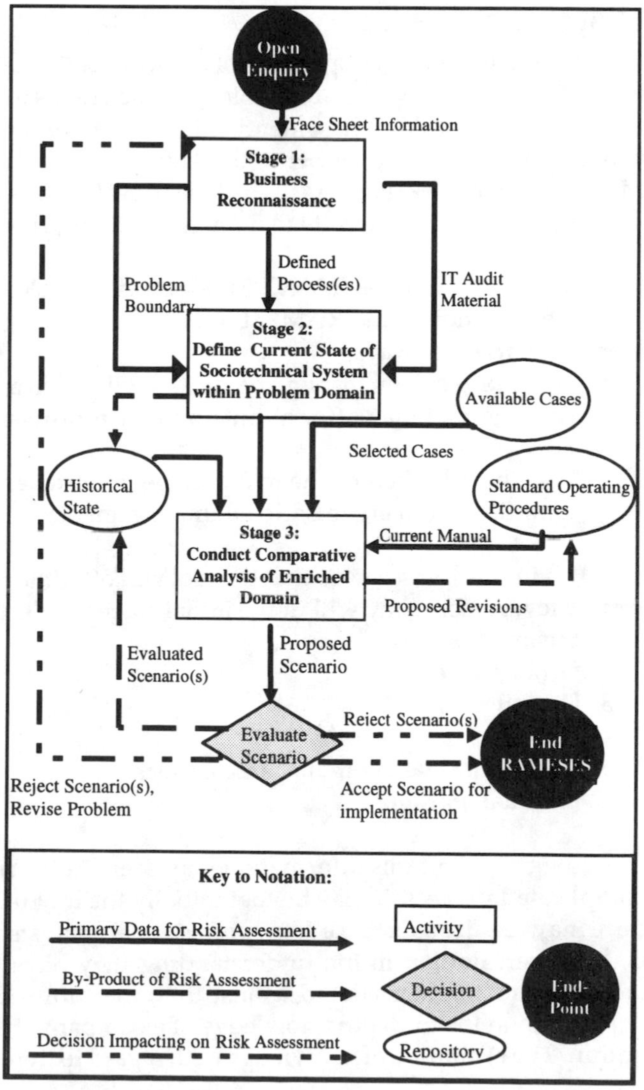

enquiry, by collecting all relevant documentation, and discussing with each employee involved what tasks they undertook to fulfill the order. This information was then plotted onto the organisational map drawn from the first round of interviews. The objective here was to seek points of complexity, bottlenecks or smooth processes from the comparison of the two sets of data. This analysis again raised the issue of the complexity surrounding the technical director's function, as he became a bottleneck for progress as so much work had revolved around his contribution.

Phase Three was to study in-depth the issues raised by the first two investigations although in this particular study it would have been politically difficult to carry out the required work due to the seniority of the person involved.

# OUR RESULTS

Taking the three perspectives of the socio-technical system as a starting point has led to the development of ontology, which seeks to represent all three of these aspects. This ontology has identified issues relating to organisation, business process and IT system as being the key to socio-technical understanding. The Method Framework (Figure 4), which has developed as a result of the research, has a matrix of information as its tool for undertaking risk analysis.

### Using the RAMESES Method of Risk Assessment

The adoption of the RAMESES tool for informing strategic decisions can be seen in a variety of ways:

- That a one-off run through of the tool will aid in a specific problem situation.
- That the tool may offer a route by which problems may be identified then assessed
- That the adoption of the tool may be undertaken with a view to long-term commitment to organisational improvement.

It is in this last scenario that the tool will offer the most effective information. At this level a company will in the initial stages undertake to log all:

1. Business processes.
2. IT hardware.
3. IT software.
4. IT skills.
5. Organisational internal characteristics.
6. External markers.

Logging all of this information may seem in the first instance a tedious and complicated process. It may be that initially the tool requirements capture procedure may require assistance from professional analysts. The usefulness of analysts is, however, limited in the understanding they have of the company. External advisors must be considered as just that; the future usefulness of the tool will depend upon the in-depth knowledge of a company that is only understood from within. The elicitation of knowledge with regard to the external world is a different matter, as this position becomes clear by comparison and knowledge of benchmarking of some such similar technique is most appropriate with external aid. This is the macro/micro viewpoint of the organisation (Walsham, 1997). The combination of all this information enables a complex and comprehensive portrait of the organisation to evolve. The evolution of the organisational portrait will require regular iterations. The development of an organisational history in conjunction with an organisational memory will enable rigorous analysis of potential changes. The history of change will allow the organisation to learn more effectively the methods and techniques which are most successful within their unique position. The case based reasoning element of the tool—which learns by the experience of consultants, business advisors and academics, as well as by other organisations will offer information—which will be complemented further tailored by the techniques which the company has most benefited from in the past.

# CONCLUSIONS

### The Problem Shape Corresponds to the Solution Shape

At the start of the RAMESES project, it was not known which factors would prove relevant to the relationship between an organisation, its business processes and its IT. In that sense, the problem was not well defined. However, the aim of the project was to provide a tool which would allow small-to-medium sized enterprises (or consultants working with them) to perform their own assessment of the risk involved in changing either a business process or a legacy IT system. They would have to get to know themselves in just the same way as we got to know the companies in our case study. The ways in which the tool would ask them to assess themselves is directly derived from the factors which assumed significance during the case studies. This is then a very clear case of interaction between solution and problem as advocated by the wicked problem literature (Rittel & Webber, 1984). The notion of assessing risk allowed us to focus on the problem, whilst the mechanism of a tool by which enterprises could assess themselves led us to draw out the factors that they needed in order to do this.

### Viewpoints on an Organisation

An organisation may be examined from an infinite number of viewpoints, but where the researchers stand is determined by what they are looking for. In observing, interviewing and mapping, the researcher has always to consider that the questions are *about* something. This 'aboutness' is a viewpoint. Grounded theory advocates a very open and inductive style, but each study must have its focuses, its 'abouts' and its viewpoints. Our viewpoints were set to reveal the parallax and the gaps between business processes, IT processes, and the usage of both, because a gap was taken to represent a risk. As we were looking for risk, we stood in the best place to see it. To the furtherment of our aims, our solution space determined the problem space that we were prepared to look at. Had we not taken this teleological approach to the project, we would have found that it ramified too widely ever for analysis to have been concluded. Instead, our investigations have been undertaken with a consistent and useful perspective, and a highly usable tool is emerging.

## ACKNOWLEDGMENTS

The University of Sunderland has given permission for the case studies from the RAMESES project to be used in this chapter, to illustrate the concept of a wicked problem. Further details about this work are accessible from the RAMESES Web site (http://osiris.sunderland.ac.uk/rameses). The RAMESES project is funded by EPSRC, as part of its 'Software Engineering for Business Process Change' programme.

## REFERENCES

Budgen, (1993). *Software Design.* Wokingham, England: Addison Wesley.

Churchman C.W. (1967). Wicked Problems. *Management Science 14,* 141-142.

Conklin, E.J., & W. Weil, (1998). Wicked Problems: Naming the Problems in Organisations:

*3M Meeting Network:*_http://www.mmmco.de/...work/readingroom/gdss_wicked.html, last accessed 6/7/98.

Denzin, N. K. and Y. S. Lincoln (1994). *Handbook of Qualitative Research.* Thousand Oaks California, Sage.

Giddens, A. (1984). *The Constitution of Society: An Outline of the Theory of Structuration.* Oxford, England: Polity Press.

Glaser, B. and Strauss, A. L. (1967). *The Discovery of Grounded Theory: Strategies for Qualitative Research.* Chicago: Aldine Publishing Co.

Hammer, M and Champy, J (1993). *Reengineering the Corporation: A Manifesto for Business Revolution.* London, England: Nicholas Brearley.

Mumford & Beckman, (1994). *Tools for Change and Progress: A socio-technical approach to business re-engineering.* Netherlands: CSG Publications.

Rittel H.J., Webber, M.M., (1984). *Planning problems are wicked problems. In Developments in Design Methodology.* Cross N., Ed, pp. 135-144. Chichester, England: Wiley.

Royce, W.W. (1970). *Managing the development of large software systems: Concepts and Techniques.* Proceedings of WESCON.

Shurville *et al,* (1997). *A development methodology for composer: a computer support tool for academic writing in a second language.* In: Jakobs and Knorr (eds.) 1997, The production of scientific texts in the age of the computer,

Strauss & Corbin, (1997). *Grounded Theory in Practice.* London: Sage.

Walsham, G., (1997). Micro-Studies and Macro-Theory. *Bit97 Conference Proceedings,* CD-ROM, Cambridge, England.

Winch, P., (1958). *The Idea of a social Science: and its Relation to Philosophy.* London: Routledge & Kegan Paul.

## Chapter X

# A Measure of Task-Technology Fit for Computer-Mediated Communication

E. Vance Wilson and Joline P. Morrison
University of Wisconsin-Eau Claire

A key determinant in the success of computer-mediated communication systems (CMCS) and group support systems (GSS) is the task they are used for (Huber, 1984; DeSanctis & Gallupe, 1987). Task models and theories exist in the domain of non-mediated groups (e.g., McGrath, 1984; Wood, 1986) but application of these to GSS and CMCS has been spotty and the results equivocal (Zigurs & Buckland, 1998). Although research findings repeatedly suggest that the fit between task and computer-mediated communication technology is important, researchers have not yet been able to comprehensively describe or measure the dimensions of appropriate fit.

This chapter describes the development and initial testing of an instrument to measure the perceived effectiveness of CMCS based on task type (hereafter *PE measure*). The PE measure extends prior research in several ways. First, it operationalizes the four major dimensions of McGrath's task circumplex (McGrath, 1984; McGrath & Hollingshead, 1994), a model which frequently is used as a conceptual framework for studying GSS and CMCS (Dennis & Gallupe, 1993). Thus, it will be straightforward to integrate findings from studies that use the PE measure into the existing literature. Second, all four task types are incorporated into the PE measure, where prior research has focused primarily on generation tasks and, to a lesser extent, choice tasks. This comprehensive view of the overall task construct should benefit the process of theory-building as well as prediction in practical applications. Third, the PE measure has been tested successfully within heterogeneous task domains, suggesting that the instrument has validity and is relatively robust.

In the following sections we discuss the background and assumptions of our research and develop a set of hypotheses. Then we describe our research method, which involves developing and testing the PE instrument. Finally we discuss our findings and present our conclusions.

## BACKGROUND

The task circumplex model is based on the assumption that all group tasks can be categorized within four main types (McGrath, 1984). These types are distinguished by two components: conceptual vs. behavioral orientation and cooperation vs. conflict emphasis (see Figure 1). The task types are:

- *Generation tasks*, including creativity tasks, e.g., idea generation and brainstorming, and planning tasks, e.g., planning and scheduling;
- *Choice tasks*, including intellective tasks or solving structured problems, i.e., solution of problems that have a correct answer and similar logic problems, and decision-making tasks or solving problems that require consensus among group members;
- *Negotiation tasks*, including cognitive conflict tasks or resolving conflicts of viewpoint, and mixed-motive tasks or resolving motivational conflicts; and
- *Execution tasks*, including performance tasks where there is some objective standard, i.e., *excelling*, and contest/battle tasks where there is competition for victory, i.e., *winning*.

The first assumption of our research is that the different task types require distinct task-technology fit conditions, i.e., one task type might benefit from one particular technology feature, such as text-only messaging, while another task type might benefit more from a different technology feature, such as graphical message attachments. Support for this assumption arises from theoretical and empirical bases. McGrath and Hollingshead (1994) theorize that three task types—generation, choice, and negotiation—are distinguished respectively by increasing information requirements. This idea parallels certain equivocal results that GSS research reports between generation and choice task types. In their review of the GSS literature, Dennis and Gallupe state:

> We are convinced that GSS technology can dramatically improve group performance and member satisfaction for generation tasks, where the group's objective is to draft a project plan, or produce a set of ideas, alternatives, opinions, information, and so forth.... We are less convinced that GSS technology can help groups facing a choice task, where the objective is to choose an alternative(s) from a pre-specified set (1993, p. 74).

Our second assumption is that we can define a task-technology fit construct that is appropriate to CMCS. For this we turn to the related GSS domain, where Zigurs and Buckland define task-technology fit as "ideal profiles composed of an internally consistent set of task contingencies and GSS elements that affect group performance" (1998, p. 323). Part of this definition is directly applicable to our research as we propose, first, to develop a profile of task variables based upon McGrath's task circumplex and, second, to develop a technology profile comprising a controlled CMCS feature set. The use of group performance as a measure is less relevant to CMCS than to GSS research. GSS and CMCS are distinct system

*Figure 1: Group Task Circumplex (McGrath, 1984, p. 61).*

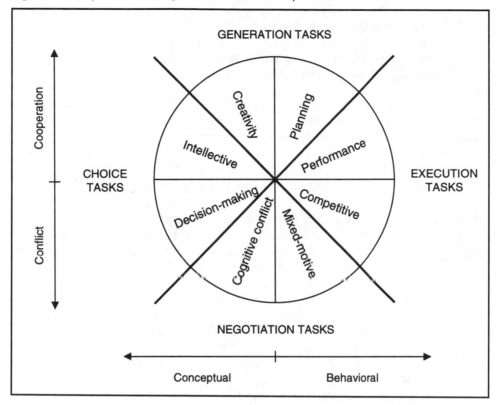

types that, we argue, should be measured using different standards. The purpose of GSS is to increase overall group effectiveness (Huber, 1984), which is accomplished by supporting computer brainstorming, option-ranking, voting, etc. In contrast, CMCS emphasize support for effective communication (Turoff, Hiltz, Bahgat, & Rana, 1993), which is only one of the overall factors that contribute to group performance. Thus, we propose to adapt Zigurs and Buckland's definition to the CMCS context by using *communication effectiveness* as the primary criterion of task-technology fit in the present study.

## HYPOTHESIS

Subsequent to a recommendation by DeSanctis and Gallupe (1987), McGrath's task circumplex frequently has been employed as a conceptual framework for task classification in GSS research. However, only two task types—generation and choice—have been used extensively in empirical studies, and even these have not been tested systematically. Zigurs and Buckland note:

There is one problem with how researchers have applied the circumplex, based on the fact that tasks typically have elements of both the creativity

(Generate type) and problem-solving (Choose type). In empirical work, even if authors classified a task in multiple categories of McGrath's circumplex according to the task's different phases, the subsequent analysis and discussion of results were typically combined across the entire group session. This practice makes it difficult to unravel task-technology fit issues. (1998, p. 323)

To answer these and related concerns, it would be valuable to develop an objective methodology for categorizing task types as they relate to task-technology fit.

A recent study of software development teams took initial steps toward creating such a methodology (Wilson, Morrison, & Napier, 1997). Subjects in this study used a combination of computer-mediated communication and face-to-face (FTF) communication to complete a team project. Subjects were then asked to describe in their own words the activities for which they perceived the two communication channels to be most effective and least effective. Researchers organized this list to consolidate redundant items and categorized the list into six logical factors: the generate, choose, and execute task types of the McGrath task circumplex (subjects produced no comments that fit the negotiation task type category); socialization; communication speed; and communication completeness. They then returned the reduced list of activities to the entire subject pool and asked them to rate how effective they perceived each communication channel to be for supporting each activity relating to their team project. Analysis of the ratings showed relatively high reliability among items within each of the three tested task types and indicated that,

> for the three investigated task types the communication methods pro-
> duced different hierarchies of perceived effectiveness. FTF communica-
> tion supported execution tasks better than generation tasks ($p < .001$), but
> CMCS supported generation tasks better than both execution tasks ($p < .01$) and choice tasks ($p < .05$). Comparison between the hierarchies
> suggests that distributed software development teams may be able to
> create, plan, and coordinate fairly well. (Wilson et al., 1997, p. 4)

These results support the idea that a comprehensive measure of perceived effectiveness can be successfully operationalized based upon McGrath's task circumplex. However, there are several issues that may thwart development. First, it is not known whether survey items created within the domain of software development will generalize well to other task domains. Second, in the Wilson et al. study, relatively high intercorrelations of items between task types were found along with correlations reported *within* the tested task types, and it is not clear whether the survey items employed actually formed independent factors. Finally, it is only speculative that the negotiation task type can be represented successfully in such an instrument, since this was not previously tested. These issues could be addressed by developing a generalized PE measure that incorporates the negotiation task type and can be subjected to more rigorous analysis, leading to the following hypothesis:

*H1: Perceived effectiveness of computer-mediated communication can be distinctly measured for the four major task types of the McGrath task circumplex.*

In order to be useful either as a basis for theory-building or for prediction in practical settings, a PE measure should provide similar outcomes for task domains that share similar characteristics and different outcomes between task domains that have different characteristics. This ability is a key test in establishing construct validity of the instrument, also called instrument validity (Davis, 1989). Cook and Campbell state, "assessing construct validity depends on two processes: first, testing for a convergence across different measures or manipulations of the same 'thing' and, second, testing for a divergence between measures and manipulations of related but conceptually distinct 'things'" (1979, p. 61). These criteria form the bases for Hypotheses 2 and 3.

*H2: Groups with similar task domains will perceive the effectiveness of computer-mediated communication similarly across the four task types.*

*H3: Groups with different task domains will perceive the effectiveness of computer-mediated communication differently across the four task types.*

In the remaining sections of the chapter, we describe our research methodology and results, followed by a discussion of the findings.

## RESEARCH METHOD

Our research design tested how communication effectiveness is affected by task-technology fit between two task domains (software development team project vs. general communication) and a controlled CMCS feature set. The research proceeded in two phases: instrument development and instrument testing. Procedures used for each phase are described in the following sections.

### Instrument Development

To test Hypothesis 1, an instrument was developed to measure perceived effectiveness of computer-mediated communication. *Perception* of effectiveness was chosen in place of alternative primary attributes, e.g., objective evaluation of communication effectiveness. In this decision, we followed the suggestion of Moore and Benbasat, who justified their choice of perception measures of adoption of information technology innovation in this way:

Primary attributes are intrinsic to an innovation independent of their perception by potential adopters. The behaviour of individuals, however, is predicated by how they perceive these primary attributes. Because different adopters might perceive primary characteristics in different ways, their eventual behaviours might differ. This is the root of the problem of using primary characteristics as research variables. Furthermore, studying the interaction among the perceived attributes of innovations helps the establishment of a general theory. (1991, p. 194)

In our study, subjects' perceptions were judged to be particularly relevant antecedents to a variety of important outcomes relating to effectiveness, e.g., satisfaction with the CMCS for a given task and subsequent decisions to use the CMCS for the task.

Items in the instrument were drawn initially from the instrument developed by Wilson et al. (1997). This instrument used nine generation task items, four choice task items, and six execution task items. Several items were specific to software development, e.g., the execution task item *debugging program code,* and these were rewritten prior to inclusion to be appropriate to general communication or were eliminated. With the objective of ensuring content validity through adequately representing each task type, the items were augmented by the two authors. The overall list was reviewed to verify that the emergent inventories fit within and were representative of the McGrath task type definitions through several review and reduction cycles. From the review a test instrument containing eight generate task items, eight choice task items, eight negotiate task items, and eleven execute task items was developed.

The test instrument asked subjects to rate each task item through a single question in one of the following forms, depending on the subject's task domain:

Software development team project task domain question: *Based on your experiences with computer-mediated communication in your project team, how **effective** do you feel this communication method is for the following activities?*

General communication task domain question: *Based on your general experiences with computer-mediated communication, how **effective** do you feel this communication method is for the following activities?*

Test items were operationalized as a list of activities, e.g., "Resolving conflicts" and "Making difficult decisions." Subjects rated their perceptions of effectiveness for each item using a five-position Likert scale ranging from (1) Very Ineffective to (5) Very Effective.

## Instrument Testing

In the second phase of the research, the test instrument was administered to subjects, final inventories of items representing the task types were developed, and mean responses on the task type dimensions were analyzed between groups.

### Subjects

Subjects were 167 undergraduate students enrolled in three different information systems courses at a university located in the U.S. Midwest. Participation in the study was a part of course requirements as reviewed and approved by the University Human Subjects Committee.

### CMCS

Computer-mediated communication was implemented using the controlled set of CMCS features provided by Eudora Pro software running under Windows 95/NT on Pentium PC computers. Eudora Pro is a popular text-based communication application that supports file attachments and features a graphical user interface that conforms to Microsoft Windows standards.

### Procedure

The test instrument was administered during the final week of a 15-week course schedule. In one of the courses, students had used computer-mediated communication both for general communication with the instructor and other students and for receiving course materials. Of the other two courses, one focused on 3GL programming and the other addressed database concepts and application development. In both of these latter courses, students participated in project teams of approximately four members. Projects were conducted over a three-month period during which team members used both FTF communication and computer-mediated communication to support their team projects. As previously discussed, the test instrument for students in the first course asked about perceived effectiveness of CMCS for "general" communication and for the latter two courses asked the same question about communication "in your project team."

# RESULTS

## Data Screening

Data from the 167 subjects were analyzed for completeness in response to test items. Of these subjects, 12 did not mark responses to all the items, and these were removed from subsequent analysis. The remaining data were screened for outliers, particularly for those indicating reverse marking on the Likert scale, i.e., consistently marking 1 instead of 5 to indicate "Very Effective". No extreme outliers or reverse-marked scales were found in the data.

## Item Evaluation and Reduction

A practical objective of instrument development is to achieve a parsimonious representation of the convergent underlying constructs. Thus, we conducted a *post hoc* analyses of correlation in the pooled data to eliminate items that showed low intercorrelations within the task type. This analysis resulted in the reduced instrument shown in Table 1. In its final form, the PE measure uses four items to measure each of four task types. Correlations among these items are shown in Table 2, and results from reliability analysis and exploratory factor analysis of the pooled data for these items are shown in Table 3. Although some intercorrelation was found between choice and negotiation task factors, generally the results suggest the PE measure satisfies the criterion of Hypothesis 1 by distinctly measuring perceived effectiveness in factors corresponding to the four major task types of the McGrath task circumplex.

*Table 1: The PE Measure\*.*

| | | | | |
|---|---|---|---|---|
| **Circle a number from 1 to 5** to answer your response to **ALL** of the following questions for each of the listed activities. *Please take your time and read the instructions completely.* The numbers are used in this way: | | | | |

| 1 | 2 | 3 | 4 | 5 |
|---|---|---|---|---|
| Very Ineffective | Somewhat Ineffective | Neither Effective Nor Ineffective | Somewhat Effective | Very Effective |

Based on your experiences with computer-mediated communication in your project team, how **effective** do you feel this communication method is for the following activities?

| | |
|---|---|
| Planning what tasks need to be done | 1 2 3 4 5 |
| Planning a meeting agenda | 1 2 3 4 5 |
| Planning when tasks need to be completed | 1 2 3 4 5 |
| Planning meetings | 1 2 3 4 5 |
| Making difficult decisions | 1 2 3 4 5 |
| Choosing when all of the alternatives seem about the same | 1 2 3 4 5 |
| Choosing when none of the alternatives seem very good | 1 2 3 4 5 |
| Making complex decisions | 1 2 3 4 5 |
| Negotiating who will be responsible for something | 1 2 3 4 5 |
| Resolving differences of opinion | 1 2 3 4 5 |
| Negotiating who will pay for something | 1 2 3 4 5 |
| Negotiating how to pay for something | 1 2 3 4 5 |
| Developing a presentation with other people | 1 2 3 4 5 |
| Improving a group presentation | 1 2 3 4 5 |
| Writing a report with other people | 1 2 3 4 5 |
| Editing a report developed with other people | 1 2 3 4 5 |

*Item presentation order is randomized in actual administration

Table 2: Correlation Among Items in the PE Measure.

| Task Type | Survey Item | 1 | 2 | 3 | 4 | 5 | 6 | 7 | 8 | 9 | 10 | 11 | 12 | 13 | 14 | 15 | 16 |
|---|---|---|---|---|---|---|---|---|---|---|---|---|---|---|---|---|---|
| Choice | 1. Making difficult decisions | 1.000 | | | | | | | | | | | | | | | |
| | 2. Choosing when all of the alternatives seem about the same | 0.394 | 1.000 | | | | | | | | | | | | | | |
| | 3. Choosing when none of the alternatives seem very good | 0.469 | 0.447 | 1.000 | | | | | | | | | | | | | |
| | 4. Making complex decisions | 0.673 | 0.357 | 0.444 | 1.000 | | | | | | | | | | | | |
| Negotiation | 5. Negotiating who will be responsible for something | 0.313 | 0.374 | 0.215 | 0.399 | 1.000 | | | | | | | | | | | |
| | 6. Resolving differences of opinion | 0.354 | 0.382 | 0.374 | 0.468 | 0.537 | 1.000 | | | | | | | | | | |
| | 7. Negotiating who will pay for something | 0.355 | 0.377 | 0.233 | 0.377 | 0.437 | 0.467 | 1.000 | | | | | | | | | |
| | 8. Negotiating how much to pay for something | 0.308 | 0.352 | 0.223 | 0.361 | 0.506 | 0.403 | 0.514 | 1.000 | | | | | | | | |
| Generation | 9. Planning what tasks need to be done | 0.314 | 0.385 | 0.224 | 0.304 | 0.348 | 0.347 | 0.376 | 0.438 | 1.000 | | | | | | | |
| | 10. Planning a meeting agenda | 0.243 | 0.286 | 0.209 | 0.278 | 0.322 | 0.187 | 0.231 | 0.394 | 0.488 | 1.000 | | | | | | |
| | 11. Planning when tasks need to be completed | 0.244 | 0.285 | 0.221 | 0.370 | 0.367 | 0.320 | 0.349 | 0.380 | 0.501 | 0.629 | 1.000 | | | | | |
| | 12. Planning meetings | 0.157 | 0.267 | 0.134 | 0.152 | 0.275 | 0.179 | 0.229 | 0.296 | 0.362 | 0.484 | 0.466 | 1.000 | | | | |
| Execution | 13. Developing a presentation with other people | 0.454 | 0.320 | 0.363 | 0.506 | 0.284 | 0.314 | 0.358 | 0.442 | 0.342 | 0.359 | 0.259 | 0.161 | 1.000 | | | |
| | 14. Improving a group presentation | 0.422 | 0.314 | 0.357 | 0.470 | 0.299 | 0.367 | 0.331 | 0.367 | 0.343 | 0.373 | 0.317 | 0.173 | 0.579 | 1.000 | | |
| | 15. Writing a report with other people | 0.402 | 0.311 | 0.351 | 0.395 | 0.217 | 0.304 | 0.275 | 0.328 | 0.314 | 0.281 | 0.290 | 0.036 | 0.587 | 0.532 | 1.000 | |
| | 16. Editing a report developed with other people | 0.255 | 0.280 | 0.275 | 0.293 | 0.231 | 0.311 | 0.321 | 0.326 | 0.278 | 0.252 | 0.258 | 0.121 | 0.477 | 0.442 | 0.566 | 1.000 |

*Table 3: Reliability Analysis and Factor Analysis Results for the PE Measure.*

| Task Type | Item | Factor Loadings | | | |
|---|---|---|---|---|---|
| | | 1 | 2 | 3 | 4 |
| Generation | Planning what tasks need to be done | | | | .418 |
| α = .77 | Planning a meeting agenda | | | | .736 |
| | Planning when tasks need to be completed | | | | .782 |
| | Planning meetings | | | | .524 |
| Choice | Making difficult decisions | | .733 | | |
| α = .81 | Choosing when all of the alternatives seem about the same | | .430 | | |
| | Choosing when none of the alternatives seem very good | | .807 | | |
| | Making complex decisions | | .588 | .357 | |
| Negotiation | Negotiating who will be responsible | | | | |
| α = .76 | for something | | | .644 | |
| | Resolving differences of opinion | | | .639 | |
| | Negotiating who will pay for something | | | .584 | |
| | Negotiating how to pay for something | | | .542 | |
| Execution | Developing a presentation with other | | | | |
| α = .83 | people | .708 | | | |
| | Improving a group presentation | .561 | | | |
| | Writing a report with other people | .746 | | | |
| | Editing a report developed with other people | .670 | | | |

Kaiser-Meyer-Olkin (KMO) measure of sampling adequacy for this analysis = .878. Factor extraction via Generalized Least Squares method and rotation via Varimax with Kaiser Normalization (Norusis, 1993); for clarity, factor loadings less than .35 are not shown.

results. Although some intercorrelation occurs between the choice and negotiation task factors; this seems reasonable since choice is often intertwined with negotiation. Initial empirical testing indicates the PE measure has instrument validity as determined through convergent validity, which addresses whether items comprising a measure behave as if they are measuring a common underlying construct, and discriminant validity, which addresses whether the measurement item differentiates between objects being measured (Davis, 1989). These findings suggest the PE measure, as presently constituted, will be useful to CMCS researchers in providing descriptive analysis of communication effectiveness. In particular, the PE measure could facilitate task-based comparisons between alternative CMCS feature sets to help choose those features that are most effective in supporting specific group tasks.

*Table 4: Means Testing Among Subject Subgroups*

| Task Type | Group* | N | Mean | S. D. | Analysis Results |
|---|---|---|---|---|---|
| **Generation** | GC | 62 | 4.08 | .74 | ANOVA $F = .405$, p = .667 |
| | 3GL | 57 | 4.07 | .85 | *No significant differences among* |
| | DB | 36 | 3.94 | .82 | *groups at $\alpha = .05$* |
| **Choice** | GC | 62 | 3.31 | .82 | ANOVA $F = 19.33$, p < .001 |
| | 3GL | 57 | 2.46 | .90 | Post Hoc |
| | DB | 36 | 2.38 | .87 | GC <> 3GL, p < .001 |
| | | | | | GC <> DB, p < .001 |
| | | | | | 3GL = DB, p = .960 |
| **Negotiation** | GC | 62 | 3.27 | .74 | ANOVA $F = 2.90$, p = .058 |
| | 3GL | 57 | 2.95 | .94 | *No significant differences among* |
| | DB | 36 | 2.91 | .92 | *groups at $\alpha = .05$* |
| **Execution** | GC | 62 | 3.23 | .91 | ANOVA $F = 4.65$, p = .011 |
| | 3GL | 57 | 2.77 | 1.13 | Post Hoc |
| | DB | 36 | 2.67 | .98 | GC <> 3GL, p = .048 |
| | | | | | GC <> DB, p = .019 |
| | | | | | 3GL = DB, p = .960 |

\* GC = general communication; 3GL = 3GL programming project team; DB = database development project team

## Means Testing

Three subgroups were represented in the subject pool. Two of these groups had a similar task domain, i.e., project teams conducting software or database development. The third group's task domain was generalized communication that did not include a team project with specific deliverables. Means testing was conducted across the groups using one-way ANOVA and *post hoc* multiple comparisons were conducted using the Dunnett T3 method. Results of these analyses are shown in Table 4 and Figure 2.

Perceived effectiveness was very similar across all task types between the two project team subgroups, 3GL programming and database development. This finding suggests that where task domains are similar the PE measure converges appropriately, supporting Hypothesis 2. Significant differences do appear between the general communication group and both divergent groups on the Choice and Execution task types. This finding supports Hypothesis 3 and suggests that the PE measure is capable of discriminating between dissimilar task domains.

# DISCUSSION, LIMITATIONS AND CONCLUSIONS

Overall, the findings are encouraging. The PE measure proved capable of distinguishing between distinct constructs as evidenced in the factor analysis

*Figure 2: Perceived effectiveness of computer-mediated communications.*

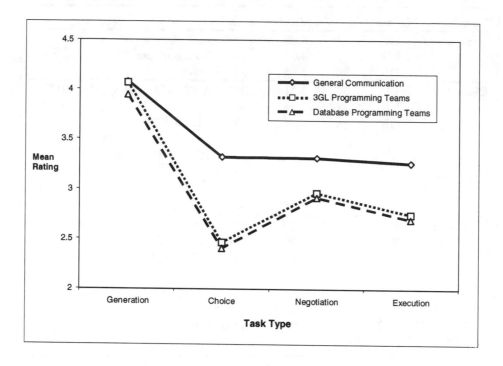

Figure 2 provokes some interesting discussion points regarding the task domains that were studied. Subjects in all three tasks gave equivalent effectiveness ratings of CMCS for generation tasks. However, subjects in project teams reported significantly lower ratings for the choice and execution tasks and marginally lower for negotiation tasks (p = .058). One explanation is that, in general communication, subjects are more free to choose which tasks they will use CMCS to support and which they will save for FTF situations. Our subjects that were involved in team projects were required to produce specific deliverables within strict deadlines, which may have reduced their options and forced them to use CMCS. This initial finding suggests caution in the way we interpret results from different task domains. Substantial differences arose in our subjects' perceptions of CMCS effectiveness based on the task they performed.

Another interesting aspect is the range among the task ratings for the subjects in the various task domains. As predicted in previous research (Dennis and Valacich, 1993; Wilson et al., 1997), the generation task was the best task type supported by CMCS technology and the choice task was not supported as well overall (paired $t$ test of pooled subjects, two-tailed, 154 df, $t = 16.51$, p < .001). However, within the team project task domains, negotiation and execution also were rated higher than choice (paired $t$ test of pooled project team subjects, two-tailed, 92 df: negotiation vs. choice, $t = 5.63$, p < .001; execution vs. choice, $t = 3.09$, p = .003). Future work needs to investigate why CMCS falls down in supporting the choice task in this task domain, why it is perceived to support the negotiation and evaluation tasks better, and how the technology could be changed to support all three tasks at a higher level.

Although our hypotheses were supported by the results, several questions emerged from the research. First, although we can measure differences in communication effectiveness between task domains, it is not clear how to relate these measurements to specific task characteristics. If a choice task involves voting, for example, is this equivalent to an alternate choice task that involves development of consensus? Development of theory—along with theory's predictive and explanatory capabilities—likely will be hampered until research reveals more specific relationships than was possible in our research design. Potentially, this issue could best be addressed by studying perceptions of task characteristics in the same manner that we studied perceived effectiveness. However, this idea is speculative at present.

Second, some areas within McGrath's task circumplex are not represented in the PE measure. For example, all the generation task items involve planning rather than creativity-oriented activities. This might have occurred because the CMCS being evaluated did not support simultaneous input or input feedback, but it also is possible that other causes exist, e.g., that creativity and planning are fundamentally distinct constructs. Future research needs to explore this issue by testing additional instrument items and using CMCS with different feature sets than the system we studied.

Finally, our study does not address individual or group differences among subjects. Although all subjects were enrolled in information systems classes on the same campus and during the same time period, it is possible that those who participated in an extended team project in which e-mail was used extensively were sufficiently changed by the task that their views toward CMCS and their use of CMCS in general were altered. Because of concerns about experimental handling bias and learning effects, our research did not take measurements that could answer this question. However, it is well documented that such effects can occur. Future research should attempt to address this issue through employing different research designs, e.g., repeated measures.

This chapter has described the development and validation of an instrument to measure perceived effectiveness in computer-mediated communication based on the tasks identified in McGrath's task circumplex. It provides a methodology that researchers can use to determine the impact of different task domains on perceived effectiveness of a CMCS, as well as the perceived effectiveness of different CMCS when addressing similar tasks. Our research also raises questions for future research, in particular the question of how CMCS can support choice, negotiation and execution tasks more effectively.

# REFERENCES

Cook, T. D., & Campbell, D. T. (1979). *Quasi-experimentation*. Boston: Houghton Mifflin Co.

Davis, F. D. (1989). Perceived usefulness, perceived ease of use, and user acceptance of information technology. *MIS Quarterly*, 13(3), 319-340.

Dennis, A., & Gallupe, R. B. (1993). A history of group support systems empirical research: Lessons learned and future directions. In L. M. Jessup & J. S. Valacich (Eds.), *Group support systems: New perspectives* (pp. 59-77). New York: MacMillan.

DeSanctis, G., & Gallupe, R. B. (1987). A foundation for the study of group decision support systems. *Management Science, 33*(5), 589-609.

Galegher, J., & Kraut, R. E. (1994). Computer-mediated communication for intellectual teamwork: An experiment in group writing. *Information Systems Research, 5* (2), 110-138.

Huber, G. P. (1984) Issues in the design of group decision support systems. *MIS Quarterly, 8*(3), 195-204.

McGrath, J. E. (1984). *Groups: Interaction and performance.* Englewood Cliffs, NJ: Prentice-Hall, Inc.

McGrath, J. E., & Hollingshead, A. B. (1993). Putting the "group" back in group support systems: Some theoretical issues about dynamic processes in groups with technological enhancements. In L. M. Jessup & J. S. Valacich (Eds.), *Group support systems: New perspectives* (pp. 78-96). New York: Macmillan.

Moore, G. C., & Benbasat, I. (1991). Development of an instrument to measure the perceptions of adopting an information technology innovation. *Information Systems Research, 2*(3), 192-222.

Norusis, M. J. (1993). *SPSS for Windows professional statistics release 6.0.* Chicago: SPSS Inc.

Turoff, M., Hiltz, S. R., Bahgat, A. N. F., & Rana, A. R. (1993). Distributed group support systems. *MIS Quarterly, 17*(4), 399-417.

Wilson, E. V., Morrison, J. P., & Napier, A. M. (1997). Perceived effectiveness of computer-mediated communications and face-to-face communications in student software development teams. *Journal of Computer Information Systems, 38*(2), 2-7.

Wood, R. E. (1986). Task complexity: Definition of the construct. *Organizational Behavior and Human Decision Processes, 37,* 60-82.

Zigurs, I. & Buckland, B. K. (1998). A theory of task-technology fit and group support systems effectiveness. *MIS Quarterly, 22*(3), 313-334.

# Chapter XI

# The Metaphorical Implications of Data Warehousing

Elizabeth J. Davidson
University of Hawai'i Manoa

Metaphors have long pervaded the discourse around information technology (IT) design (Johnson, 1994), helping developers to conceptualize technological features and functions, to design human-computer interfaces (Rechtin, 1997; Golovchinsky and Chignell, 1997; Rauch, Leone, and Gillinhan, 1997), and to articulate application requirements (Boland and Greenburg, 1992; Davidson 1996a). Metaphors also play an important role in conveying what Swanson and Ramiller (1997) call the organizing vision for IT innovations. An organizing vision, which develops through the discourse of a community of technology producers, information systems (IS) professionals, business managers, and other stakeholders, provides an interpretation of the applications of an IT innovation and the rationale for its use. Buzzwords are labels or names that come to be identified with an organizing vision and "may serve as a potent metaphor" (Swanson and Ramiller, 1997, p. 463) for conceptualizing the roles, relationships, control mechanism, and work processes associated with the IT innovation.

Data warehousing is one such metaphor. Drawn from practices for materials management in manufacturing and distribution operations, this metaphor has been used to conceptualize organizational processes for gathering, storing, and distributing firm-wide data for business analysis and to define the applications of technologies such as multidimensional and relational databases and on-line analytic processing software in these processes. In the last decade, this IT innovation has become a key area for information systems development as many firms have undertaken the construction and operation of so-called data warehouses. Design concepts for data warehousing and experiential reports on their development have received considerable attention in the business press (Sakaguchi and Frolick, 1997) and from professional associations such as the Data Warehouse Institute. Data warehousing has also become a subject of academic research, where research has focused primarily on technology design issues.

The data warehousing metaphor has undoubtedly served as a valuable cognitive device for conceptualizing the technical design of corporate-wide, informational databases. However, this metaphor also has implications for the meaning and utility of data used by business analysts and for end users' relationships with IS staff, that have not been fully explicated and debated. As more companies commit to a data warehousing strategy, it becomes increasingly important to balance the technological design perspective with a human-centered perspective in order to facilitate our understanding of the value, limitations and consequences of adopting this IT innovation. The objectives of this chapter are to explore data warehousing from the human centered perspective, first by examining the data warehousing metaphor and its implications for organizing IT support of business analysis activities. Then, the consequences of relying on the data warehousing metaphor as a conceptual model for designing the social aspects of business analysis processes are considered in a review of findings from a field study of a data warehousing project. Finally, the chapter considers the limitations of the data warehousing metaphor and explores alternative metaphors to highlight the human dimensions of this IT innovation.

## BACKGROUND: THE METAPHORICAL IMPLICATIONS OF THE DATA WAREHOUSE

Metaphor is a central cognitive mechanism that enables human beings to create and comprehend abstract concepts (Lakoff and Johnson, 1980). A metaphor provides a set of conceptual mappings between a source domain of knowledge and experience and the target domain that are expressed in idiomatic expressions and used to communicate thoughts and interpret events (Lakoff, 1993; Ortony, 1979). Metaphors are particularly helpful when new phenomena are encountered, providing a vocabulary drawn from familiar circumstances to facilitate discourse in the new domain (Weick, 1979; Morgan, 1986).

The data warehousing metaphor is drawn from experiences with the management of physical materials in manufacturing and distribution processes. In its original context, warehousing is the management of materials while they are in storage, including storing, dispersing, ordering, and accounting for all materials (Gaither, 1992). Warehousing ensures materials are available when needed by providing an inventory buffer between material suppliers and production processes, while reducing inventory costs through efficient purchasing and materials handling operations. Similarly, one of the primary motives for creating a data warehouse is to provide a data buffer between operational systems and business analysis activities, allowing each process to run efficiently and independently (Hathathorn, 1995; Orr, 1997; Sakaguchi and Frolick, 1997). Data warehousing concepts are also drawn from related materials management activities such as purchasing. The mission of purchasing is to develop and implement purchasing plans for each major product or service, select suppliers, negotiate contracts, and act as the interface between the company and supplier (Gaither, 1992). Analogously, a key rationale for warehousing data is to improve the quality of data used in business analysis by collecting operational data from "preferred vendors" and forcing data to conform to a single set of standards (Gray and Watson, 1998; Sakaguchi and Frolick, 1997). The IS development team assumes purchasing-like responsibilities for determining what types of data are needed for business analysis, locating acceptable suppliers among operational systems, and establishing supply channels for data.

The implied cognitive mappings from materials warehousing to the target domain of data management for business analysis are easy to discern. In data warehousing, operational data (materials) are collected from transaction processing systems (suppliers) for storage until needed in business analysis (production). Data files from operational systems or external data sources (shipments) are received and stored in relational or multidimensional databases (warehouses). Incoming materials are inspected for compliance to quality standards and may be standardized by converting fields to a common code or format. Data may be assigned to lots via a timestamp and packaged for storage and retrieval in summarized form (Inmon, 1995; Orr, 1997). End-user analysts or management information systems carry out the information production process, transforming data requisitioned from the warehouse via queries or scheduled data file transmissions, or feeds, into analytical reports (products) for use by managers (customers).

In the discourse on materials warehousing, much attention is given to optimizing the design and layout of the physical warehouse (Gaither, 1992). Similarly, discussions of data warehousing focus on topics such as how to design and build multidimensional or relational databases to efficiently store and access data (Gray and Watson, 1998; Orr, 1997). Warehouse design and layout issues are, of course, critically important, because large volumes of data are loaded and accessed in a typical data warehouse. However, the data warehousing metaphor has become more than a guide for the physical design of data bases or data handling processes. It has become the buzzword for an organizing vision (Swanson and Ramiller, 1997) that has broad implications for the social aspects of this IT innovation as well. For example, the data warehousing metaphor suggests that information systems personnel have two primary roles: purchasing agents who establish the data supply lines and warehouse operational staff who manage the receipt, storage, and distribution of data. Business analysts, on the other hand, become production workers who transform raw materials (operational data) into information products (analytical reports).

Also implicit in the data warehousing metaphor are assumptions about the nature of operational data and its utility in business analysis. For example, warehousing operational data implies that data can be treated like any physical material – collected, stored, repackaged, and distributed – without their value or meaning being altered or reduced. In fact, warehousing data is expected to increase data value, by creating "a single version of the truth" (Gray and Watson, 1998, p. 19) or a single image of business reality by integrating various data sources (Sakaguchi and Frolick, 1997). However, data have little utility until they are interpreted in ways that reflect events, actions, or objects of interest in the real world, in other words, until they are transformed into information. Boland (1987) characterized the notion that information is the same thing as structured data, a fantasy, maintaining that "information is not a resource to be stockpiled as one more factor of production. It has meaning, and can only be achieved through dialogue in a human community" (p. 377). With its focus on the collection and distribution of data, the warehousing metaphor provides few insights into how humans achieve such dialogues.

The organizing vision for data warehousing is compelling. The business press cites many anecdotal reports of successful applications, and hardware and software vendors extol the advantages of warehousing data. However, no metaphor can adequately represent all aspects of a complex social reality. If fact, a metaphor may raise false expectations about how an actual information technology will operate (Rechtin, 1997). Undue adherence to one metaphor for an IT innovation may also have undesirable consequences, as Mason (1991) illustrated in his analysis of the limitations of the IT-as-competitive-weapon metaphor. On the other hand, explicit consideration of the cognitive mappings inherent in a metaphor can bring to light both its strengths and limitations (Boland and Greenberg, 1992; Mason, 1991; Morgan, 1986) and may stimulate creative thinking about IT development and use (Couger, Higgins, and McIntyre, 1993).

With these issues in mind, the next section reviews findings of a case study of a data warehousing project to illustrate how reliance on this metaphor can mask important concerns about how users make sense of and use operational data in business analysis and about the complementary roles and responsibilities of IS personnel and business analysts.

## ISSUES AND PROBLEMS: DATA WAREHOUSING IN PRACTICE

The case study discussed in this chapter was conducted as part of a research project which investigated the ways in which IT developers, users, and managers conceptualize technology use in organizations and how differences in conceptualization affect requirements definition processes and outcomes (Davidson, 1996b). Data were collected on two systems development projects during a longitudinal field study at one research site. The research site, Group Health, Inc. (GHI) is a healthcare insurance company in the United States. The company utilized a variety of operational systems running on different hardware and software platforms, ranging from its mainframe to various mid-sized computers. Several years before the research project began, the company began a multi-year project to transfer all transaction processing to a single, unified set of enrollment and claims processing systems. While the move to a single transactional system was expected to reduce problems with inconsistent operational data, the new system did not support multi-year, multi-product line business analysis.

The findings discussed in this chapter relate to one of the projects studied at GHI, the INFOSYS project. This project began as a pilot project to install a software package (INFOSYS), which had a graphical user interface (GUI) for end-user generation of reports and ad-hoc queries. The initial goal was to populate the package's insurance claims database with several years of data for GHI's largest customer. Over several years, the INFOSYS project evolved from the initial idea of providing a limited end-user computing tool to a plan for building a corporate-wide warehouse of claims and enrollment data. The evolution of the INFOSYS application into data warehousing provided an opportunity to study how data warehousing concepts affected users' and IS developers' roles and relationships, practices, and expectations for the system.

Data on the INFOSYS project were collected in semi-structured interviews with INFOSYS developers (15), business analysts (13), and IS managers and executives (3). Observational data on user/developer interactions were collected during several requirements interviews and in training sessions. Systems documentation, project proposals, training materials, memos, and meeting notes were also examined. These data were examined for evidence of developers' and users' interpretations of the application and value of the INFOSYS system and of their expectations for the system's operation and use. Special attention was given in this analysis to the influence of data warehousing concepts on users' and developers' understanding of the system and what it would take to integrate the system into business analysis processes. Through this analytic process, four key areas were identified in which data warehousing concepts appeared to influence users' and developers' expectations for the INFOSYS applications, and which were sources of unresolved differences or potential problems. The first three areas discussed concern the meaning users attribute to operational data in business analysis. The fourth area related to differences in users' and developers' expectations for each other's roles and responsibilities. Quotations from study informants are presented throughout the discussion to demonstrate and substantiate the author's analysis. These quotations are representative of comments from key informants, which include most development team members and those business analysts who had had direct experience with the INFOSYS system.

## Issue 1: The Importance of Data Access Versus Contextual Cues in the Operational Context

Essential functions of data warehousing include extracting data from operational systems, cleansing and structuring data to make them more uniform, and storing data in the warehouse database for later use. The need to do so and the advantages for business analysis activities were readily apparent to developers at GHI. Not only were data strewn among diverse operational systems, these systems were difficult for business analysts to access. To secure appropriate data sources, IS developers had to search amid this confusion of operational systems. Deciding what data to stock in the INFOSYS database was no easy task. Project files contained many memos describing the intricacies of data definitions, indicating the extent to which data structure and content reflected the complexity of business processes and the context of business practices encoded in these operational systems.

To create a data feed file containing uniform data, IS developers developed standard definitions and searched for the perceived best source for each data field. They relied on users' detailed knowledge of data sources, acquired through their exposure to operational systems, to verify data sources. A systems analyst observed:

> When somebody says they need an element, the first thing we say to
> them, I think, is, 'Well, are there any oddities associated with this
> element?'

Cleaning up, or scrubbing, operational data and standardizing them to fit
INFOSYS formats did remove some anomalies. However, extracting data for
storage in the data warehouse also meant losing cues, and clues, embedded in the
operational context about the meaning, validity and interpretation of data. Business analysts relied on their familiarity with existing databases and their operational context to detect major problems with the data they used, as this analyst
explained:

> If I see something wrong, I'll know it's wrong, probably just from looking
> at this clinical data over and over and getting to know what it means and
> seeing things.

Commenting on this issue, a business analyst observed that to effectively use
a database, he needed to know the history of the company. To illustrate his point,
he cited fluctuations in the volume of claims processed several months earlier,
caused by a processing backlog in the operational system. Without his knowledge
of this operational problem, acquired through his close association with the
transactional system and its business context in the conduct of his job, the analyst
might have made the wrong assumptions about the meaning of increased transaction volumes. Although buffering business analysts from operational processes by
warehousing data lessened data access and standardization issues, analysts anticipated losing some of the knowledge and understanding about the idiosyncrasies,
the oddities of data, needed to interpret them correctly.

### Issue 2: Transforming Raw Operational Data into Analytic Categories for Business Reporting

To be of value in business analysis, transactional data from operational
systems have to be transformed into summary records, indices, or measurements
that depict real-world events and outcomes. In data warehousing terms, this
transformation refers to the shift from process-oriented to subject-oriented databases (Inmon, 1995). One business manager commented on the inherent difficulties
of doing so:

> You're dealing with numbers and a computer [system] that are struc-
> tured in any of a number of different ways, and you want to put all those
> numbers together in some way that equates to what happens in the real
> world. There's a lot of different ways you can do that. People don't agree
> on the best way to do it.

Some analysts believed that, since the INFOSYS GUI reports and queries had
defined algorithms and standardized reports, it would be more feasible to have

agreed-upon definitions. An account reporting analyst voiced his hope about INFOSYS use:

> If I want the top 300 providers, and somebody else wants the top 300 providers, we're going to get the same report ... there's going to be a lot more standardization, and I think that's a nice piece of it.

However, other analysts complained that INFOSYS's algorithms differed from algorithms they had traditionally used when interpreting data to produce business analysis reports, as this analyst commented:

> The people who brought INFOSYS into the company knew there were differences in the definitions, and they hadn't kept the standards that the company had.

Though INFOSYS provided a potential standard, its use could not easily be enforced, as this business manager observed:

> As long as they [analysts] have other ways of getting information the way they choose to view it, it's going to be very hard to get them to buy into using a tool like INFOSYS.

As the development team promoted INFOSYS's use as a corporate-wide data warehouse, such disagreements over the proper methods of interpreting raw, operational data were likely to continue, unless management could effectively dictate INFOSYS's use.

### Issue 3: Understanding Data Quality Versus Data Legitimacy

Developers and business analysts agreed there were data quality problems in existing reporting systems. By finding reliable data suppliers, patching up data quality problems, and standardizing and integrating data in the warehouse database, IS developers assumed the INFOSYS database would be more accurate and complete. They realized some data quality problems would continue, due to problems in the underlying operational systems, and that this might cause users to question the INFOSYS database. The INFOSYS project manager noted this in an interview:

> People who are using the data will not understand that this particular record looks crazy because of something that happened at claims processing.

Business analysts did understand that the quality of data in informational systems depended on the transactional systems from which data was derived. However, beyond questions about data quality, business analysts had concerns about data legitimacy. Account reporting analysts, for example, had an existing data source from which they obtained both ad-hoc reports and periodic, standard reports for customers. In some cases, reports had been produced continually over a period of years to monitor trends. Not only were the embedded schemes for summarizing and reporting claims data different from those in INFOSYS, but it was difficult to know whether the same sets of raw data were used in calculations in both systems. Analysts were concerned that reports produced from INFOSYS gave different results than the periodic reports and ad-hoc reports produced using existing procedures, algorithms, and data files. An analyst commented that this was a problem for her when she used INFOSYS to produce an ad-hoc report for GHI's largest customer, because the customer compared the INFOSYS report to earlier reports she had provided and found discrepancies which the analyst was at a loss to explain.

Developers, assuming they had done all they could to enhance data quality, didn't acknowledge that data legitimacy was an important issue separate from data quality that required intervention to increase users' confidence in INFOSYS. Instead, they interpreted business analysts' concerns about differences in results from these reporting systems in terms of data quality. Assuming INFOSYS had a higher quality database, they expected business analysts to willingly switch to this source, as the INFOSYS trainer commented:

> The way I'm trying to promote this to users is that you have a baseline that probably wasn't a reliable one. Make this your baseline, make this the new standard.

However, with other sources of data available, INFOSYS's role as the single source of data for business analysis could not be taken for granted. Unless all other information sources were eliminated, a process that would take some time to complete, questions of data legitimacy were likely to persist.

### Issue 4: Building the Warehouse Versus Supporting End-Users in Business Analysis

The INFOSYS project began as a solution to a specific problem, that is, providing a reporting tool to end users who produced analytical reports from health insurance claims for GHI's largest customer. However, key project sponsors anticipated that the INFOSYS package might serve as the basis for creating a broad, end-user programming environment. As part of this larger goal, data for other large customers were added to the database after the first pilot was completed. Later, GHI management determined that the package could be used for business analysis of a new HMO product line. Eventually, developers mapped out a strategy for building a corporate-wide database for business analysis that would include all of GHI's enrollment and claims data. In this way, the INFOSYS project evolved from a focused, end-user computing system into a data warehousing project, and IS developers' focus shifted from INFOSYS's GUI interface, which they believed would facilitate end-user programming, to the claims database they were building.

One of the interesting aspects of this evolution was team members' adoption of the term "data warehouse" to describe INFOSYS. This term was not evident in early project documentation; instead, the system was described as an MIS system that would support end-user computing. Later, these ideas merged, as the project sponsor's interchangeable use of the terms data warehouse and MIS system suggested:

> We had been talking for years about a data warehouse, an MIS system, for probably going on a decade pretty soon.

Other team members began to use the terminology of data warehousing to describe INFOSYS, as these systems analysts did to describe their expectations for INFOSYS:

> I would like to see it become the center of some sort of information warehouse, some sort of data warehouse, that everyone comes to for claims data.

> You're going to take and see a single repository of information that will be used to meet reporting needs.

As the project evolved into a data warehousing project, the goal of promoting end-user reporting remained, as the project sponsor indicated:

> I think the perception is still what it was originally, and that was to be a way to access information so that the end users don't have to depend on the programmers to get at most of their data.

Calling INFOSYS a data warehouse further emphasized the role of business analysts as report producers by highlighting the importance of expanding the INFOSYS database. Developers came to view their primary responsibility as expanding and operating the warehouse database, believing that their critical task was to get more data loaded as soon as possible. Little time could be spared for training or support, as a project leader commented:

> We are still in a constant implementation mode .... and we are often torn between our desire to go out and help use the product on a production basis and our need to continue to implement data so that more and more business units can use it.

Instead, a full-time trainer was hired to conduct half-day sessions focused on the mechanics of the system, such as moving through the menu of reports and queries, with little discussion of the meaning of data elements and none of practices for using the system.

Business analysts, on the other hand, expected that, beyond classroom training, they needed to play with the system, that is, to experiment in work situations with its features and data in order to understand its limits and capabilities. Through their efforts to locate data sources and design database extract and load programs, IS developers had acquired a deep knowledge of the oddities of data fields stockpiled in the warehouse – knowledge that would have been very beneficial to business analysts struggling to understand the INFOSYS system. To help them over this hurdle, business analysts wanted more than documentation, demonstrations, and brief training sessions. They expected in-depth support from the development team, as this analyst commented:

> Adults don't learn in the classroom. They learn by doing. When I try to use INFOSYS, I need one of the developers by my side .... If I had this for a week, I would know the system.

Given the priority developers placed on building the warehouse, it is not surprising adequate support was lacking in another analyst's opinion:

> What they were doing was just leaving people in the lurch, I think, on how to practically use it.

The INFOSYS trainer's views on the situation contrasted sharply with users' perspective. Expressing the developers' assumption that business analysts could function independently as information producers and should not expect the kind of assistance they had received in the past from programmers, she commented in an interview:

> They've all come to us asking us to do their work for them ... They want to be spoon fed.

If users were to accept INFOSYS as the preferred data source and utilize it for business analysis, such support issues had to be addressed. When the research project concluded, developers were waiting for users to specify standard reporting packages that IS staff would then code and operate using the INFOSYS database. However, questions about technical support for ad-hoc reporting remained unacknowledged and thus unresolved.

## Summary: Lessons from INFOSYS

After three years of development, excitement about INFOSYS was high among developers and business managers in many parts of GHI, with plans in place to add all claims and enrollment data to the warehouse over the next several years. On the other hand, business analysts were actually making little use of the two pilot databases, in large part because questions about the meaning and legitimacy of data in the warehouse and the difficulties they were having learning how to use INFOSYS remained unresolved. Project sponsors and developers had not acknowledged business analysts' reluctance to adopt INFOSYS as anything more than typical resistance to change. The data warehousing metaphor, which focused IS developers' attention on the physical construction of the database and the process of extracting and storing data, inhibited their recognition of latent problems with users' acceptance of the system. These problems were caused by users questions about the meaning, interpreting, and legitimacy of warehoused data and with their expectations for and need of IS developers' support to learn about and become comfortable with the new data source. Without positive action on their part to address analysts' questions about warehoused data and to help establish a core group of knowledgeable end-users who could comfortably use the system, it seemed likely that INFOSYS would be underutilized for some time and might never live up to its potential.

These types of problems are not unique to data warehousing projects, of course, and INFOSYS developers might have lessened the consequences with a stronger marketing and implementation effort. However, this analysis suggests that relying on the warehousing metaphor as a design guide put undue emphasis on technical design aspects while masking important social issues. The next section elaborates on this proposition by highlighting two areas in which the data warehousing metaphor is inadequate for understanding key social dimensions of business analysis systems.

# SOLUTIONS AND RECOMMENDATIONS: LIMITATIONS OF THE DATA WAREHOUSING METAPHOR

The data warehousing metaphor focuses attention on the tangible task of collecting and storing data created by diverse computerized systems and stored in electronic formats. Fundamental to the ontological mappings of the warehouse metaphor is the notion that data can be treated in much the same way that physical materials are treated, i.e., they can be collected, transported, stored, and used in production processes without losing their value. While value ultimately depends on utility, quality is a key component of value, and data warehousing is promoted as a way to improve data quality. However, data quality is a multidimensional concept that includes factors such as believability, reputation, accuracy, relevancy, completeness, interpretability, representational consistency, and accessibility (Wang and Strong, 1996). The potential for trade-offs between quality dimensions may be intrinsic to the data warehousing concept.

For instance, extracting data from operational systems and consolidating them in a warehouse can improve data accessibility. On the other hand, data interpretability may be diminished when data are abstracted from the operational context that provides cues for appropriate interpretation, or when analysts, buffered from operational systems by the warehouse, lose their understanding of complex operational realities encoded in data. Information about data formats and contents can be stored as metadata in data dictionaries or recorded in documentation, but this information cannot capture all the knowledge analysts develop through their experience with and exposure to operational processes. Uniform definitions and algorithms for processing data can be implemented in a data warehouse, but requiring common definitions may decrease the relevancy or the believability of data for those groups forced to acquiesce to warehouse standards.

In the organizing vision for data warehousing, a key rationale is to create a single source of data, and in this way, a single version of business realities (Gray and Watson, 1998). In this regard, the warehouse metaphor masks important aspects of the organizational data management problem and suggests unrealistic expectations for data warehousing outcomes. Simply building a warehouse does not guarantee a single source of data. At a minimum, there will be a transition time during which the data warehouse is built, other information systems are dismantled, and users are persuaded or compelled to abandon alternative data sources. Even if all preexisting MIS systems are eradicated after a data warehouse is implemented, data legitimacy problems can reoccur in a warehousing model. Unlike physical products that can be consumed only once, the same data set can be used many times, stored in multiple locations, and processed through more than one system. The data warehouse may be the official storehouse, but there is little to prevent users from creating local stockpiles of data in desktop applications for later use. Furthermore, business analysts who extract data from a warehouse may select, process, and interpret data differently, arriving at different versions of reality. The warehousing metaphor, which focuses attention on acquiring, storing and dispersing data shipments, offers limited insight on how to control data and data interpretation once data are shipped out of the warehouse database. Reaching consensus on the interpreted meaning of warehoused data remains a human accomplishment, not a technological feature of data warehousing.

The data warehousing metaphor, by focusing attention on the benefits and rationales for stockpiling corporate-wide data, may also mask the need for ongoing IS staff support for users engaged in business analysis. The warehousing metaphor specifies IS staff members' roles as purchasing agents or warehouse operators and business analysts' roles as producers of information products. In fact, expectations for end-user computing pervade the organizing vision for data warehousing, with the promise that IS staff will finally be freed from fulfilling mundane report requests from users. Spending time supporting users, either in one-on-one or group training sessions, can conflict with plans to continue building the warehouse, particularly when development staff resources are limited or there is strong demand for adding new data sources to the warehouse. However, developers can acquire unique knowledge of the negotiated meanings of data in a warehouse in their roles as purchasing agents and warehouse builders. Metadata contained in data dictionaries might suffice to convey basic information about data fields, but it cannot replicate the in-depth knowledge of warehouse developers nor eliminate the need to help business analysts develop their own knowledge and understanding of the new data sources, not only in training courses but also through on-the-job practice.

# FUTURE TRENDS: ALTERNATIVE METAPHORS FOR BUSINESS ANALYSIS

Undoubtedly, gathering data from diverse operational systems, standardizing their form, and maintaining a stockpile of historical data addresses numerous, long-standing problems with corporate-wide business analysis. Data from across the organization are more accessible, more accurate, and more complete. Organizations developing and using warehouses to good advantage attest to the value of this approach. However, relying too heavily on warehousing as the metaphor to guide the social organization of IT support for business analysis can also raise false expectations about what can be achieved with this approach and divert attention from important social concerns with system and process design. The fact that business press accounts of warehousing projects report that users often have difficulty agreeing on data definitions and with understanding warehoused data and that training and support requirements are frequently underestimated (Sakaguchi and Frolick, 1997) suggests this may be the case. Comparing and contrasting the warehouse metaphor with other potential metaphors, on the other hand, can stimulate creative thinking about how IT support for business analysis might be organized from a more human centered perspective. Here, two alternative metaphors are briefly considered.

### The Data Department Store

The term warehouse carries with it mental images of a large, cavernous building, crammed with piles of materials, located along the train tracks or at the harbor. Customers do not poke around a warehouse with a shopping list, looking for items that might be useful or interesting. Instead, they go to a retail store, where a variety of related products have been selected and arranged for easy access, convenience and appeal, and there are service people ready to help them find items and make purchases. The need for and advantages of retailing to enhance customer service are not evident in the warehousing metaphor. Instead, end-users are treated as producers who are expected to find their way, with the aid of the data dictionary, through multidimensional or relational databases containing terabytes of data. While some users are comfortable doing so, many might prefer a visit to a data department store. If IT support for business analysis were organized according to this metaphor, users might find a variety of data brands to select from and knowledgeable IT staff to explain differences in the features of each brand. They would probably find a broad selection of related data in the department store, with less raw data and more finished informational goods.

A shift towards data retailing is evident to some extent in the use of smaller, more focused data marts. Ideally, data marts draw data from the larger warehouse, process the data into summaries or "views" targeted for specific business uses and users, and present a more user-friendly, simpler interface to the user. However, in practice, data marts tend to be merely scaled-down versions of data warehouses rather than true data department stores. The metaphorical implications of data retailing, which emphasize information products and customer service, have yet to be fully developed.

### The Data Library

Perhaps because data warehousing deals with structured operational data, the focus in building warehouses has been on finding and maintaining a single, best source of data, on supplying the right facts to represent organizational truth, on once and for all settling disputes about "who has the right numbers." Knowledge, on the other hand, involves experience, interpretation, learning, opinions and diverse viewpoints. The discourse around IT support for knowledge management takes this into consideration. A metaphor that has been helpful in conceptualizing how to apply IT in knowledge management activities is that of a library. Borrowing this metaphor to think in terms of a data library might be a useful way to explore alternative social and technical designs for IT support of business analysis activities.

In a data library, data-as-knowledge might be available at different levels of abstraction, from structured, raw data files to completed analysis. Data sources might present a variety of viewpoints on an issue, and patrons of the library would resist efforts to restrict the library's contents to one version of the truth. Instead, users might search for information from various perspectives that would offer insights into a problem area. For example, the library might contain not only raw operational data, but also data interpretations from operational personnel as well as corporate analysts, who might have differing interpretations of the meaning and relevance of operational data. Librarians would select useful data for the library's collection, and reference experts would help patrons locate good sources of information, pointing out limitations in each source and suggesting alternative sources.

To the data warehouse practitioner or theorist, the notion of a data department store or data library may seem abhorrent, a step backward from the gains achieved through data warehousing. However, these metaphors are not proposed as a replacement for the data warehouse metaphor, but merely as alternative perspectives that illuminate some of the social aspects of managing data for corporate-wide business analysis. The first metaphor points to the need to build information distribution channels to enhance support and service for business analysts, who become customers, not producers, of information products. The second metaphor implies that the quest to establish one source for "business reality" is unrealistic and may be detrimental if it limits the organization's flexibility and openness to alternative interpretations of operational data. Exploring the cognitive mappings of these and other metaphors and contrasting them with the mappings of the warehousing metaphor can stimulate creative thinking about the social aspects of business analysis.

Further research will be needed to investigate the ways in which the data warehousing metaphor has shaped the discourse and influenced development of IT products and IS support services related to this innovation, including organizational practices in this area. Such research would consist of process-oriented, historical studies focused on the evolving text of practitioner conferences, exhibitions, and publications as well as developments in academic areas (Swanson and Ramiller, 1997). Studies may bring to light areas of overlap and conflict between organizing visions, such as between data warehousing and knowledge management. Further research into possible organizational consequences of using the warehouse metaphor as a guide for designing and structuring IT support is also needed. The case study reviewed in this chapter suggested two areas of particular interest. First, investigating how different organization members, such as operational users, business analysts, or mangers assess the legitimacy of warehoused data will improve understanding of the dimensions of data quality and may suggest ways to increase the utility of warehoused data. Second, examining the roles of end users and IT staff implied by the warehousing metaphor, studying the ways in which roles are enacted in practice, and assessing whether these groups have different expectations for IT support will help to identify factors that contribute to users' acceptance of data warehousing and the types of roles and skills that IT departments will need to develop and maintain.

## CONCLUSION

This chapter considers the influence of the data warehousing metaphor on the social design of IT support for business analysis. It takes as a starting point the existence of an organizing vision for the IT innovation represented by the buzzword data warehousing. While acknowledging that data warehousing offers many benefits, this chapter argues that the warehousing approach has been applied without critical reflection on the cognitive mappings implied by the underlying metaphor or the possible consequences of its use in practice. In particular, the data warehousing metaphor appears to have focused attention on technical design issues, while masking issues related to how human beings in organizational settings make sense of operational data used in business analysis. The metaphor also de-emphasizes the need for intensive support for end-users of the warehouse by emphasizing the role of IS staff as warehouse builders. Findings of a case study of a data warehousing project illustrated how attention was diverted from business analysts' questions about the meaning and legitimacy of warehoused data and from their expectations for support from IT staff. A critique of the warehouse metaphor highlighted inherent limitations of the metaphor for conceptualizing key aspects of the data management problem in business analysis. The insights from two alternative metaphors for supporting business analysis, that of a data department store and a data library, were also considered.

Business managers and data warehousing practitioners may find this critique useful in several respects. Explicitly examining the conceptual mappings of the data warehousing metaphor points out where data warehousing outcomes can differ from the results achievable with materials management, and thus may indicate where expectations for the data warehouse are unrealistic. Asking users and developers to explore the metaphorical implications of data warehousing may unearth areas of disagreement and problems with user satisfaction. Finally, exploring other metaphors to guide development and design can stimulate creative thinking about requirements for IT support of business analysis.

## REFERENCES

Boland, R., Jr. (1987). The In-formation of information systems. in R. Boland, Jr. and R. Hirschheim (eds.),*Critical issues in information systems research*. New York: John Wiley & Sons, Ltd., 363-379.

Boland, R., Jr., & Greenberg, R. (1992). Method and metaphor in organizational analysis. *Accounting, Management and Information Technology*, 2(2), 117-137.

Couger, J., Higgins, L., and McIntyre, S. (1993). (Un)Structured creativity in information systems organizations. *MIS Quarterly*, 17(4), 375 - 397.

Davidson, E. (1996a). Negotiating requirements: A social cognitive perspective on the systems development process. *Proceedings of the Second Annual AIS Americas*

*Conference on Information Systems*. Phoenix, Arizona, 422-424.

Davidson, E. (1996b). *Framing information systems requirements: An investigation of social cognitive processes in information systems delivery*. MIT Sloan School of Management: unpublished doctoral dissertation.

Gaither, N. (1992). *Production and operations management (fifth edition)*, Orlando, Florida: The Dryden Press, 548-570.

Golovchinsky, G. & Chignell, M. (1997). The newspaper as an information exploration metaphor. *Information Processing and Management, 33(5)*, 663-683.

Gray, P. & Watson, H. (1998). *Decision support in the data warehouse*. New Jersey: Prentice Hall.

Hathathorn, R. (1995). Data warehouse energizes your enterprise. *Datamation, 41(2)*, 38-45.

Inmon, W. (1995). Tech topic: What is a data warehouse? *Prism* [Online], 1(1). Available: http://www.cait.wustl.edu/cait/papers/prism/vol1_no1 [1999, September 27].

Johnson, G. (1994). Of metaphor and the difficulty of computer discourse. *Communications of the ACM, 37(12)*, 97 - 102.

Lakoff, G. (1993). The contemporary theory of metaphor. In A. Ortony (Ed.) *Metaphor and Thought (second edition)*. Cambridge University Press, New York, NY, 201-251.

Lakoff, G. and Johnson, M. (1980). *Metaphors we live by*. Chicago: University of Chicago Press.

Mason, R. (1991). The role of metaphors in strategic information systems planning. *Journal of Management Information Systems, 8(2)*, 11-30.

Miles, M. and Huberman, A. (1994). *Qualitative data analysis*, Thousand Oaks, CA: Sage Publications.

Morgan, G. (1986). *Images of organization*. Newbury Park, California: Sage Publications.

Orr, K. (1997). *Data warehousing technology*. [Online] The Ken Orr Institute. Available: *http://KenOrrInst.com* [1999, September 27].

Ortony, A. (1979). *Metaphor and thought*. Cambridge: Cambridge University Press.

Rauch, T., Leone, P., & Gillinhan, D. (1997). Enabling the book metaphor for the World Wide Web: Disseminating on-line information as dynamic web documents. *IEEE Transactions on Professional Communications, 40(2)*, 111-128.

Rechtin, E. (1997). The synthesis of complex systems. *IEEE Spectrum*, July, 51 - 55.

Sakaguchi, T. & Frolick, M. (1997). A review of the data warehousing literature. *Journal of Data Warehousing, 2(1)*, 34-54.

Swanson, E. & Ramiller, N. (1997). The organizing vision in information systems innovation. *Organization Science, 8(5)*, 458-474.

Wang, R. & Strong, D. (1996). Beyond accuracy: What data quality means to data consumers. *Journal of Management Information Systems, 12(4)*, 5-33.

Weick, K. (1979). *The social psychology of organizing (second edition)*. New York: Random House.

## Chapter XII

# Critical Thinking and Human Centred Methods in Information Systems

Lorraine Warren
The University of Lincolnshire and Humberside

## PERSPECTIVE

Over the last four decades, information technology (IT) has permeated almost every aspect of our lives. From its origins in the data processing (DP) departments of large organisations, where bureaucratic operations were automated on mainframe computers, IT has penetrated ever further into all kinds of organisational activity, largely due to the accessibility of the personal computer (PC) in the 1980s and the 1990s. Beyond that, IT is also involved in many aspects of our everyday lives, such as education, leisure and entertainment, now that the boundaries between traditional telecommunications technologies and computer-based systems effectively no longer exist. This permeation has meant that the range of people now closely involved with IT on a regular basis has expanded far beyond the white-coated experts in the early DP departments, with terms such as 'the information society' in common parlance. It is therefore hardly surprising that the discipline of information systems (IS) emerged and is now evolving to meet the challenge of analysis and design in this complex and dynamic social environment. Nor is it surprising that IS is moving on from its early emphasis on highly structured formal methods of analysis and design, designed to cope with the machine-like preoccupations of the data processing world, to a far softer, human-centred focus. There is clearly an agenda for improvement for IS; although the notions of success and failure may be problematic in themselves, we hear of IS 'failures' which make the evening news at depressingly regular intervals — Y2K, the UK air traffic control project at West Drayton, the recent Passport Agency fiasco, for example. More generally, a wide-ranging (14,000 organisations) survey in the UK carried out by the Economic and Social Research Council and the Department of Trade and Industry (OASIG, 1996) concerning the outcomes of IT investments makes worrying reading, reporting that:

- 80-90% do not meet their performance goals;
- about 80% of systems are delivered late and over budget;
- about 40% of developments fail or are abandoned;
- less than 40% fully address training and skills requirements;
- less than 25% properly integrate business and technology objectives;
- only 10-20% meet all their success criteria.

In the study, it is concluded that the problems are rarely caused by the technology itself, but instead to the lack of attention paid to the people who have to use the technology and also to broader organizational factors. The following far-reaching concerns were identified, *inter alia*:

- the complexity of interaction between humans and technological artifacts;
- the heterogeneity of interests and agendas which exist in organizations;
- the lack of (consistent) user involvement with the design and implementation process;
- the (perceived) association of IT developments with redundancies;
- the turbulent economic environment which organizations face.

The emergence of the social character of technology as a focal point for study has led those working in IS to draw on the disciplines of psychology, linguistics, sociology and anthropology for theoretical sophistication to guide and inform the human-centred design agenda — after all, IS is essentially an *applied* discipline. The trawl for useful strands of theory has been wide: the first part of this chapter begins by presenting an overview of how this is changing research and practice in IS; the second discusses an information systems design project where the application of one particular strand of social theory, critical systems thinking, is illustrated.

## INTRODUCTION

IS has inherited a dominant technocentric positivistic orthodoxy from its early origins when 'computer science' was regarded as a subbranch of engineering. The work of Simon (1981) was influential in ensuring that this agenda was maintained in the organisational arena, through his vision of a 'Unified Science' of complexity and information processing. The idea of organisations as formal decision-making structures under conditions of bounded rationality was a key notion in the development of classical Artificial Intelligence (AI), which seemed to hold so much promise in the 1970s. Orlikowski and Baroudi (1991) concluded on studying the approaches and underlying assumptions in research papers in IS that 95% were based on a positivist epistemology. In a similar vein, Iivari (1991) identifies seven major schools of thought in IS design: software engineering, database management, management information systems, decision support systems, implementation research, the socio-technical approach and the infological approach. He suggests that all seven schools adhere to positivism as their underlying epistemology, with only the school of decision support systems laying claim to any anti-positivistic notions — an interesting move away from classical AI!

Notwithstanding the conclusions reached by the authors referred to above, few would argue that this orthodoxy is being challenged and indeed being supplanted by a range of different perspectives, which increasingly place the human being at the centre of the IS design process, rather than the technology. This change is in some part due to the influence of Burrell and Morgan's four-paradigm framework (1979) in the field of organisational analysis, which clearly identifies a range of approaches to sociological research in terms of the underlying ontological and epistemological approaches employed. Burrell and Morgan's framework is just one indicator of the diversity of traditions which have developed in social theory as the dominance of orthodox science have been called into question. For IS, the most notable contributions have been from two of these traditions: the critical theory of the Frankfurt School, most associated with the work of Max Horkheimer and Jurgen Habermas, and the hermeneutics of Schutz and Gadamer. 'Critical theory' took a different stance to that of the 'traditional theory' — in short, that the processes of knowledge production had a socially and politically constitutive context and therefore, findings of such processes were not neutral and timeless, but should be understood and interpreted against their background. Hermeneutics has many manifestations, all of which are concerned with interpretation of meaning, with the perspective of individual actors in social situations. The spirit of these developments has been taken on board to a significant extent by the IS community, resulting in a heterogeneity of approaches to IS research and practice which have been reviewed by: Hirschheim (1985), who presents a useful history of IS episte-mology; Hirschheim and Klein (1989) and Hirschheim et al. (1995), who classify approaches to IS activity in terms of Burrell and Morgan's sociological paradigms (1979); Checkland and Holwell (1997) who classify IS schools of thought in terms of functionalist ('hard') and interpretative ('soft') approaches; and Mingers and Stowell (1997) who focus on the notion of IS as an emerging discipline. Key theoretical milestones include the work of Markus (1983) and Robey and Markus (1984), who focus on the interplay (at the micro level) between power, politics and ritual in the IS design process. Klein and Lyttinen (1985), criticise the engineering agenda inherent in the prevailing 'scientism' in IS for its lack of attention to social factors. Boland (1985, 1987, 1991) calls for the use of phenomenology as an approach to research in IS, with a view to supporting the emergence of meaning during the IS design process. Winograd and Flores (1986), laying claim to Heidegger, argue that organizations are constituted as networks of conversations in which commit-ments are generated — and that computers can only support such conversations if there is a break with the rationalist tradition. Stamper (1997) also contributes to the linguistic turn by promoting the use of semiotic frameworks for IS research and design. The use of metaphor as a tool for analysis and interpretation has been developed by Kendall and Kendall (1983) and Walsham (1991) who point out the limitations for IS of the predominance of the metaphors of the organization as a machine and as an organism.

There is certainly ample evidence that the theoretical shift in IS has led to shifts in practice. By and large, the result has been the development of participative IS design programmes, where it is intended that those participating are enabled to take control of the design process themselves, away from domination by experts or managerial agendas — obviously with varying degrees of success. From the early days of the pioneering work of Mumford (1983) in socio-technical participative design, fully fledged action research programmes have emerged, notably Baskerville and Wood-Harper (1996), Checkland and Holwell (1997), Lau (1997) and Stowell et al. (1997). Walsham (1995) and Myers (1997) demonstrate that interpretive methods have become increasingly mainstream since being kick-started by Checkland's Soft Systems Methodology (SSM) in 1981. In line with these developments have been calls for methodological pluralism in IS (Avison and Myers, 1995; Galliers, 1992; Jackson, 1997a; Landry and Banville, 1992; see also Brinkkemper et al, 1996), on the grounds that the complexity of organisational activity could never be captured or addressed by one single method, and that a diversity of approaches was required.

Some of the most powerful lobbyists for change in IS at present are those who advocate systems-based approaches to participative development programmes. Jackson (1997b) summarises the case for systems thinking in general as a theoretical prop for IS on the basis of four interrelated arguments. Firstly, that systems thinking has made extensive progress in questioning the nature of the 'systems' it seeks to understand and intervene in. Second is the fact that systems thinking has undergone, and managed to come through, a period of crisis when different conceptualisations of the field of study fought one another for hegemony. The third argument is that systems thinking has demonstrated great potential for linking theory and practice. Finally, there is the utility of the 'boundary' concept, which surely must be a fundamental notion for IS developers given the all-pervasive nature of IT referred to at the beginning of this chapter.

While systems thinking can be traced to its scientific roots in the general systems movement of von Bertalanffy and Boulding (and, from social theory, the work of Parsons and Luhmann), more recent developments have explicitly taken account of the critical and interpretative schools of thought, as the systems movement has seen its traditional, 'rational', 'hard' models unable to cope with the increasingly complex and turbulent organisational world, with its conflicting human perspectives — partly in response to Silverman's (1970) attack on the traditional approach. During the late 1970s and 1980s, organisational cybernetics and soft systems thinking evolved as important strands of systems thinking, with Beer's Viable System Model (VSM) (1981, 1985) and Checkland's Soft Systems Methodology (SSM) (1981), as notable milestones. In terms of Burrell and Morgan's sociological paradigms, the functionalism of hard systems thinking was being challenged by the structuralism of organisational cybernetics and the interpretivism of soft systems thinking. Both these approaches have been used for IS analysis and design, so there is clear evidence of long-time synergy between the IS and the systems communities (see Espejo and Harnden, 1989 for the cybernetic perspective, and Checkland and Holwell 1997 for the most developed version of SSM in IS). Notwithstanding the emergence of these newer perspectives, systems thinking was still subject to a barrage of radical critique for being inherently managerialist in its outlook (Ulrich, 1981; Rosenhead, 1976; Jackson, 1982). It was also acknowledged that the plethora of systems methodologies now available all had strengths, weaknesses and limitations, there was little guidance on which to choose, or how to match a given methodology to a particular problem or situation. These criticisms led to the emergence of critical systems thinking (CST) in the late 1980s and the 1990s. A similar situation pertained in IS, apart from Avison and Wood-Harper's Multiview (1990), which is an attempt at fusing a range of hard and soft methodologies in the context of an overall hermeneutic philosophy. These parallels make the time ripe for a consideration of how IS might benefit form CST, that is, if we can define what CST is and what its potential benefits to IS might be! CST is still an evolving phenomenon with different manifestations. Although there are two main strands, here we concentrate on the one arising from direct attempts to develop systems thinking through Habermas' theory of knowledge constitutive interests, that is to address the technical, the practical and the emancipatory interest by means of pluralistic combinations of existing methodologies. This strand of thinking produced a number of authors arguing for explicit fundamental commitments for CST, albeit using different definitions and terminologies. Jackson (1991a) lists five; Schecter (1991), Flood and Jackson (1991a) and Midgley (1996) list three. Jackson's commitments are critical awareness, social awareness, complementarism at the methodological and the theoretical levels and dedication to human well-being and emancipation. Critical awareness primarily concerns understanding the strengths and weaknesses and the theoretical underpinnings of available systems methods, techniques and methodologies. It is here that CST has drawn most heavily on social theory. Social awareness concerns considering the organisational and societal climate which prevails at any stage in an intervention. Methodological complementarism originates from the idea of somehow orchestrating the use of different methodologies within an intervention; to gain any benefits from the diversity of approaches available, this must necessitate complementarism at the theoretical level also, even if that does raise the spectre of paradigm incommensurability. Emancipation seeks to achieve for all individuals the maximum development of their potential. The intention is that these commitments are considered as of equivalent importance and as interdependent themes, yet clearly, the commitments raise complex (and still debated) questions for both theory and practice. An earlier strand of CST can be found in Ulrich (1983, 1996), who builds on the philosophy of Kant in an attempt to make explicit and enable challenge to 'boundary judgements' in social systems design; it operates through Critical Systems Heuristics, a mode of questioning intended to reveal the normative content of design processes. Although CSH is not followed here, the importance of the boundary concept is of key importance to IS designers, and its value is unquestioned.

Jackson (1997b) has argued that information systems researchers have, at one time or another, shown an interest in each of the commitments of CST. The argument can be further developed to infer that CST can yield an integrated programme of research and practice for IS. As yet, there are few documented instances of the application of CST to IS-related problems beyond Jackson's own account (in 1997b, and Green, 1992 and 1993a,b) of an intervention in North Yorkshire Police, and a report of an intervention then underway concerning the student record systems at the University of Luton (Lehaney and Clarke, 1997). What then, are the expected benefits and drawbacks which we can expect from using CST over other IS methodologies, such as Checkland's SSM, Mumford's ETHICS, or other action-research oriented programmes, to guide an IS-related intervention? One difficulty in identifying these is that there is as yet little in the literature focusing directly on the practical benefits of CST, rather hope and optimism that the drawbacks of earlier modes of systems thinking (hard, soft and cybernetic) will be overcome, whilst their benefits will be realised and overall, a spirit of human improvement should prevail. Typically, one reads fairly brief discussions around CST's own underpinning philosophical commitments (Clayton and Gregory, 1997; Jackson, 1997b; Warren and Ellis, 1997): Were we critical? Did we use complementarism? Was our practice emancipatory? This is useful, but rather inward looking, particularly when terminology is used in different ways (with emancipation meaning anything from traditional notions of personal libera-tion, to the much more nebulous, 'local improvement'). Midgley (1997) goes a little further, arguing for more emphasis on exposing boundary judgements and in-creased awareness of the interdependency of the three commitments in evaluations of interventions. He defines improvement as "when a desired consequence has been realised through intervention, and a *sustainable* improvement has been achieved when this looks like it will last into the indefinite future without the appearance of undesired consequences (or a redefinition of the original conse-quences as undesirable)"(p. 340) . Whilst advocates of CST evidence great concern and deep reflection on these issues, it is all still rather vague, particularly where convincing practitioners is concerned, and is clearly an area which warrants further research!

CST has been subject to critique at both the practical and the theoretical levels. Practically, CST presents a complex set of commitments for researchers or practi-tioners to operationalise. One of the best-known attempts to put CST into practice is Total Systems Intervention (TSI). This was established by Flood and Jackson (1991b; presaged by Jackson and Keys (1984) and Jackson (1987)). TSI was designed as a meta-methodology, the first version of which consisted of three phases[1] — Creativity, Choice and Implementation. In the Creativity phase, managers are encouraged to "think creatively" about their organisations using various meta-phors as "lenses" to provide insight into different aspects of organisational prob-lem situations. The metaphors of "machine", "organism", "brain", "culture", "team", "coalition" and "coercive system", derived largely from Morgan (1986), are recommended[2] . In the Choice phase, the metaphors generated in the Creativity phase are mapped to the 'System of Systems Methodologies' (SOSM) in order to match methodology to problem situation. In the SOSM, problem situations are mapped according to two axes: *simple/complex* and *unitary/pluralist/coercive*, accord-ing to the degree of (dis)agreement between participants. The implementation phase consists of the application of the chosen methodology(ies) to yield change.

This early version of TSI has been subjected to considerable critique at both the theoretical and practical levels, not least by one of its creators (Jackson, 1999). Other examples include Tsoukas (1993a,b), Spaul (1997), Brocklesby (1994,1995), Mingers and Brocklesby (1996), Ormerod (1992,1996) and Cummins (1994). In brief, the concerns centre on practical unwieldiness, that it can be used as a 'recipe', incom-mensurability where methodologies from different paradigms are concerned, and a lack of methodologies to deal with coercive situations. Although this latter difficulty cannot be laid at the door of TSI, nonetheless it rather undermines TSI's claim to support emancipatory practice. There are however, some positive accounts in the literature, including Green (1993a, b), and Ho (1994), and notwithstanding his own critique, Jackson (1999) still favours the 'spirit' of TSI and calls for its further development as "critical systems practice (CSP)

" (p. 19), to underscore that this must be a research vehicle for CST and not a consultants' charter (a recipe). In the mooted CSP, a meta-methodology is called for which seeks to manage the paradigms not by aspiring to meta-paradigmatic status, but by mediating between paradigms. Paradigms are allowed to confront one another on the basis of 'reflective conversation' (Morgan, 1983). Critique is therefore managed between the paradigms and not controlled from above the paradigms. How such a conversation between paradigms can best be orchestrated need further research.

Theoretically, CST's claimed linkages to Habermas are now acknowledged to be not entirely successful (Spaul, 1997; Jackson, 1999); secondly, postmodernism presents challenges to the very notions or "grand narratives" of critique, emancipation and pluralism. Several authors in the systems community are looking to postmodernism as a source of inspiration for further development of CST, for example, Flood, 1996; Flood and Romm, 1996; Ormerod, 1996, 1997; Taket and White, 1995, 1997. At present, these efforts are largely directed towards the orchestration of diversity through (methodological) pluralism in a spirit of contextual sensitivity.

Whilst the word 'postmodernism' often elicits knee-jerk horror reactions, nonetheless the endeavour has made a significant contribution to IS, and if CST is going to prove useful to IS, it is worthwhile exploring this contribution for potential synergy for future development. Unfortunately, the work does not come in a neatly delineated IS-labelled package: the literature body is very diffuse; sometimes the ontological and epistemological assumptions are made explicit, sometimes they are implicit, in which case the reader is relying upon his/her own interpretation of the text. However, bearing this in mind, if one identifies postmodern approaches with relativist ontology—that is denial of one or all of the theses of universalism, objectivism and foundationalism (Harre & Krauss, 1996) it is possible to see a contribution at both the theoretical and the methodological level.

There are few developed treatises relating solely to the theoretical issues which may link postmodernism and IS. Exceptions to this are Poster (1990), who links the changes in contemporary communication patterns enabled by IS/IT to the themes of Foucault, Derrida and Lyotard. More recently, Crowe et al. (1996) focus on the notion of IS as social constructs. Finally, Law et al. (1996) provide a memorable challenge to orthodoxy in the title of their paper, *Read this and change the way you feel about software engineering*! The opening gambit in the abstract to this paper hints at its usefulness, for in the words of the authors, the paper is "concerned with the bridging the interdisciplinary divide between the technical and social aspects in the enterprise of software engineering".

Outside these specific instances, the most significant theoretical contribution comes from sociology, particularly developments emerging from sociological studies of science, applied science and technology. Within this field, the key postmodern accounts are represented by constructivist studies which explicitly claim a relativist ontology. While few examples are specific to IS, there are many examples which refer to technological systems and so raise issues for constructivist studies of IS as instances of technological systems. In terms of constructivist approaches to studying technological systems, there are a number of seminal texts: Law (1986; 1991), Bijker and Law (1992) and Bijker et al. (1987). These edited collections are broad and, while clearly developing constructivist theory, are also empirically informed. The value of these collections is twofold, firstly in establishing frameworks for thinking about human-technology relations and secondly for exploring both heterogeneous interpretations of technological systems and the processes through which technologies become stabilised. Alongside the edited collections, there are a number of notable individual contributions: for example Callon (1986), Latour (1993), Law (1988), and Grint and Woolgar (1997). While the collected editions demonstrate variety within constructivist approaches, these individual contributions represent two currently powerful, yet distinct, foci in technology studies—namely the notion of artifacts as social agents represented in actor-network studies (Latour, Callon and Law ) and discourse-based approaches (Grint and Woolgar).

At the methodological level, there is a richer vein, although in these works, ontological and epistemological assumptions are less likely to be made explicit - sometimes it is more a question of the spirit of postmodernism inhabiting the work. One of the most powerful studies is that of Anderson (1994). In reviewing the use of ethnography in Human-Computer Interaction (HCI), Anderson suggests that most instances of ethnography in HCI demonstrate a *mis*understanding of ethnography—the focus being ethnography as data collection rather than analytical tool. Anderson locates this misunderstanding in a failure to recognise the textuality of ethnographic practice. In this study he draws on the debates of meta-ethnography in order to develop a sophisticated discussion linking material from HCI, sociology and anthropology. By relating contemporary issues in HCI concerning user contexts and boundary (see for example Suchman, 1988; Luff et al., 1992) with the sociology of translation (Latour, 1992) and reflexive ethnographies of programming practice (Button and Sharrock, 1994) Anderson provides a sound review of ethnography in systems design and argues for the use of analytic ethnography in design. His purpose in so doing is that analytic ethnography will serve to counterpoise "a summary logic of organizational structure such as that associated with the calculus of efficiency and productivity with the local logics of daily organizational life."

In pursuing this approach in practice, Forsythe et al. (1992) and Forsythe (1995) use ethnography to examine the meaning of information needs in a specific context (medical infomatics) and, following a similar line, Hughes et al. (1993) focus on the social construction of experience, revealing hidden knowledge of specific (work) communities. A further study by Despres (1996) takes a slightly different problem scope when he undertakes "an ethnography of information technology and modernist business organization." Although once again he is exploring the contextual nature of information he relocates his discussion in a meta (socio-economic) context; this study is less concerned with design issues than exploration of technology in context.

The usefulness of constructivist approaches to thinking about IS is quite clear —they address the issues of complexity, heterogeneity and difference; slightly less clear is the usefulness of constructivist accounts to the IS agenda of improvement. The significant texts tend to have relevance to only in as much as they raise awareness and sensitise readers to the constructed nature of IS; there is little that can be taken forward as theoretical grounding for policy development or practice, which raises the charge of impotence — although the benefits are much clearer at the methodological level. There is clearly synergy to be gained from dialogues between the systems and postmodern communities, particularly at the method-ological level, where discourse-based analysis, or reflexive ethnographic practice may reveal meaning and political difference in social situations — this may be one area which could provide insights into the 'conversation between paradigms' which Jackson speaks of in regard to Critical Systems Practice, referred to earlier. However, a theoretical state of ontological relativity would clearly be problematic for systems thinkers as this would require abandoning the notion of 'system' itself! Nonetheless, this is clearly a fruitful area for future research.

## A CASE STUDY

This case study is presented to demonstrate the usefulness of CST to guide and inform an IS design project. The original reporting on this project appears in more detail in two papers currently in press (Warren and Adman, 1999 for the CST/TSI methodology, and Adman and Warren, 2000 for the adaptation and discussion of the ETHICS and QUICKethics methodologies used within the intervention). In this account, I am attempting to highlight and emphasise where CST seems to have made its greatest contribution to the IS design process. The full articles should be consulted for more detailed discussions.

The setting is a medium-sized university in the UK where the student population has grown from 6,000 to around 12,000 students in recent years; there are around 900 academic staff. The Academic Computing Services Unit (ACSU) is staffed by between 30 and 40 staff, including academic-related, technical and clerical grades. Collectively, they provide campus-wide IS support to all academic staff and students from a central location (the 'Centre'). The ACSU offers a wide range of IS services to support teaching, research and administrative activities. In brief, the ACSU was finding it increasingly difficult to respond favourably to an ever-increasing demand for user support. Nationally, the growth in popularity of end-user computing over the past decade has placed pressures on IS support services; both user numbers and the diversity of applications in use tend to increase, often without concomitant increase in support service resources. There was a recognition within the management of the ACSU that these national pres-sures were causing a local problem of increased demand, as manifested by queues at public access points in the Centre. Various reports from ACSU staff and comments from service users suggested that the organisation of the ACSU's 'front end', that is the way in which users' requests, queries and problems were handled did not help the situation. The 'front end' consisted of the following elements. There were two official physical user access points in the Centre—the 'Reception Desk' and a separate 'Help Desk'. The Reception Desk was publicised as the first point of contact; its staff dealt directly with a wide variety of simple enquiries including small sales. More complex enquiries were referred to the Help Desk, or a specialist member of the ACSU staff could be brought in to assist. Phone enquiries to Reception were also dealt with. At peak times however, the volume of demand could lead to queues building up, of both users seeking information/help and incoming phone calls needing attention. The Help Desk was intended to process more complex enquiries and could be accessed in person, by telephone, or by referral from the Reception Desk; again, lengthy queues often built up. As queues lengthened, response times became unpredictable and users often began to get agitated and even aggressive. To complicate matters, hardware-related problems were investigated by a separate group of technicians who operated in a mobile fashion. They could be contacted by telephone on a separate line from the Reception Desk, or via the Help Desk. The user had to decide who or which service to contact for best results, which sometimes meant queuing twice. To avoid queues, many academic staff would bypass both the Reception Desk and the Help Desk by telephoning individual ACSU staff directly in their offices. Sometimes the same user would try several different ACSU staff one after another until they were satisfied. From the ACSU staff's viewpoint these ad-hoc and unscreened interruptions were disruptive and frustrating. Unfortunately, there was no system of call-logging or follow-up monitoring of enquiries, which often led to 'black holes' for users. Another difficulty was that powerful users of the ACSU would sometimes expect to 'jump the queue', regardless of the urgency of other problems in hand at the time. ACSU staff also commented on the unrealistic expectations of some users, who were often unaware of the inherent complexity of what might appear on the surface to be a "simple" problem.

All in all, a fairly typical problem set was experienced by most IS support services as demand has mushroomed in line with technical and social change. The trigger for this particular project was the opportunity for change presented when the long serving Director of Computing Service retired; this led to the creation of a new post, Dean of Information Systems (DIS), who was keen to make the ACSU more customer driven. It was decided that this could be achieved by redesigning the ACSU's activities around its front-line service; and so the project was initiated, under the direction of a steering group comprising the DIS and senior members of the ACSU, including the Project Director who kindly permitted me to work with him on this project. My role was not to take part in the mechanics of the intervention, but to act, using Baskerville and Wood-Harper's term (1996), as a 'monitor' to act as a sounding board for discussion and consultation as and when required during the intervention. And at the end of the day, a new system was designed, accepted and implemented, with, it would seem, a considerable degree of success, although formal evaluation is still underway. To briefly describe the new system, it involved a physical redesign of the ACSU reception area, to make better use of space, to make it more welcoming for visitors by introducing a seating area and plants, and to make it more efficient for staff. Call-handling was completely overhauled, with the introduction of a 'one-stop shop'; call logging, tracking and ownership procedures were established, and a computer-based support system accessible to all staff was installed. To prevent queue jumping and unrealistic expectations, task priorities (transparent to all) were established, response levels and performance indicators established. Naturally training sessions for all those involved were delivered.

Looking back to the problem situation and examining the new system, it would be easy to say, "well surely that's obvious! I could have got there without any elaborate CST / TSI process to help me!". Whilst no-one can determine whether that is true or not, such a response rather misses the point. It *was* clear to most people concerned right from the outset that as part of becoming more customer centred, information flows within the ACSU and between the ACSU and its customers would have to be improved, and that the reception area was rather chaotic in appearance and function. What was important was that the new design was analysed, designed and implemented by all the ACSU staff for themselves, to give a sense of ownership, and a stake in the success of the new system. There were early calls from some staff to just install some proprietary logging software and train staff in the use of that — but that seemed like a very reductionist, 'firefighting' response, which would not yield the benefits of a more systemic intervention. Talking of which, where should the boundary for the project be drawn? Although the system of interest is obviously the ACSU, it is contained within the wider system of the university, the staff and students who are the customers of the ACSU. The nature and frequency of interaction with the users of the ACSU—who might be physically present in the building, or communicating from outside by phone, fax or e-mail - presented a highly permeable system boundary. They were seen from the ACSU almost as part of the system — *almost*. A weakness at the outset of this project was that whilst broad consultation with the users (or 'customers' now) would have been very desirable, this was limited to minutes of IT user committee meetings and fairly *ad hoc* informal conversations with members of the ACSU staff.

Having decided to carry out the project in a systemic manner, the question arose of how we would reflect on our own practice. It is clear from the literature that TSI is flawed, we accepted that much, but felt that, to echo Jackson, it still had some value in enabling the *spirit* of CST to come through in our efforts. So to a brief description of the project.

TSI begins with a creativity phase, which goes on from general information gathering, through standard techniques such as observation, interviews, focus groups, documentary search and so on. This was carried out, in large part by the researchers, and is reflected in the description of the problem situation given above. Project planning meetings were used however, to give the ACSU staff an early opportunity to become involved by discussing their perceptions of the problem situation. It was fairly clear from these discussions that there was overall general agreement that the project needed to be undertaken, and that there was a need to make improvements. There were different views over how the project should proceed, particularly between different groupings within the ACSU staff, but no serious disagreements were evident — just the everyday fairly jocular 'rough and tumble' of organisational life! TSI also calls for the use of metaphor analysis to gain insights for both participants and researchers into problem situations. We spent a little time as researchers considering the neurocybernetic, machine, and organism metaphors; the insights gained from this exercise were not profound, although the resonance of the neurocybernetic metaphor with the poor quality of information flows was fairly evident. This concept was not pursued at any length beyond, no it's not like a machine, and yes, it's a bit like an organism, particularly as the participants did not seem to find it especially helpful. On reflection, a different approach to the metaphor analysis might have yielded benefits—this is discussed later.

We were now on to the Choice phase of TSI, in which methodologies are mapped onto different aspects of problem situations. During this phase, critical analysis allowed us to recognise that while the relationships between the participants in this project was unitary—that is there were few disagreements among them, nonetheless the situation was complex in nature and it would be as well to use a participatory methodology to ensure that lines of communication were kept open and that everyone continued to be involved. In line with the SOSM, we selected Mumford's ETHICS methodology (Mumford, 1995) (Effective Technical and Human Implementation of Computer-Based Systems). ETHICS belongs to the socio-technical school of thought, and is a participative methodology which claims to attach equal importance to human and technical factors during systems development. Although it has been criticised for its somewhat managerialist goal-driven outlook, and its positivistic search for cause-and-effect relationships to solve problems, nonetheless our analysis of the problem situation suggested it would suit us well; the use of a more pluralist methodology such as SSM would have run the risk of "let's get on with it!" frustration breaking out. Going through the steps of ETHICS, a 'working model' for the new system emerged and was refined through further discussions. New roles, tasks and responsibilities were identified and defined. We also used QUICKethics (Quality Information from Considered Knowledge), a companion model for ETHICS (see Avison and Fitzgerald, 1995 for further discussion) to generate information requirements for the new design. QUICKethics claims to be based on Beer's Viable System Model (1981, 1985), but this claim has been disputed by Adman and Warren (1998). The final stage of TSI, implementation, took place over a six-week period.

So how did we do, and how did CST/TSI help our IS design project? In Jackson (1997b), a case study involving a similar project by North Yorkshire Police (NYP) is described. Although different methodologies were used in the project (SSM and VSM; the desired outcome of this project was by no means as clear as in the ACSU project), the overall TSI project went through similar phases. Overall, Jackson concludes that the NYP project was successful, and brought about considerable change in NYP which was well-received and brought offers of future involvements with the force. There is some self-critique, in that it is reported that the endeavour almost failed because the researchers had not been critical enough of how the weaknesses of the VSM would detract from its value to the project; this was linked to a lack of social awareness. In spite of this setback, it is argued that the project made full use of CST and that it would not have been as successful had it not made use of CST.

On balance, the researchers in this project reached the same conclusions, although the difficulties in evaluating CST interventions must be borne in mind. Our success criteria, given below, were generated, summarising Flood (1996) and Midgley (1997):

1. Achievement of a desired consequence, as understood by the actors in the situation
2. Sustainable improvement, locally and temporarily defined, as understood by the actors in the situation
3. Improvement achieved through critical awareness and methodological pluralism

Looking at each of these in turn, firstly, the answer to date is an unqualified yes, in that the design was derived, accepted and implemented with the unanimous agreement of all involved in the project. The reception environment is more relaxed, complaints have decreased and informal feedback from ACSU staff and staff and students of the university has been good. As to the second question, is the improvement sustainable as locally and temporally defined, again all the indicators so far are positive. Midgley (1997) advises that all understandings of improvement are bounded in that a limited set of actors consider a limited set of variables in making those judgments: hence, there is a need to be critically aware of what boundary judgments are being made. Here, there was the boundary between the ACSU and the university to consider, and although as stated earlier, participation by customers was somewhat limited, this does not seem to have generated any difficulties. Secondly, there were hierarchical boundaries to consider, between the steering group and the ACSU staff, between the Project Director and everyone, and among different groupings within the ACSU staff. The flexibility built into the participative design process mediated against conflicts arising, even though time spent was often constrained. No serious issues concerning coercion or power issues arose, so it would be foolish to extrapolate from our notion of 'understanding' — and indeed, project ownership—to that of emancipation. Naturally, preexisting tensions were noticeable among staff, it would be naive to assume otherwise, but the everyday 'jockeyings for position' were dealt with by sensitive management as they occurred (and that sounds really easy if you say it fast!). Finally, was improvement achieved through critical awareness and methodological pluralism? Well, we did use different methodologies at different stages in the project as appropriate, and were aware of their strengths, weaknesses and underlying assumptions — and the use of ETHICS militated against a hasty leap to a technological solution. It is impossible to say how much of this could be attributed to the CST/TSI process and how much to the considerable experience of the Project Director — even so, it is hard to imagine that the rigour of this process would not engender some degree of critical awareness.

Overall, our enthusiasm for TSI was much more muted than for CST, which is hardly surprising given the existing critiques referred to earlier, most of which were borne out during this project. Even so, a number of authors, including Ellis (1995), Herrscher (1996), Hutchinson (1996) and Warren et al. (1998) have noted a lack of acceptance of (critical) systems thinking outside the academic community.

More research into identifying clear practical benefits of these approaches needs to be carried, and it is hoped that the successes reported here will contribute in some small way to that endeavour. Furthermore, although CST is theoretically flawed, it can still be regarded as a useful position or philosophy which has not yet developed the *modus operandi* of the CSP mooted by Jackson. As noted earlier, the employment of discourse-based analysis or reflexive ethnographic practice may reveal meaning and political difference in social situations by focusing on the *process* of intervention, rather than the *technology* of intervention (procedurally speaking) which the CST/TSI journey certainly encouraged for me. One example of where these ideas have been taken forward is in Warren (1999) where textual analysis of user-generated metaphors in a focus group situation is used to explore how a group of female owners of rural SMEs make sense of technology in their everyday working lives; this approach seemed to yield far greater insight than challenging users with 'alien' metaphors. I would conclude that the future development of CST for IS, theoretical and practical, needs to take place through working with practitioners 'in situ' to gain this degree of understanding at the micro-level.

## CONCLUDING REMARKS

This chapter began by identifying the agenda for improvement in the IS arena of work and the emergence of the social character of technology as a focal point for study. An overview of how various strands of social theory had been taken up by the IS community to challenge and now increasingly supplants the dominant positivist orthodoxy which has been in place since the early days of 'computer science. Critical theory, hermeneutics and constructivist studies of technological systems were all identified as having made key contributions to the changing nature of IS research and practice, as human-centred design methods came into increasing usage. The tensions between the systems movement and the postmodern endeavour were highlighted, but positive suggestions for potential synergies through discourse-based analysis were made. Critical Systems Thinking (CST) was introduced as the most theoretically developed strand of the systems approach and the one which had therefore the most potential for responding to the challenge of coping with the complexity of human interaction with technology. CST was offered as an integrated programme of research which could potentially bring benefits to IS design and address the agenda for improvement. Finally, a case study was presented where the benefits (and drawbacks!) of a CST approach to an IS-related design situation were illustrated.

## ACKNOWLEDGMENTS

First to Dr. Peter Adman of the University of Hull, for permitting me to work with him on the case study referred to in this chapter. Secondly, to Linda Hitchin of the University of Lincolnshire and Humberside, for introducing me to the material on postmodernism and developing the understanding printed here.

# ENDNOTES

1  A later form (Flood 1995, 1996) adds a further recursive structure to these phases, but this is rather unwieldy, a view echoed by Tsagdis (1996)
2  Although TSI does not preclude the use of other metaphors.

# REFERENCES

Adman, P. and Warren, L. (1998). The use of ETHICS for Organizational and IS Design, in D. Avison and D. Edgar-Nevill (Eds.) *Matching Technology with Organizational Needs*, Proceedings of the 3rd UKAIS Conference, University of Lincolnshire and Humberside, 15-17 April, 194-205, Wiley: London.

Adman, P. and Warren, L. (March 2000). Participatory Socio-technical Design of Organizations and Information Systems - An adaptation of ETHICS Methodology, *Journal of Information Technology*, in press.

Anderson, R. J. (1994) Representations and Requirements: The Value of Ethnography in Systems Design, *Human Computer Interaction*, 15, 5-18.

Avison, D. and Fitzgerald, G. (1995). *Information Systems Development*, McGraw-Hill: London.

Avison, D. E. and Myers, M. D. (1985). Information systems and anthropology: an anthropological perspective on IT and organisational culture, *Information Technology and People*, 8 (3) 43-56.

Avison, D. E. and Wood-Harper, A. T. (1990). *Multiview: An Exploration into Information Systems Development*. Blackwell Scientific: Oxford.

Baskerville, R. L. and Wood-Harper, A. T. (1996). A critical perspective on action research as a method for information systems research, *Journal of Information Technology*, 11, 235-246.

Beer, S. (1981). *The Brain of the Firm*. Wiley: Chichester.

Beer, S. (1985). *Diagnosing the System for Organizations*. Wiley: Chichester.

Bijker, W. and Law, J. (eds.) (1992). *Shaping Technology/Building Society : studies in sociotechnical design*. MIT Press : Cambridge Mass.

Bijker, W., Hughes, T. P. and Pinch, T. (eds.) (1987). *The Social Construction of Technological Systems*. MIT Press: Cambridge Mass.

Boland, R. J. (1985). Phenomenology: a preferred approach to research on information systems, in *Research Methods in Information Systems*, R. J. Boland and R. A. Hirschheim (Eds.), Elsevier: Amsterdam.

Boland, R. J. (1987). The in-formation of information systems, in *Critical Issues in Information Systems Research*, Boland, R. J. and Hirschheim, R. (eds.) Elsevier: Amsterdam.

Boland, R. J. (1991). Information systems use as a hermeneutic process, in *Information Systems Research: contemporary approaches and emergent traditions*, Nissen, H-E., Klein, H. K. and Hirschheim, R. (eds.), Elsevier: Amsterdam.

Brinkkemper, S., Lyttinen, K. and Welke, R. (Eds.) (1996) *Method Engineering*. Chapman and Hall: London.

Brocklesby, J. (1994). Let the Jury Decide: Assessing the Cultural Feasibility of Total

Systems Intervention, *Systems Practice,* 7 (1), 75-86.

Brocklesby, J. (1995). Intervening in the cultural constitution of systems — methodological complementarism and other visions for systems research, *Journal of the Operational Research Society,* 46, 1285-1298.

Burrell, G. and Morgan, M. (1979). *Sociological Paradigms and Organizational Analysis.* Heinemann: London.

Button, G. and Sharrock, W. (1994). The mundane work of writing and reading computer programs in Ten-Have, P. and Psathas, G. (eds.) *Situated Order: Studies in the social organization of talk and embedded activities,* University Press of America: Washington.

Callon, M (1986). The Sociology of an Actor Network in Callon, M., Law, J. and Rip, A. (eds.) *Mapping the Dynamics of Science and Technology,* Macmillan: London

Checkland P. B. (1981). *Systems Thinking, Systems Practice.* Wiley, Chichester

Checkland, P. B. and Holwell, S. (1997). *Information, Systems and Information Systems: Making Sense of the Field.* Wiley: Chichester.

Clayton, J. and Gregory, W. (1997). A Practical Project at HM Prison Hull: Total Systems Intervention or Total Systems Failure? in *Systems for Sustainability: People, Organizations and Environments,* Proceedings of the 5th International Conference of the United Kingdom Systems Society, July 7-11, Milton Keynes, F. A. Stowell, R. L. Ison, R. Armson, J. Holloway, S. Jackson and S. McRobb (Eds.), Plenum: London.

Crowe, M. Beeby, R. and Gammack, J. (1996). *Constructing Systems and Information,* McGraw-Hill: London

Cummins, S. (1994). An open letter to Total Systems Intervention (TSI) and friends, *Systems Practice,* 7, 575-583.

Despres, C, J-N. (1996). Information, technology and culture: an ethnography of information technology and modernist business organization, *Technovation,* 16(1) : 1-20.

Ellis, R. K. (1995). The Association of Systems Thinking with the Practice of Management. In *Systems for the Future,* Proceedings of the 1st Australian Systems Conference, September 9-11, Hutchinson, W., Metcalf, S., Standing, C. and Williams, M. (Eds.), 17-22, Edith Cowan University: Perth.

Espejo, R. and Harnden, R. (eds.) (1989). *The Viable System Model: Interpretations and Applications of Stafford Beer's VSM.* Wiley: Chichester.

Flood, R. L. (1995). *Solving Problem Solving: A Potent Force for Effective Management.* Wiley: Chichester.

Flood, R. L. (1996). Total Systems Intervention: Local Systemic Intervention, *Critical Systems Thinking: Current Research and Practice,* R. L. Flood and N. R. A. Romm (Eds.), Plenum: New York.

Flood, R. L. & Jackson M. C. (1991a). (Eds.) *Critical Systems Thinking: Directed Readings,* Wiley: Chichester.

Flood, R. L. & Jackson M. C. (1991b). *Creative Problem Solving: Total Systems Intervention.* Wiley: Chichester.

Flood, R. L. and Romm, N. R. A. (Eds.) (1996). *Critical Systems Thinking: Current Research and Practice,* Plenum: New York.

Forsythe D. E. (1995). Using ethnography in the design of an explanation system,

*Expert Systems with Applications* 8(4) :403-417.

Forsythe, D. E., Buchanan, B. G., Osheroff, J. A. and Miller, R. A. (1992). Expanding the concept of medical information: an observational study of physicians information needs, *Computers and Biomedical Research* 25(2) : 181-200.

Green, S. M. (1992). Total Systems Intervention: organisational communication in North Yorkshire Police, *Systems Practice*, 5, 585-603.

Green, S. M (1993a). Total Systems Intervention: A practitioner's critique, *Systems Practice*, 6, 71-79.

Green, S. M. (1993b). Total Systems Intervention: A trial by jury, *Systems Practice*, 6, 295-299.

Grint, K. and Woolgar, S. (1997). *The machine at work : technology, work and organization*, Polity Press in association with Blackwell : England.

Harre, R and Krauss, M (1996). *Varieties of Realism*, Blackwell: Oxford UK.

Herrscher, E. G. (1996), An Agenda for Enhancing Systemic Thinking in Society, *Systems Research*, 13 (2), 159-164.

Hirschheim, R. (1985). Information systems epistemology: an historical perspective, in *Research Methods in Information Systems*, Mumford, E., Hirschheim, R., Fitzgerald, G and Wood-Harper, A. T. (Eds.). Elsevier: Amsterdam.

Hirschheim, R. and Klein, H. K. (1989). Four paradigms of information systems development, *Communications of the ACM*, 32: 1199-1216.

Ho, J. K. K. (1994). Is Total Systems Intervention no better than common sense and not necessarily related to Critical Systems Thinking (CST)?, *Systems Practice*, 7, 569-573.

Hughes, J. A., Somerville, I., Randall, B. and Bentley, R. (1993). Designing with ethnography: making work visible, *Interacting with Computers* 5(2): 239-253.

Hutchinson, W. E. (1996), Making Systems Thinking Relevant, *Systemist*, 18 (4), 196-201.

Iivari, J. (1991). A paradigmatic analysis of contemporary schools of IS development, *European Journal of Information Systems*, 1(4): 249-272.

Jackson, M. C. (1982). The Nature of Soft Systems Thinking: The work of Churchman, Ackoff and Checkland, *Journal of Applied Systems Analysis*, 9, 17-42.

Jackson, M. C. (1987) Present positions and future prospects in management science, *Omega*, 15, 455-466.

Jackson, M. C. (1997a) Pluralism in Systems Thinking and Practice, in Mingers, J. and Gill, A. (Eds.) *Multimethodology: The Theory and Practice of Combining Management Science Methodologies.* Wiley: Chichester

Jackson, M. C. (1997b). Critical Systems Thinking and Information Systems Research, in *Information Systems: An Emerging Discipline.* McGraw-Hill: London

Jackson, M. C. (1999) Towards Coherent Pluralism in Management Science, *Journal of the Operational Research Society*, 50(1), 12-22.

Jackson, M. C. and Keys, P. (1984). Towards a system of systems methodologies, *Journal of the Operational Research Society*, 35, 473-486.

Kendall, J. E. and Kendall, K. E. (1993). Metaphors and Methodologies, *MIS Quarterly*, 17(2), 149 - 171.

Klein., H. K. and Lyttinen, K. (1985). The poverty of scientism in information systems, in *Research Methods in Information Systems*, Mumford, E., Hirschheim,

R., Fitzgerald, G and Wood-Harper, A. T. (Eds.). Elsevier: Amsterdam.

Landry, M. and Banville, C., (1992) A disciplined methodological pluralism for MIS research, *Accounting, Management and Information Technologies*, 2 (2) 77-97

Latour, B (1992). Where are the missing masses? The sociology of a few mundane artefacts, in Bijker, W. and Law, J. (eds) (1992) *Shaping Technology/Building Society: Studies in sociotechnical design*, MIT Press: Cambridge, Mass.

Latour, B. (1993). *We have never been modern.* translated by Catherine Porter, Harvester Wheatsheaf : Hemel Hempstead.

Lau, F. (1997). A review on the use of action research in information systems studies, in Lee, A., Liebenau, J. and DeGross, J. (Eds.), *Information Systems and Qualitative Research*, Chapman and Hall: London.

Law, J. (1988).The anatomy of a socio-technical struggle, in Elliott, B. (ed.) *Technology and Social Process*. Edinburgh University Press: Edinburgh.

Law, J. (ed.) (1986). *Power, Action and Belief: A New Sociology of Knowledge?* Routledge Keegan Paul: London.

Law, J. (ed.) (1991). *A Sociology of Monsters: Essays on Power, Technology and Domination*. Routledge: London.

Law, J., Johnson, J., Hall, P., Hovenden, F., Rachel, J., Robinson, H. and Woolgar, S. (1996). Read this and change the way you feel about software engineering, *Information and Software Technology*, 38(2), 77-87.

Lehaney, B. and Clarke, S. (1997). Critical Approaches to Information Systems Development: Some Practical Implications, in *Systems for Sustainability: People, Organizations and Environments*, Proceedings of the 5th International Conference of the United Kingdom Systems Society, July 7-11, Milton Keynes, F. A. Stowell, R. L. Ison, R. Armson, J. Holloway, S. Jackson and S. McRobb (Eds.), Plenum: London

Luff, P., Heath, C., and Greatbatch, D., (1992). Tasks in interaction: paper and screen based activity in collaborative work, *Proceedings of the Conference on Computer Supported Co-operative work*, ACM : NY 163-170.

Markus, M. L. (1983). Power, Politics and MIS Implementation, *Communications of the ACM*, 26(7), 430-444.

Midgley, G. (1996). What is this Thing Called CST?, in *Critical Systems Thinking: Current Research and Practice*, Flood, R. L. and Romm, N. R. A. (Eds.), Plenum: New York .

Midgley, G. (1997). Critical Systems Criteria for Evaluating Interventions, in *Systems for Sustainability: People, Organizations and Environments*, Proceedings of the 5th International Conference of the United Kingdom Systems Society, July 7-11, Milton Keynes, F. A. Stowell, R. L. Ison, R. Armson, J. Holloway, S. Jackson and S. McRobb (Eds.), Plenum: London

Mingers, J. and Brocklesby, J. (1996) Multimethodology: towards a framework for critical pluralism, *Systemist*, 14, 101-132.

Mingers, J. and Stowell, F. (1997). (Eds.) *Information Systems: An Emerging Discipline?*, McGraw Hill, UK.

Morgan, G. (1983). *Beyond Method*, Sage: California.

Morgan, G. (1986). *Images of Organization*. Sage: California.

Mumford, E. (1983). *Designing Participatively.* Manchester Business School: Manchester.

Mumford, E. (1995) *Effective Systems Design and Requirements Analysis: The ETHICS Approach*. MacMillan Press Ltd: Hampshire

Myers, M. (1997) Interpretive research in information systems, in *Information Systems: An Emerging Discipline?* Mingers, J. and Stowell, F. (Eds.), McGraw-Hill: London

OASIG Study (1996) Why do IT Projects so often Fail, *OR Newsletter* 309, 12-16

Orlikowski, W. J. and Baroudi, J. J. (1991) Studying IT in organisations: research approaches and assumptions, *Information Systems Research*, 2 (1), 1-28

Ormerod, R. J. (1992) *Combining Hard & Soft Systems*. Warwick Business School Research Papers

Ormerod, R. J. (1996) Combining Management Consultancy and Research, *Omega*, 24, 1-12

Ormerod, R. J. (1997) The Design of Organisational Intervention: Choosing The Approach, *Omega*, 25, 415-435

Poster, M. (1990) *The Mode of Information: Poststructuralism and Social Context*, Polity Press: Cambridge

Robey, D. and Markus, M.. L. (1984) Rituals in Information System Design, *MIS Quarterly*, 8(1), 5-15

Rosenhead, J. (1976) Some further comments on "The Social Responsibility of OR", *Operational Research Quarterly*, 17, 265-283

Schecter, D. (1991) Critical systems thinking in the 1980s: a connective summary, in *Critical Systems Thinking: Directed Readings*, Flood, R. L. and Jackson, M. C. (Eds.), Wiley: Chichester

Silverman, D., (1970) *The Theory of Organisations*, Heinemann: London

Simon, H. A. (1981) *The Sciences of the Artificial*, Free Press, New York

Spaul, M. (1997) Multimethodology and Critical Theory: an Intersection of Interests, in Mingers, J. and Gill, A. (Eds.) *Multimethodology: The Theory and Practice of Combining Management Science Methodologies*. Wiley: Chichester

Stamper, R. (1997) Organisational Semiotics, in *Information Systems: An Emerging Discipline?* Mingers, J. and Stowell, F. (Eds.), McGraw-Hill: London

Stowell, F., West, D. and Stansfield, M. (1997) Action Research as A Framework for IS Research, in Mingers, J. and Stowell, F. (Eds.) *Information Systems: An Emerging Discipline*. McGraw-Hill: London

Suchman, L. (1988) *Plans and situated action*. Cambridge University Press: Cambridge.

Taket, A. and White, L. (1995) Working with heterogeneity: A pluralist strategy for evaluation, In Ellis, K., Gregory, A., Mears-Young, B. R. and Ragsdell, G. (Eds.), *Critical Issues in Systems Theory and Practice*, Plenum: New York

Taket, A. and White, L. (1997) Critiquing multimethodology as metamethodology: working towards pragmatic pluralism, in Mingers, J. and Gill, A. (Eds.) *Multimethodology: The Theory and Practice of Combining Management Science Methodologies*. Wiley: Chichester

Tsagdis, D. (1996) Systems methodologies, reference systems and science, in *Cybernetics and Systems '96*, Austrian Society for Cybernetics, Trappll, R. (Ed.) 784-788, Vienna

Tsoukas, H. (1993a). The Road to Emancipation is through Organizational Development: A Critical Evaluation of Total Systems Intervention, *Systems Practice* 6, 53-70.

Tsoukas, H. (1993b). By their fruits ye shall know them: a reply to Jackson, Green and Midgley, *Systems Practice*, 6, 311-317.

Ulrich, W. (1981). A critique of pure cybernetic reason: The Chilean experience with cybernetics, *Journal of Applied Systems Analysis*, 8, 33-52.

Ulrich, W. (1983). *Critical Heuristics of Social Planning*. Haupt: Bern

Ulrich, W. (1996). Critical Systems Thinking for Citizens, *Critical Systems Thinking: Current Research and Practice*, , R. L. Flood and N. R. A. Romm (Eds.), Plenum: New York.

Walsham, G. (1991). Organizational metaphors and information systems research, *European Journal of Information Systems*, 1: 83.

Walsham, G. (1995). The emergence of interpretivism in IS research, *Information Systems Research*, 6 (4), 376-394.

Warren, L. (1999). *IT/IS in Rural SMEs: A Qualitative Study of the Metaphors Generated by Females in SMEs in a Rural County in England*, Proceedings of the 4th UKAIS Conference, to be held at York University, April 7-9 1999, 43-51

Warren, L. and Adman, P. (1999). The use of critical systems thinking in designing a system for a university information systems support service, *Information Systems Journal*, 9, 58-78 (in press).

Warren, L. and Ellis, R. K. (1997) Reflections on Achieving Sustainability in a Complex Situation, in *Systems for Sustainability: People, Organizations and Environments*, Proceedings of the 5th International Conference of the United Kingdom Systems Society, July 7-11, Milton Keynes, F. A. Stowell, R. L. Ison, R. Armson, J. Holloway, S. Jackson and S. McRobb (Eds.), Plenum: London.

Warren, L., Ellis, K. and Adman, P. (1998). Reflections on Systems Theory and Systems Practice, *OR Insight*, 11(2), 14-19.

Winograd, T. and Flores, F. (1986). *Understanding Computers and Cognition*, Addison-Wesley: Reading, MA.

## Chapter XIII

# Rethinking Stakeholder Involvement: An Application of the Theories of Autopoiesis and Boundary Critique to IS Planning

José Rodrigo Córdoba and Gerald Midgley
University of Hull

Diego Ricardo Torres
Javeriana University

## INTRODUCTION

Current practice in strategic information systems (IS) planning seems to be focused on surfacing an organisation's vision and goals, exploring the potential offered by information technology (IT), and designing information systems to support the fulfillment of the stated goals using the most appropriate technology available (García, 1993; Currid, 1994; Lewis, 1994; Andreu et al., 1996). Methodologies for IS planning usually involve the training and participation of individual employees—but only in so far as they contribute to furthering the pre-set organisational agenda.

These methodologies also tend to assume a 'standard' role for IS experts: providing expertise in IT/IS management. Most of the literature and the practice of IT/IS development in organisations seem to be focused upon technical issues (Davies and Wood-Harper, 1989), where computer science experts play an important role (Winograd and Flores, 1987). They are expected to provide knowledge to solve problems.

These assumptions about how IS planning should work are as prevalent in educational institutions as they are in other kinds of organisations (Galvis, 1998). Of course, failures and delays in IS implementation and use occur just as much in the arena of education as elsewhere, and these failures are mostly attributed to 'people problems' (Solloway, 1991; Tarrago, 1993; Carr et al., 1998). When problems appear, they tend to be tackled in a reactive manner, putting the responsibility for the effective adoption of IS on teachers and students (Carr et al, 1998; Spitzer et al, 1998). However, it is the role of experts to say what teachers and students should do. Therefore, it is little wonder that 'user resistance' is so often encountered, both in educational IS projects and more widely (Lyytinen and Hirschheim, 1987).

To us, the phenomenon of resistance points to the need for a rethink of the assumptions underpinning many IS planning methodologies. In the words of Kearsley (1998), "We need to develop a framework that allows for the patterns and relationships among people and organisations that will allow educational technology to be successful" (p.2). In other words, the technology will only be successful if its development and implementation takes into account, and helps people build upon, human relationships and ideas. There should not be an expectation that human relations will be determined by the needs of the technology.

Of course, the implications of this statement for IS design are profound: "...any statement of design is a statement that the designer makes about desirable actions, beliefs and values" (Kozma, 1994, p.17). Therefore, designing an IS without first understanding the details of human relations in a local context will result in the imposition of the designer's value system on users, and will most likely produce resistance. IS planners need to look on IS as *serving* the purposeful activities of individuals, groups and organisations, and this means taking account of the various different perspectives that might inform wider activity planning (Lewis, 1994; Checkland and Holwell, 1998).

This chapter is concerned with IS planning in an educational context (a Colombian University), but we take a different perspective to most IS planning methodologists—including some of the methodologists who are already critiquing the traditional 'expert' approaches to IS planning. We argue that the majority of methodologies fail to consider the diversity of users' social contexts, and that IS planning should involve the participation, right from the start, of a variety of stakeholders, each of whom inhabit multiple domains of action. Each domain of action involves people playing a different 'language game' (Wittgenstein, 1953), which brings forth specific concerns about other people as human beings. For example, a person may play one language game when interacting with her family, and then switch to another at work. The two language games will imply different expectations and duties of both the self and others. Indeed, within the work context alone, people may be able to identify several domains of action, and several different language games (or rationalities) that they draw upon. Even many of the IS planning methodologies based on user involvement define involvement in terms of a single, pre-set purpose to be pursued by the participant group—and this is usually set by senior management. However, the experience of many people is that they have to juggle multiple (sometimes conflicting) purposes and rationalities in the course of managing their lives (Shotter, 1993).

As people are involved in multiple domains of action, pursuing multiple purposes, they also have multiple (and sometimes conflicting) concerns for others. Therefore, stakeholders (including IS 'experts') should not be confined to a single role within IS planning, or be expected to conform to a single rationality. Rather, the spectrum of their (sometimes contradictory) lives should be swept in. Within an extended IS planning process, founded upon genuine stakeholder involvement (that is, sweeping in a range of stakeholders and their multiple concerns, with only minimal constraints from an organisational agenda), a variety of questions about what is meaningful in different domains of action can arise. These questions can be dealt with by considering the different values and boundaries that are assumed in different domains of action, and debate can be fostered between stakeholders on the implications of choosing any one boundary, or set of boundaries, for IS planning.[1] We argue that working like this will ensure that IS planning deals with the effects of change on as many as possible of the domains of action that people participate in. We also believe that IS *implementation* will be improved, because the factors that cause user resistance will be accounted for from the start.

Of course, this approach collapses the distinction between people's 'working' and 'private' lives. This is deliberate: we argue that these two supposedly separate domains are actually interlinked. When people have problems at work, it affects their family life, and when they have problems at home they can bring these to work. More perniciously, people can get into vicious cycles in which problems at home and work affect each other until all aspects of their lives begin to crumble simultaneously. We therefore follow Lleras (1995) in arguing that it is in the interests of both individuals *and* organisations to sweep in all possible domains of people's lives.

In the next section of this chapter, some background is provided on current trends in the uses of IT and IS in education. It will be argued that, while great claims have been made for the value of IS-based teaching, most IS applications simply support the dominant model of education which has been widely criticised. This dominant model is what Freire (1972) calls the "banking" method, where the teacher attempts to deposit his or her own learning and experience into the student as if the latter were a passive, empty vessel that simply needs to be filled. This analysis will lead into a critique of the banking method: we will argue that it is more appropriate to see students as active learners, building on their past knowledge and experience. If this is accepted, then it makes no sense to exclude students from the IS planning process: students are the primary users, and need to participate in order to ensure that IS are appropriately tailored. Also, like all people, students participate in multiple domains of action. Education can support them in many of these domains, not just those associated with the workplace, so the form of participation needs to allow students the freedom to explore a variety of meanings of education before IS are debated.

Following the discussion of IS-based teaching and our critique of the dominant model of education, this chapter explores two theories that we believe could usefully support the future development of IS planning methodologies: these are the theories of *autopoiesis* (Maturana 1981, 1988a,b; 1997a,b, Maturana and Varela, 1992; Mingers, 1995) and *boundary critique* (Churchman, 1970, 1979; Ulrich, 1983, 1986, 1988a,b, 1994, 1996a,b; Midgley, 1992a, 1994, 1996; Midgley et al., 1998; Yolles, 2000). We then propose a critical methodology for engaging stakeholders in IS planning and briefly describe one application of it in a Colombian University.

# THE USE OF IT/IS AND THEIR IMPACT IN EDUCATION

It appears that the use of information systems (IS) and information technologies (IT) has become essential for survival in a world characterised by continuous change, especially as organisations rely more heavily than ever before on the use of information (Reyes and Zarama, 1998). Over the coming years, within the so-called 'information society', it is predicted that almost every aspect of life will become dependent on electronic data (Information I, 1996a). It is generally assumed that this will improve the quality of people's lives (ISC, 1998). However, it is anticipated that the benefits will be greater for some countries than others (Senker, 1992; Friis, 1997), and there are worries that the increasing reliance on information systems will have negative effects on relationships between individuals (Wickham, 1997).

In the area of education, the use of IT to support IS has been given a huge impetus. In the UK and the Republic of Ireland, for example, there are plans to train thousands of teachers and provide computers to schools in order to create a critical mass of IT-literate people (Grid, 1997; Information I, 1996b). Around this, an educational software industry will be created. However, critics of this strategy stress the need to be aware of the social implications of technological change in education (Levrat, 1992). It is relationships between people that provide the social contexts in which IS are introduced: technology cannot simply be imposed from above without creating significant problems of 'inappropriate' applications (from the points of view of people on the ground), together with user resistance (Kearsley, 1998; Carr et al., 1998).

There is also an issue of the global context of introducing IT and IS into education. In Latin America, there are particular infrastructure and resourcing issues. For example, the average number of computers available for students in Latin American countries is ten times lower than in developed nations like the U.S. (Murray-Lasso, 1992). However, the use of IS is seen as essential in Latin America to maintain competitiveness within the global economy, while simultaneously providing more access to education for marginalised groups (Educación XXI, 1998).

In Colombia, there are communications infrastructure problems that need to be addressed: there are still marginalised sectors which have no access at all to computers or even telephone lines (Telecomm, 1997; Video Conferencia, 1999). In 1997 there was a concerted effort to elaborate a National Informatics Plan (PNI, 1997; PNE, 1998) for introducing IS into the Colombian education system: different groups of people (IT providers, consultants, government ministers and teachers) gathered together and diagnosed a range of problems to be addressed. These included an unreceptive culture, an inadequate communications infrastructure, poor educational resources, and the absence of local IT industries. A plan was devised to overcome these problems. However, obstacles to implementation are now being experienced: many teachers are reluctant to use IS in their jobs; most students have no experience of using computers, so a basic IT-literacy programme is needed; and insufficient resources are available to provide the necessary infrastructure to the various regions of the country (El Tiempo, 1999).

There are therefore big questions about whether adoption of the same technologies being used in the most developed nations is feasible, or even desirable. As a consequence, we agree with Checkland and Holwell (1998) that IS should be defined in terms of systems of information flow, not the technologies that may (or may not) be used to support this. It should not be taken for granted that IS development means using state-of-the-art technology, or even a computer of any kind. Depending on the situation, lower-tech solutions may be more appropriate.

Nevertheless, in just about all countries, people have argued that a significant reduction of costs could be achieved by making interaction between teachers and students more efficient using systems of computer-aided learning (Fischer, 1996; Thomas et al., 1998; Whetzel et al., 1998). Also, there can be improvements in learning, shown by better scores obtained by students in tests. However, in most educational establishments, there is a strong focus on the achievement of a limited range of 'results' (e.g., examination results), which obscures the contexts in which education is given and the associated needs and desires of students. Measuring the effectiveness of IS in terms of this limited range of results could therefore further erode the capacities of educational institutions to respond to the contingencies of local contexts. Also, the rhetoric of IS as a learning medium could actually have negative consequences for learning: media do not have any learning attributes, only students do (Clark, 1983). Dependency on the medium to improve learning could constrain the development of new education methodologies (Clark, 1994; Thompson and Bates, 1998). This is an observation that is supported by research which shows that very often students do not see the same benefits of IT-based resources as their designers: the technology may change, but the education methodology remains the same (Solloway, 1991; Tarrago, 1993; Carr et al., 1998).

However *efficient* interactions between teachers and students become, a question mark still hangs over the *value* of traditional education methodologies, and the effects on students of the use of IS to enhance these traditional methodologies needs to be considered (Clark, 1994; Russell, 1994; Bostock, 1998). This issue will be discussed in more detail in the next section.

# A CRITIQUE OF THE TRADITIONAL MODEL OF EDUCATION

Traditional models of education based on a one-way information transfer between the teacher and students have been criticised on a variety of grounds. First, they impose a 'hidden curriculum'. Students forget about 90% of what they study within weeks of taking an examination, so what they are *really* learning appears to be their place in society. Generally speaking, 'successful' students learn to be passive recipients of the views handed down by figures of authority (Postman and Weingartner, 1969; Illich, 1971; Reimer, 1971). It is interesting to note that this is not only a criticism levelled at the education system by those interested in fostering participative democracy (for participative democracy to work, citizens would need to be effective questioners of received wisdom)—it has also been a bone of contention for industrialists who would like to employ more managers with a greater capacity for critical and creative thought. Creativity and critical thinking are necessary for people to deal effectively with rapid social and organisational change (see Burgoyne and Reynolds, 1997, for a variety of perspectives on the need for critical thinking in management education).

Of course, many educational specialisations are now introduced according to the needs of a productive system, yet these specialisations (especially in the areas of IT and IS) rapidly become out of date. Technical knowledge can always be provided through on-the-job training, but the capacity for creative problem solving is a resource that takes more time to develop. Indeed, the same point can be made with regard to the transmission of values: the values of the teacher, if transmitted unreflectively to students, will not necessarily be relevant to the 'brave new worlds' encountered by students (Postman and Weingartner, 1969).

Another problem with traditional methodologies of education is that getting a certificate or a degree becomes the main goal of many students. The subject they study is less relevant than holding the piece of paper at the end, which is one reason why the information transmitted by teachers is so easily forgotten. Of course, in order to give students the opportunity to gain a range of certificates, different subject areas have to be created. Thus, the disciplines are divided from one another on an artificial basis creating fragmentary compartmentalisation in the transmission of knowledge. The traditional model of education is not sufficiently systemic (Banathy, 1992), and this creates problems further down the line when the boundaries between disciplines obstruct the effective development of scientific knowledge (von Bertalanffy, 1956; Lovelock, 1988; Banathy, 1992; Midgley, 1999).

Also, while being 'educated', people are relatively isolated from social and economic life. This reinforces the message that what is worth learning comes from a teacher. In contrast, if schools and universities were built around the lives of students as participants in their communities, learning might be more varied, 'grounded' and meaningful to both the students and others they interact with (North, 1987; Weil, 1999). One of the consequences of perpetuating the traditional model of education is that people are less aware of their own social contexts than they might otherwise be (Freire, 1970, 1972). The education system does not encourage self-directed (and collective) critical reflection on personal, social and ecological issues (except within a pre-determined framework), but prefers to subordinate critical thinking to the pursuit of a centrally designed curriculum (Gregory, 1993).

The final criticism levelled at the "banking" system of education, "...in which the scope of action allowed to the students extends only as far as receiving, filing and storing the deposits (of information)" (Freire, 1973, p.7), is that it is based on an inadequate understanding of human learning. For some years now, the consensus in the discipline of psychology has been that individuals are *active* learners, not passive recipients of information: people can only assimilate what is meaningful in terms of the understandings they have already developed through their previous experiences (e.g., Kelly, 1955; Vygotsky, 1978, 1986; Maturana, 1988a,b; Giddens, 1991; Shotter, 1993). As students come to educational institutions with a variety of experiences already in place, they will inevitably use different "interpretive frameworks" (Midgley et al, 1996) to understand what is presented to them as knowledge. Therefore, their assimilation of this knowledge will vary widely. Some students, whose interpretive frameworks are similar to the teacher's, may find no difficulty in assimilating what the teacher views as knowledge; others may end up with partial or different understandings; and some will assimilate nothing from the teacher—they will simply learn that 'education' is a useless and alienating experience.

Indeed, it is not simply that individual students are active learners. It is also the case that modern psychology is challenging the view that individuals operate with a *single* interpretive framework (or worldview) through which everything is filtered. A more recent emphasis has been on the idea that each individual uses *multiple* interpretive frameworks—or, to draw upon Wittgenstein's (1953) terminology, individuals participate in multiple 'language games' (Vygotsky, 1978, 1986; Maturana, 1988a,b; Shotter, 1993; Harré and Gillett, 1994). As people move from one context (domain of action) to another, they use different 'rationalities'—and some of these may conflict with one another.

There are major implications of this for both education and IS planning. For education, it means that there is a need to build upon the active learning capacity of the individual (Greene and Ackermann, 1995; Fischer, 1996; Carr et al, 1998), recognising that students engage in many different domains of action, requiring the use of a variety of interpretive frameworks or language games. It will never be possible to define just one purpose for education without imposing a single interpretive framework on students: if the multiple interpretive frameworks of students are to be taken into account, there will be as many educational purposes as domains of action—and only the individuals who engage in those domains of action can specify what they are in a manner that is meaningful for their own learning.

For IS planning to support a form of education that acknowledges these changes in our understanding of learning, it makes absolutely no sense to adopt an 'expert' (top-down) methodology. Not only will it be vital to involve both teachers and students (plus other stakeholders) in determining the role(s) of IS, but the process of involvement needs to emphasise the multiple domains of action that individuals engage in. From here we can begin to specify what an IS planning methodology that is responsive to the new understanding of learning will look like.

# TOWARDS A NEW METHODOLOGY FOR INFORMATION SYSTEMS PLANNING

The purpose now is to use the above reflections to propose a set of principles that should inform processes of IS planning, particularly in the education sector. These principles are:
- Processes of IS planning should consider the multiple expectations of different stakeholders, accepting that the stated purpose(s) of the organisation(s) funding the IS initiative could be subject to review as part of this.
- An IS planning expert not only needs technical knowledge, but also facilitation skills to enable dynamic stakeholder participation.
- Responsibilities for implementation should be widely discussed. Tradition-

ally, planning has been seen as the responsibility of IS experts, and implementation has been left to teachers and students (see, for example, Grid, 1995; PNE, 1998; Galvis, 1998). IS planning should extend to the *planning of implementation*.

- The outcomes of IS planning should be evaluated through a reflective, dialogical process (a written output may be useful, but is not essential). Traditionally, an expert report has been viewed as enough, but this is insufficient to allow full participation.[2]

- IS planning should facilitate debate on the meaning(s) of education (or whatever other service or product is being produced), and the values flowing into these. It should not be isolated from wider debates about policy and practice, but should be an integral part of them.

- A match between student-centred approaches to education and the new, interactive ITs should not be taken for granted. There is a danger that this match, which has been proposed by a variety of educational technology experts, will become a new orthodoxy resulting in the imposition of yet another single interpretive framework for education. Local solutions involving local actors always need to be the primary focus of IS planning (local actors, engaged in constructive discussion together, can decide whether or not an 'imported' model of education will be useful, or whether they should design something new for themselves).

Based on these principles, we have developed our own approach to IS planning. This is influenced by the theories of autopoiesis and boundary critique. It combines systems thinking ideas with a critical view of the role of the expert in the process of IS planning.

The theory of autopoiesis provides an understanding of the individual human being as a self-producing system, with her own unique set of interpretive frameworks, who interacts with her environment—and within the environment are the language games relating to various domains of action that the individual participates in. It is therefore just one example of the new breed of psycho-biological theory that pictures people as actively constructing multiple meanings—but it is a particularly well-elaborated example, which is why we have chosen it as the basis for our own methodology.

Complementing the theory of autopoiesis, the theory of boundary critique provides an understanding of how interpretive frameworks (understandings) are bounded, and how values are implicated in this. It also provides a model of social inclusion, exclusion and marginalisation, explaining how and why some stakeholders and issues come to be devalued in social relationships. The theory of boundary critique is needed in addition to the theory of autopoiesis because it would be naive to assume that relationships between stakeholders, and between the different perspectives even a single stakeholder brings to IS planning, will always be unproblematic. The theory of boundary critique supports reflection on difficult relationships and conflicting ideas.

Before proceeding to discuss these two theories, we should note that they do not absolutely *require* one another. They are simply both useful in the context of this discussion of IS planning. Indeed, the theory of boundary critique has been linked to an argument for theoretical pluralism (Midgley, 2000): it does not need to be underpinned by any one understanding of human nature (e.g., the theory of autopoiesis)—movement between different theories, or the (temporary) suspension of theorising about human nature, is quite acceptable when engaging in boundary critique[3].

## THE THEORY OF AUTOPOIESIS

According to Maturana and Varela (1992), human beings are autopoietic systems. Essentially, the term 'autopoiesis' means *self-producing*. An autopoietic system is one which acts to maintain its internal organisation and, when it interacts with its environment to maintain itself, the actions it takes are determined by its current structure (Maturana and Varela, 1992). The *structure* of a system is its arrangement of components in such a way that its *organisation* (that which gives it identity) is maintained. The structure of a system changes over time, but within limits laid down by its organisation (which cannot change without the system losing its identity as a self-producing entity—in other words, without it dying). The implications of this are profound, especially the observation that interactions with the environment are determined by a system's structure. While it is common to hear talk about people being *caused* to act in particular ways, Maturana and Varela (1992) say that the environment cannot be a cause, only a *trigger*. The environment produces perturbations that may or may not be received as meaningful information by a human being. If the perturbation is meaningful, it is because the person's internal structure allows it to be received as such. Even if the perturbation is life-threatening (if it will disrupt the organisation of the system), the person will not be able to react unless her internal structure is receptive to the perturbation—i.e., if it is meaningful to her.

Like Wittgenstein (1953) before him, Maturana (1988a,b) explicitly considers the role of language. As social animals, human beings do not only *act*, we also strive to *coordinate* our actions. Language helps in this process: it allows us to *coordinate our coordinations of actions*. The "coordination of coordinations of actions" is a rather obscure phrase, but it summarises Maturana's position quite neatly: we act in coordination with others, and language supports the coordination of these coordinations.

Interestingly, when Maturana talks about coordinations of actions, he has something very specific in mind. While a person can only react to outside forces on the basis of her current structure (maintained by, and maintaining, her organisation or identity as a system), she is organisationally predisposed to identify recurrent patterns of interaction and adapt her structure accordingly, thereby giving rise to habitual responses. When a person and an aspect of her environment (which may or may not be another person) have a recurrent relationship, sufficient adaptations occur, and sufficient habitual responses are set up, to allow us to describe the relationship between the person and the aspect of her environment as *structurally coupled*. Structural coupling, when taking place amongst a group of people, allows the working out of coordinations of actions in ways that are of mutual benefit to all those concerned. Of course, language may facilitate and strengthen this process.

Language is socially shared only in as much as each individual who develops and uses it implicitly understands the relationship of language with the coordinations of her own actions and those of others. When the use of language gives an unexpected result in terms of a person's perception of the actions of others, it is evidence that the language was inappropriate for that event of social coordination. This is an unusual understanding of language in two respects: (i) language does not describe a 'real world' external to subjective realities, but only the coordination of actions; and (ii) it can never be taken for granted that words mean exactly the same to all people (they are always dependent for meaning on their use by acting subjects appreciating a local context).

Language also forms "rational domains" in which people participate. Over time, a particular use of language to coordinate coordinations of actions may become more and more elaborate, allowing people to exist in very subtle, well-coordinated, structurally coupled relationships. Thereby, whole human activity systems, or domains of action, are created. People may actually participate in a variety of domains of action, but the movement of individuals from one to another—and hence from the use of one form of language to another—crucially depends on the invocation of emotion. According to Maturana (1988b), emotions make individuals switch from one 'rationality' to another. All rational arguments are "braided" with emotion (in other words, forms of language come to be associated with emotional states within individuals), so when a particular emotion is experienced, this triggers a switch to the appropriate, associated rational domain (or elaborated system of language). This is why an appeal to the emotions can have such a powerful effect in terms of changing peoples' ways of thinking (Bilson, 1996, 1997). Indeed, the relationship between rational domains (forms of language) and emotion is two-way: the use of a particular 'language game' associated with an emotion will give rise to that emotion, altering the set of rational domains that become available to participating individuals at that moment.

Human beings, then, are self-producing organisms who co-construct their realities through language. It is because of the role of language in the coordination of coordinations of actions that *conversation* is so important. Individuals flow through different domains of action by moving between different networks of conversations, guided by their emotions (Maturana, 1988a,b). Conversations end when the emotional commitment to remain engaged in them ends.

In Maturana's view, people share a common emotion: love (or mutual respect for the 'other' as an equally valid human being). However, love is not universally extended to all people at all times. In conversations, the braiding of emotion and reason helps to specify who is the 'other' to be concerned about at any particular time, and what actions should be taken towards him or her. These concerns and/or actions may be loving, instrumental, exclusionary or even violent. However, a true *social* system, as defined by Maturana, is indeed based on love (mutual respect) for others.

Now, the theory of autopoiesis is descriptive (concerning the nature of human beings), but it also has a normative dimension: it is *pre*scriptive about the right course of action for human beings to follow. Because it is love that enables mutual understanding during conversations, Maturana argues that we have an ethical responsibility when we engage in conversations to do so with an attitude of love—listening to the 'other' as an equally valid person. To do anything less is to negate the value of the 'other' as a fellow human being.

It is clear that the theory of autopoiesis says something important for both educationalists and IS practitioners about the nature of human learning: people actively construct a variety of meanings that relate to different domains of action. It also indicates the attitude with which we and other participants should approach IS planning: a willingness to engage with others in an atmosphere of mutual respect. However, this is easier said than done. Does the 'other' mean every other person in the world? To engage all these others in conversation, based on mutual respect, is a self-evidently impossible task. It is for this reason that it becomes important to consider the *boundaries* of inclusion, exclusion and marginalisation of both people and issues. The theory of boundary critique comes in useful here: this offers a language of value and boundary judgements that can support reflection on setting appropriate boundaries for conversation, and it also provides a model of social marginalisation processes that can be used to explore situations where mutual respect appears to be lacking.

## THE THEORY OF BOUNDARY CRITIQUE

Our review of the theory of boundary critique will start with the work of C. West Churchman (1968a,b, 1970, 1971, 1979) who has been widely acknowledged as a major contributor to the development of systems thinking and operational research. It will then move on to examine the writings of Werner Ulrich (1983, 1986, 1988a,b, 1994, 1996a,b), Gerald Midgley (1992a, 1994, 2000) and Maurice Yolles (2000) who have built upon the foundations laid by Churchman. It should be noted that these authors talk about designing improvements through 'systems intervention' rather than IS planning, but the arguments are equally applicable to the latter.

For Churchman (1970), the business of defining improvement when conducting an intervention is a systems problem. This is because the *boundary* of analysis is crucial. What is to be included in, or excluded from, any analysis is a vital consideration: something that appears to be an improvement given a narrowly defined boundary may not be seen as an improvement at all if the boundaries are pushed out. For this reason, Churchman argues that as much information as possible should be "swept in" to definitions of improvement.

This way of thinking involves a fundamental shift in our understanding of the nature of a 'system'. Prior to the work of Churchman, many people assumed that the boundaries of a system are 'given' by the structure of reality. In contrast, Churchman made it clear that boundaries are social or personal constructs that define the limits of the knowledge that is to be taken as pertinent in an analysis. There is also another important element of Churchman's understanding of 'system'. When it comes to human systems, pushing out the boundaries of analysis may also involve pushing out the boundaries of who may legitimately be considered a decision maker (Churchman, 1970). Thus, the business of setting boundaries defines both the knowledge to be considered pertinent *and* the people who generate that knowledge (and who also have a stake in the results of any attempts to improve the system). This means that there are no 'experts' in Churchman's systems approach, at least in the traditional sense of expertise where all relevant knowledge is seen as emanating from just one group or class of people: widespread stakeholder involvement is required, sweeping in a variety of relevant perspectives.

Not only did Churchman introduce this fundamental change in our understanding of 'system', but he also discussed critique. In examining how improvement should be defined, Churchman (1979) followed Hegel (1807), who stressed the need for rigorous self-reflection, exposing our most cherished assumptions to the possibility of overthrow. To be as sure as we can that we are defining improvement adequately, we should, in the words of Churchman (1979), pursue a "dialectical process": this involves seeking out the strongest possible "enemies" of our ideas and entering into a process of rational argumentation with them. Only if we listen closely to their views and our arguments survive should we pursue the improvement.

Churchman produced a great deal of highly influential work in the 1960s and 1970s, and in the 1980s several other authors began to build upon it in significant new ways. One of these authors was Werner Ulrich. Ulrich (1983) agrees that Churchman's desire to sweep the maximum amount of information into understandings of improvement is *theoretically* sound, but also acknowledges that the need to take practical action will inevitably limit the sweep-in process. He therefore poses the question, how can people rationally justify the boundaries they use? His answer is to develop a methodology, Critical Systems Heuristics, which can be used to explore and justify boundaries through debate between stakeholders. In producing his methodology, Ulrich draws upon the later writings of Jürgen Habermas (1976, 1984a,b) concerning the nature of rationality. Habermas regards rationality as dialogical—and the tool of dialogue is language, which allows us to question. The basis of dialogue is therefore open and free questioning between human beings. However, Habermas does not take a naive line concerning dialogue: he acknowledges that it may be distorted through the effects of power. This may happen directly, when one participant coerces another, or indirectly, when participants make unquestioned assumptions about the absolute necessity for, or inevitable future existence of, particular social systems. To overcome these effects of power, we need to establish what Habermas calls an "ideal speech situation": a situation where any assumption can be questioned and all viewpoints can be heard.

However, while Ulrich (1983) accepts the *principle* of Habermas's understanding of critique, he nevertheless criticises him for being utopian. For all viewpoints to be heard, the ideal speech situation would have to extend debate to every citizen of the world, both present and future. This is quite simply impossible. Ulrich sees his task as the *pragmatisation* of the ideal speech situation, and a marriage between 'critical' and 'systems' thinking is the means by which this can be achieved. Truly rational inquiry is said to be *critical*, in that no assumption held by participants in inquiry should be beyond question. It is also *systemic*, however, in that boundaries always have to be established within which critique can be conducted. Indeed, Ulrich claims that both ideas are inadequate without the other. Critical thinking without system boundaries will inevitably fall into the trap of continual expansion and eventual loss of meaning (as everything can be seen to have a context with which it interacts, questioning becomes infinite). However, systems thinking without the critical idea may result in a "hardening of the boundaries" where destructive assumptions remain unquestioned because the system boundaries are regarded as absolute.

An important aspect of Ulrich's (1983) thinking about boundaries is that boundary judgements and value judgements are intimately linked: the values adopted will direct the drawing of boundaries that define the knowledge accepted as pertinent. Similarly, the inevitable process of drawing boundaries constrains the ethical stance taken and the values pursued. Debating boundaries is therefore an ethical process, and a priority for Ulrich is to evolve practical guidelines that can help people steer the process of critical reflection on the ethics of drawing system boundaries. For this purpose, Ulrich (1983) developed a list of 12 questions which can be used heuristically to question what the system currently is and what it ought to be. It is important to note that some of these questions relate to who should participate in discussing boundary judgements in the first place, meaning that there is always the possibility for people to enter or leave discussions.

There is a key guiding ideal embedded in this work. According to Ulrich, if rationality is dialogical, plans for improvement should, in principle, be normatively acceptable to all those participating in a given dialogue. In practice, this means (if at all possible) securing agreement between those designing an improvement and those affected by it (of course, judging who or what is actually involved and/or affected already involves making a boundary judgment). When agreement is not secured, citizens who disagree with implementing the 'improvement', and who are affected by it, may legitimately use Ulrich's 12 questions in a "polemical" mode to build an argument with which to embarrass planners in future public debate by exposing the limited nature of the expertise they lay claim to.

We have now seen how Ulrich has built on and developed the work of Churchman. In a similar fashion, Midgley (1992a) has extended the work of Ulrich. For both Churchman and Ulrich, the question of what system boundaries are to be used in an analysis is essentially an ethical question because value and boundary judgements are intimately related. Midgley (1992a) uses this insight as a starting point to ask what happens when there is a conflict between different groups of people who have different ethics (values in action) relating to the same issue, and thereby make different boundary judgements.

If one group makes a narrow boundary judgement and another makes a wider one, there will be a *marginal* area between the two boundaries. This marginal area will contain elements that are excluded by the group making the narrow boundary judgement, but are included in the wider analysis undertaken by the second group. We can call the two boundaries the *primary* and *secondary* boundaries (the primary boundary being the narrower one). This is represented visually in Figure 1.

Midgley argues that, when two ethical boundary judgements come into conflict, the situation tends to be stabilised by the imposition of either a *sacred* or a *profane* status on marginal elements. The words "sacred" and "profane" mean valued and devalued respectively. This terminology has been borrowed from the

*Figure 1: Marginalisation*

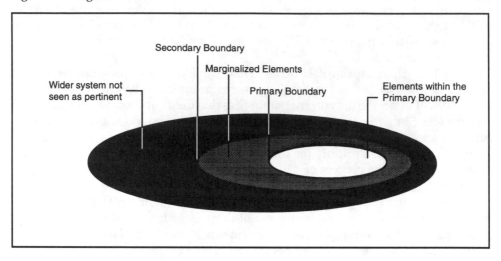

tradition of anthropology, exemplified by the work of Douglas (1966), and it should be stressed that they are not meant in an exclusively religious sense, but refer to the special status of a marginalised element. The imposition of either a sacred or profane status on marginal elements stabilises a conflicting situation in the following manner. When marginal elements become profane, the primary boundary and its associated ethic is focused upon and reinforced as the main reference for decision making. People or issues relegated to the margins are disparaged, allowing the secondary boundary to be ignored. Conversely, when marginal elements are made sacred (and thereby assume a special importance), the secondary boundary and its associated ethic is focused upon and reinforced.

However, this is not the end of the story. Not only do ethical tensions give rise to sacredness and profanity, but this whole process comes to be overlaid with social ritual. Midgley (1992a) defines ritual as "behaviour, in whatever context, that contains certain stereotypical elements that involve the symbolic expression of wider social concerns" (see Douglas, 1966, and Leach, 1976, for further thoughts on the relationship between ritual, sacredness and profanity). An observation of the presence of ritual can tell us where sacredness and profanity might lie, and hence where ethical conflicts related to marginalisation might be found. In order to make this clearer, the whole process has been represented diagrammatically in Figure 2.

To explain, in Figure 2 we see one ethic arising from within the primary boundary, and another from within the secondary. These come into conflict—a conflict that can only be dealt with by making one or other of the two boundaries dominant. This dominance is achieved by making elements in the margin (between the primary and secondary boundaries) either sacred or profane. The whole process is symbolically expressed in ritual which, in turn, helps to support the total system.

While Figure 2 shows the secondary boundary *containing* the primary boundary, creating a marginal area between the two, a similar situation of marginalisation

*Figure 2: Margins, Ethics, Sacredness, Profanity and Ritual*

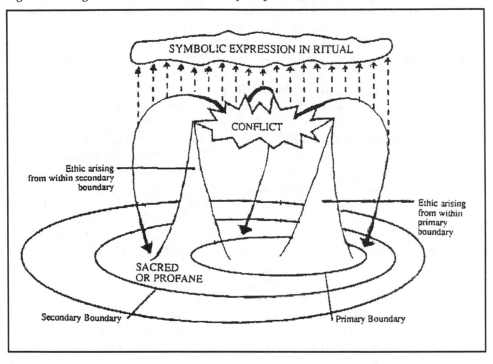

also arises when two boundaries *overlap*: the common area may be subject to dispute and can become either sacred or profane in the same manner. See Yolles (2000) for an illustration.

Of course, the 'system' represented in Figure 2 is a model, and like all models it does not fully express the complexity of the many value and boundary judgements that interact dynamically in social situations. A discussion of this complexity, and practical examples that clarify the process further, can be found in Midgley (1992a, 1994, 2000) and Midgley et al. (1998). One particularly important point about the complexity lying behind the model should be borne in mind, however: this kind of 'system' does not exist in isolation—it is 'held in place', or granted integrity, by virtue of the fact that it expresses wider struggles between competing discourses.[4]

Let us now examine the implications of this analysis for making critical boundary judgements. Ulrich (1983) stresses the importance of stakeholder involvement in the process of making such judgements: he suggests that a boundary judgement should, in principle, be normatively acceptable to all concerned citizens (even if, in practice, this is not always possible). Midgley's work problematises this in two ways. First (as Ulrich also recognises), in defining who is a "concerned citizen" it becomes particularly important not to turn ones back on those who are viewed as profane. Second, it is possible to have a consensus between a relatively diverse group of stakeholders on the boundary that they think should be adopted, yet this may be the result of processes of conflict and marginalisation that remain invisible. An example offered by Midgley (1994) is the tendency to focus uncritically on boundaries around human systems (especially in the industrial, economic and political arenas) while marginalising the non-human environment. Elements of the non-human environment are made profane, thereby justifying the narrow focus, yet the abuse they are then subject to may result in damage to human and non-human alike (note that an issue or any aspect of perceived reality may become marginalised, not just stakeholders). When all identified stakeholders share a commitment to a boundary judgement, it is still important to consider what is marginalised by this. On occasion, it may be necessary for the researcher to introduce a different perspective by widening dialogue beyond the boundary of those who are immediately identified as affected or involved. The new participants may argue for the use of a different boundary in the intervention, challenging the consensus and making visible the marginalisation that supports it.

Another important implication of the model in Figure 2 arises from its application in interventions (Midgley et al, 1997, 1998): reflections on the model can inform the appropriate design of *methods* of intervention, drawing upon a plurality of possible methods from a range of methodologies (Midgley et al., 1998)[5].

We can now summarise the main contributions of Churchman, Ulrich and Midgley to the theory of boundary critique. First, Churchman introduced the fundamental idea that the boundaries of analysis are crucial in determining how improvement will be defined during a systems intervention, and hence what actions will be taken. He also argued that pushing out the boundaries to make an intervention more inclusive may well involve sweeping in new stakeholders. Ulrich built on this by pointing out the need to rationally justify the setting of boundaries. He suggested, following Habermas, that rationality is essentially dialogical. Therefore, if boundaries are to be established rationally, they should be defined in dialogue by all those involved in and affected by the intervention. Finally, Midgley examined the systemic processes that work to stabilise conflicting situations. He demonstrated the need to be aware of how some stakeholders and issues may be stigmatised by these processes, resulting in their potential marginalisation during interventions. He also argued that it will sometimes be necessary to challenge a consensus on boundaries by seeking the involvement of people who might not be defined as directly affected or involved, but who may nevertheless have an important perspective to bring to bear on the boundaries of the intervention.

## SYNTHESIZING THE TWO THEORIES

The theories of autopoiesis and boundary critique can be synthesised. The theory of autopoiesis offers an understanding of human beings as active learners, engaged in a number of different domains of action (and corresponding 'language games' or 'rationalities'). The theory of autopoiesis also implies an ethical responsibility to engage in conversation with an attitude of love—listening to the 'other' as an equally valid person. However, given the fact that we cannot open conversation to every person in the world during IS planning, the question remains how boundaries can be established in order to demarcate which people and issues should be included at any particular moment. The theory of boundary critique provides guidance on such matters.

Both theories are concerned with social exclusion and marginalisation. In the context of IS planning, marginalisation often happens when individuals (operating in the mode of 'expert' or 'manager') impose onto others their own values concerning what is important in a design. By definition, marginalising people (and labelling them as profane) results in them not being heard in conversation as equally valid participants in debate. In short, the imposition of a profane status on people in the margins is a negation of their humanity.

The theory of autopoiesis simply asks participants in debate *not* to exclude or marginalise others (we therefore suggest it assumes that an appeal for love is sufficient to bring about social inclusion). In contrast, the theory of boundary critique suggests that exclusions and marginalisations are inevitable: it is simply impossible for participants in debate to be aware of every point of view on a particular issue, and (in a dynamically changing society) there will always be conflicts between competing discourses, giving rise to local manifestations of marginalisation. In this respect, the two theories make incommensurable assumptions. However, in synthesising them, we accept the inevitability of marginalisation and exclusion in the knowledge that this can be reflected upon and addressed on an ongoing basis. Therefore, we lose the (in our view) naive assumption that a simple exhortation to love is sufficient to bring about loving relationships, but suggest that it is still possible to *work toward* this ideal through critical reflection on situations of marginalisation. The ideal will never be perfectly realised, but more inclusive social relations will result than if processes of marginalisation are ignored.

Things *can* be done to break down patterns of marginalisation through local action, even if the wider conflicting discourses that feed local marginalisations remain (meaning that the job of promoting social inclusion is never fully completed). A variety of methods from the applied disciplines (IS planning, systems intervention, operational research, action research, management consultancy, community development, etc.) may be drawn upon to support this endeavour in IS planning and other intervention contexts (Midgley et al., 1998).[6]

With this synthesis of the theories of autopoiesis and boundary critique in mind, we will now propose a methodological framework for IS planning that embodies a different understanding of social design from the one criticised at the beginning of this chapter.

## THE NEW METHODOLOGY

There is, first of all, a need to understand the *context* of IS planning before moving toward the design of improvements. This implies thinking about the boundaries of the context, in terms of both potential participants and their multiple concerns (these people may or may not be interacting with one another, or even be aware of each other's existence, prior to IS planning). Interaction between the various participants (in single stakeholder groups and/or multi-stakeholder forums, depending on what seems most appropriate in the local context[7]) can support them in identifying relevant concerns. In facilitated interaction, people can become more aware of how they pursue their own concerns—in particular whether this is done at the expense of others. The facilitators themselves should participate in this critical reflection too: their very nature as human beings means that they cannot be neutral (they make their own boundary judgements), so they have to be careful to reflect on and counter any marginalisations introduced through their own actions.

We propose two modes of interaction that people need to embrace if the results of IS planning are to be practical, relevant to people's concerns, and informed by reflections on situations of marginalisation: *distinction* and *improvement*. These are stages in the methodology, in the sense that 'distinction' should come before 'improvement', but movements back to distinction (and again to improvement) to enable iterations of planning will often be necessary.

- *Distinction*. Here, the purpose is to distinguish, in conversation with different people involved in and affected by IS planning, their many (often interacting) domains of action and associated concerns. These conversations should involve reflections on people's daily lives (not just the work context). Some of the concerns that are distinguished will be explicitly related to IS, and others will not be. 'Questioning' methods, like Ulrich's (1983) Critical Systems Heuristics, can be valuable for surfacing concerns. Only time will tell which concerns will be important, as interactions between concerns that may not be immediately apparent need to be explored (see Midgley et al., 1997, for an example of a method for doing this). As a product of the interaction between IS planners and participants, a set of relevant people and issues come to be defined (this need not be kept unchanged for the whole project, but may be subject to revision in future iterations).

- *Improvement*. Based on the set of people and concerns identified, the purpose of interactions for improvement is to identify activities that will enable desirable change. The theory of autopoiesis implies that interactions for improvement should aim to respect other participants' ways of living, and will involve the exploration of common concerns (including participants' common concern in having respect paid to their differences) as the basis of designs for change. Interactions for improvement may or may not be limited to changes in IS, and may or may not require the use of systems methods. Importantly, it should not be assumed in advance that an IS is required (especially a computer-based system)—other needs or desires may be more urgent, and should not be ignored (facilitators should therefore not be blinkered by having the identity of 'IS planner' ascribed to them). The output from interactions for improvement will be a set of action plans that reflect the concerns identified.

### Continuous Boundary Critique

In both modes of interaction, the use of boundary critique will support participants (including IS planners) in considering possible marginalisations. We have not included boundary critique as a 'stage' of the methodology, but have said that it should be 'continuous', because it may be necessary at any point during distinction and improvement. Certainly, if distinctions are to be undertaken with

*Figure 3: Interactions between Distinction, Improvement and Boundary Critique.*

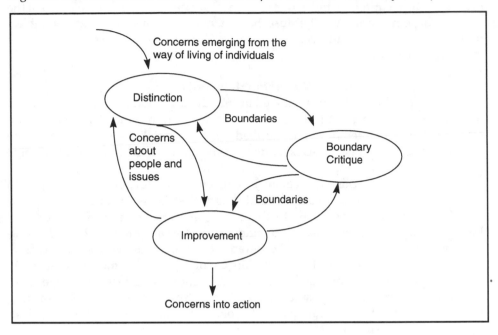

an eye on issues of marginalisation, boundary critique should be integral to them. However, the development of action plans for improvement can also be informed by boundary critique: even when a set of people and issues have been defined, problems of marginalisation may arise that were not apparent in the distinction phase. In all forms of interaction, explicit reflection on boundaries can help participants (including IS planners) identify both common concerns and ethical conflicts arising from clashes of perspectives.

The interactions between distinction, improvement and boundary critique can be seen in Figure 3.

Having described our methodology, we will now detail its first practical application.

## DEFINING THE ROLES OF INFORMATION TECHNOLOGY AND INFORMATION SYSTEMS IN A COLOMBIAN UNIVERSITY

From December 1998, we have been engaged in an IT/IS planning project in Javeriana University, Colombia. At the time of writing (June 1999), this project is still ongoing, so we cannot present a final evaluation. We can, however, show how the methodological ideas described above have informed our practice so far[8].

Inevitably, because of space restrictions, only an overview of our methods and process of application can be provided. Also, scant information can be given of the contents of people's analyses because the contents established so far may be subject to revision in future iterations of the research. However, we hope to go into much more detail in future work.

## Javeriana University

Javeriana University was founded in 1622 during colonial times in the region now called Colombia.[9] It is a Jesuit-inspired institution which first focused on teaching law and theology, and applied rules of racial discrimination in the recruitment of students: no black students were admitted, which was the norm at that time in history (Jaramillo, 1982).

Nowadays, Javeriana University's conception of education has changed to embrace a wide variety of subjects, and it admits students from all racial backgrounds. It has grown too: currently there are 3,244 lecturers and 28,250 students. Javeriana has 18 faculties offering 50 undergraduate programs; 127 taught postgraduate programs; and 4 doctoral programs. In comparison with some Universities in other countries, and even within Colombia, Javeriana has a strongly hierarchical management culture; this is a reflection of its Jesuit heritage, with priests occupying the key positions of authority. Any large-scale project seeking the involvement of a wide range of stakeholders needs the support of the priesthood if it is to be successful.

A desire to influence society as a whole has been noted in the University's last strategic plan. Inspired by the values of the Catholic faith, in the last decade there has been a continuous project of promoting 'inclusive' education that it is hoped will address some of the problems of Colombian society, such as inequalities in the distribution of wealth; the instrumental treatment of human beings; a lack of appreciation of national culture; environmental damage; intolerance; and a lack of access of some sectors to educational opportunities (Proyecto, 1992). Javeriana is striving to be an educational community with stable links inside and outside the institution to promote change toward a more egalitarian society (Proyecto, 1992; Orientaciones, 1998).

Within the above context, our project—to "rethink the role of IT and IS in Javeriana"—was seen by the senior management of the University as an interesting opportunity to build on an existing international link agreement (Javeriana and Hull have signed an accord, establishing a framework for cooperation in teaching and research), and provide a more 'human centred' vision of the uses of IT and IS by the academic community. In light of the University's mission and strategic plan, it was particularly important to the senior management that we were proposing to encourage explicit reflections on the wider social impacts of the University's IT and IS strategies.

## First Contacts

We came to be involved in this project because one of the authors, Diego Torres, took a sabbatical from his job as a lecturer in Systems Engineering at Javeriana to study for an MA in Management Systems at the University of Hull in the UK. At Hull, he met both José Cordoba (a fellow Colombian student) and Gerald

Midgley (a lecturer on the MA). On his return to Colombia, Diego Torres wanted to use some of the new systems ideas he had learned in planning an IT/IS strategy for Javeriana. He approached José Cordoba, who by this time was studying for a Ph.D. at Hull under Gerald Midgley's supervision, to see if he wanted to collaborate on this project. José Cordoba had already begun to develop the methodological synthesis of the theories of autopoiesis and boundary critique (presented earlier), and was looking for an opportunity to undertake an intervention—preferably one involving IS. We had a discussion by e-mail, and agreed to approach Javeriana University to see if it would sponsor a project that the three of us would work on— José Cordoba full time, based in Colombia; Diego Torres part time, based in Colombia; and Gerald Midgley in a supervisory capacity, based in Hull (although he travelled to Javeriana for one week to undertake another, unrelated project).

This background information is important, because it makes clear that the initiative came out of an 'overlap' between the concerns of the research team, developed in Hull, and the concerns of Javeriana University to improve its ability to influence Colombian society. In a sense, this 'overlap' was personified in Diego Torres who brought the ideas from Hull into his work in Javeriana. It is also important because, as this was a project being undertaken under the auspices of an academic link, and involved a Ph.D. student, there was no expectation of payment. For the senior management of Javeriana, it was therefore not only a good project (in terms of its relevance to the University's mission and strategy), but it was also inexpensive (which, in the Colombian context, is important).

## Starting the Project

We began by presenting the project to the vice chancellor and administrative staff. This was a necessary starting point given the hierarchical nature of the institution. In a traditional IS planning project, where the remit is handed to the planners, such a meeting might have marginalised other stakeholders. However, we went into the meeting with the intention of gaining support for wider stakeholder involvement. We set out to explain what it means to base the role of IT in the 'way of living' of Javeriana University: the 'way of living', as we define it, is the set of actions in which individuals are engaged, influenced by particular values. It is the sum total of the domains of action in which people are involved. We suggested that the uses of IT and IS should be integrated into the style of education that Javeriana wishes to pursue, and these uses should also promote the values that the University wishes to encourage in students. Of course it would be difficult to disagree with this general statement, but we argued that, to do this in an adequate manner, it would be necessary to explore the concerns of the different people involved in, and affected by, the University's activities. It should not be assumed that everybody shares the same concerns, so the work should start by clarifying all the 'domains of action' engaged in by the University's stakeholders.

There was some debate, both within the research team and with management, about the boundaries of involvement. We were very clear that students should be involved as well as academic and administrative staff, and the rationale for this was accepted by senior management. It was also agreed that a wide range of other stakeholders should be involved as well, including security guards, IT vendors, business people in the community, members of families, and members of parishes. In a strongly hierarchical institution without a culture of participation in administrative decision making, even of lecturers, we view acceptance of this level of involvement as a significant breakthrough.

## The Distinction Stage

We started the distinction stage by interviewing a small number of administrative staff (in keeping with respect for the hierarchy), but rapidly moved the boundaries out to include the full range of other stakeholders. Some of these were identified by the administrators, and some by ourselves. Interviews continued until no new stakeholder groups were identified. This is a method of 'rolling out' the boundaries of participation that was taken from Midgley and Milne (1995), and has been associated with the application of boundary critique in a previous intervention (Midgley et al., 1998).

For these interviews we used a method, developed by Weil (1998a) as part of her Critically Reflexive Action Research, which was designed to surface the widest possible range of domains of action (with their associated rationalities and emotions) that people might be involved in. Prior to the interviews, we assembled a range of pictures taken from magazines and newspapers. Some of these related to issues of particular relevance to Colombia, some to the international context, and others had no specific connotations for the research team. The idea was to invite people to select the pictures that were particularly meaningful for them, and then to reflect on this meaning to see what concerns and desires emerged.

There were three people present in each interview: the interviewee, the interviewer, and a scribe (who took confidential notes). The role of the interviewer was to facilitate by asking questions about the pictures like, "What does the picture represent for you?" "Who are the people in the picture?" "Do you see an ethical conflict in the picture?" The interviewer also supported interviewees in identifying implications for their own actions and for other people.

The interviewer intervened with questions if he noted any 'autopoietic discourse' in the interview. An 'autopoietic discourse' is one that almost has a life of its own: a network of dynamically evolving, interlinked concepts is established that is difficult for the interviewee to see beyond—each statement being justified with reference to other linked concepts, forming a complex but ultimately circular rationality. Douglas (1986) argues that religious cults provide the clearest example of this kind of self-referencing discourse, which is protected from challenge by the labelling of other rationalities as profane. However, a great deal of everyday discourse also follows the same pattern, albeit in a less obvious manner. When we thought we were encountering autopoietic discourse, we asked the following kinds of questions to support the person in reflecting on the boundaries of her rationality:

- Why do you emphasise this issue?
- Why is it so important to include this issue or these people?
- If action has already been taken along these lines, why has not it been successful?
- What or who else should be included if action is to be taken in the future?

Here we see the influence of both the theories of autopoiesis and boundary critique: an autopoietic discourse is a 'rational domain' (to use Maturana's, 1988b, terminology) that two or more people participate in. Unlike some rational domains that people can enter or leave with ease, an autopoietic discourse has strongly defended boundaries, so the means of supporting people in looking beyond such a discourse is through questioning informed by the theory of boundary critique.

As well as interviewing individuals, we also worked with stakeholder groups (e.g., we talked with a number of students in a group together, and we also worked with the IT support team as a whole). For this purpose we adapted the above method (Weil, 1998a) so that people worked in clusters of three taking on the roles of interviewee, interviewer and scribe themselves. When working in groups, we also encouraged reflection on the similarities and differences between people's outputs. The decision to involve the group participants in being interviewers and scribes was informed by the theory of boundary critique: it was designed to blur the boundary between the research team and other stakeholders, making it less likely that people would regard us as the holders of 'sacred expertise' (this might have been disempowering for participants).

Altogether, these interviews and workshops involved 30 people over a three-month period. Ten groups were run, and ten individual interviews conducted.

Also in the distinction stage, we set up a workshop with students to enable them to produce a vision of their ideal (but still feasible) education process to provide another context which could be taken into account when rethinking the role of IT and IS at Javeriana. This involved the synthesis of parts of methods drawn from two previously existing systems methodologies: Critical Systems Heuristics (Ulrich, 1983) and Interactive Planning (Ackoff, 1981). These have been synthesised previously in interventions that we regard as successful (Cohen and Midgley, 1994; Midgley, 1997a; Midgley et al., 1997, 1998). Highly summarised accounts of both methods are provided below. Because of the need for brevity, we recommend consulting the original sources for more information.[10]

Critical Systems Heuristics (CSH) gives a list of 12 questions that can be used to generate debate during planning. These focus on various issues such as whose interests ought to be served by the development of a system, whose 'expertise' should be accepted, what criteria of evaluation should be used, and who should participate in planning and management. Interactive Planning (IP) has several aspects to it (see Ackoff, 1981, for full details), but a central concept is "idealised design". Idealised design involves the generation through participative debate of a list of "desired properties" of a system, followed by the production of a design that, if implemented, should make those desired properties a reality. While implementation in its complete form might not be immediately possible, the idealised design nevertheless offers a feasible vision of the future to work towards. In this case, the "desired properties" were generated using the CSH questions, and this was followed (in the spirit of IP) by the production of a skeletal plan for a new approach to education. Again, the output from this workshop was summarised for use in the improvement stage.

The information from the individual and group interviews, together with the output from the student workshop, was summarised in two "rich pictures"

(Checkland, 1981; Checkland and Scholes, 1990): visual representations of issues linked by arrows to show how the issues are connected. Amongst other things, these pictures included common concerns about the social situation in Colombia (the guerrilla war; other violence and criminal behaviour; the phenomenon of globalisation; marginalisation of sections of society in terms of education, income and employment; etc.). They also showed that people wanted a new vision of education: while some of the students shared our own criticisms of the traditional methodology (described earlier in this chapter), the majority of stakeholders focused on using the traditional approach in new ways (e.g., aiding the redistribution of wealth through the provision of knowledge and skills to currently impoverished communities). However, all were enthusiastic about using IT and IS to enhance education by supporting new initiatives (e.g., distance learning), collecting information for monitoring and evaluation purposes, and reducing costs.[11]

## The Improvement Stage

We started the improvement stage by clarifying with a range of stakeholders within the organisation whether they still wanted to go ahead with designing a new IT/IS strategy. Their answer was "yes", but they also told us about a range of initiatives that were already going on to develop IT and IS provision, and suggested that these be taken into account. They included the commissioning of a multinational consulting company to help develop effective processes of decision making on IS issues (Javeriana Sistemas, 1999); two digital library services projects; and the purchasing of video conferencing facilities to support some distance learning programs. We were reluctant to simply take these initiatives as given, which might have considerably constrained the thinking of the various stakeholders. It was agreed that the most useful way forward, *which would enable both the existing commitments of the stakeholders and the research team to be respected* (this is an enactment of the principle of inclusion from the theory of autopoiesis), would be for the research team to actually participate in the initiatives as 'critical facilitators'—supporting people in reflecting on the boundaries of their understandings and the values flowing into them. This also involved advocating for some of the concerns identified in the distinction phase, as well as people not involved directly in the initiatives who would be affected by them (this advocacy technique has been successfully used by Midgley et al., 1998, in a previous intervention).

Apart from our participation in these initiatives (which is still ongoing), we set up a series of planning workshops: two days per week for six weeks. To these we invited a variety of internal and external stakeholders, some of whom had been interviewed in the first phase, and some of whom became involved for the first time (at the suggestion of those already interviewed). Obviously two days per week is a considerable commitment, and we had to accept people's constraints on availability—we did not expect everybody to come to everything.

The workshops started with presentations of the rich pictures and minor revisions to them. We also established the principle, right from the start, that *all* the concerns identified in the pictures should be regarded as important because they reflect people's lived experiences. While some of them might be more central than others to the IT/IS planning, each of them could be addressed in some measure—

if only by making an explicit decision to put them aside for the time being. Once again, we were conscious of the need to question any autopoietic discourses which might result in the automatic marginalisation of some concerns, but ultimately decisions on inclusions and exclusions had to be made by the group through explicit debate on the consequences for lived experience.

After this review, the research team proposed that the stakeholders should identify "relevant systems" (Checkland, 1981) that could be designed to improve the current situation, according to the concerns identified in the distinction stage. A "relevant system" is a general statement (a short phrase) about a set of human activities that, if implemented, would transform some aspect of the present reality into a more desirable state (e.g., an evaluation system may transform educational programmes that currently receive no formal feedback about quality into programmes that do receive such feedback). Each relevant system was driven by a particular set of concerns, and provided a vision of alternative actions that could be taken within Javeriana University (note that there was no push for consensus or accommodation at this stage—although we expect that participants will choose to make accommodations later). Some of the relevant systems were new and others were modifications of existing ideas. However, it was emphasised that nobody should propose a relevant system unless she personally felt responsible for under-taking the actions needed to implement it. This way utopianism was avoided, and the designs were grounded in what people felt able to pursue in the present. However, this work was not without its difficulties, which will be commented upon in the next section.

The methods from Soft Systems Methodology (SSM) were then followed (Checkland, 1981; Checkland and Scholes, 1990; Checkland and Holwell, 1998). The adequacy of the ways in which people defined their relevant systems were tested by use of Checkland's mnemonic, CATWOE, each letter of which refers to a different facet of the relevant system that should be explored. CATWOE stands for: Customers (those who might be harmed, as well as beneficiaries), Actors (those who will be involved in making the system work), Transformation process (an identification of a 'raw material' that the system will transform into an 'end product'; e.g., undergraduates may be transformed into graduates by a system for awarding degrees), Weltanschauung (the world view, or concerns, underlying the wish to make a transformation), Owners (those who have the power to stop the system from working), and Environmental constraints (things that have to be taken as given by the system). By exploring the possible customers, actors, transformation process, weltanschauung, owners and environmental constraints of a relevant system, participants in debate began to elaborate their understandings.

A "conceptual model" was then produced for each relevant system. A concep-tual model is a 'map' of the specific human activities that would need to be undertaken if the system were to become operational (Checkland and Scholes, 1990). Activities are first listed, then arrows are used to link them to show which ones need to be done first, and how the activities support one another. A conceptual model does not express the full complexity of the necessary activities, it simply highlights key points that may act as a focus for debate (Checkland, 1997).

Throughout the process of elaborating the relevant systems and producing the conceptual models, Ulrich's (1983) 12 questions from Critical Systems Heuristics were asked of participants in order to maintain a focus on what Javeriana University *ought* to be doing. Here we seen the influence of the theory of boundary critique. Every time a conceptual model was produced, the team who produced it was required to make a presentation to other stakeholders and the research team. The latter then acted as critical facilitators to enable any last revisions to be undertaken. The following are examples of the kinds of questions asked by the critical facilitators:

- What would [insert name of stakeholder] think of this activity?
- Why do you want to include these actions/people?
- What about [insert name of stakeholder or issue] that is now excluded?
- What are the wider implications for society?
- Hasn't this been tried unsuccessfully before? Why should it work now?
- Who should participate if more discussions on these actions is needed?

Again, these are mostly boundary questions.

### Future Plans

At the time of writing, we are coming to the end of the process of generating these conceptual models. According to Checkland and Scholes (1990), once conceptual modelling is complete, a comparison can be made with the rich pictures to make a judgement about whether the activities would indeed make a difference to the problem situation. Then a plan for making desirable and feasible changes can be developed, leading to action for improvement.

However, we are currently reviewing our methods. Some problems were encountered in the process of generating relevant systems that are making us question whether we have supported people in exploring a sufficient variety of ideas in the improvement stage, and it appears that we have lost commitment from some key players. We found that the IS administrators, who would be key personnel in implementing any new plans, resisted the whole idea of defining relevant systems. When we explored the reasons with them, they said that, while they welcomed participation in the first stage (making distinctions), they had expected us to act as 'experts' in the improvement stage. They felt that we should prepare our own recommendations which they could then either accept or reject. This was a misunderstanding which we had not anticipated. Participation from these key administrative personnel began to fall away. However, other stakeholders—most notably the students—were still very keen to be involved. It was for this reason that we did not change direction when resistance from the IS administrators was first encountered; we thought we would be able to overcome the problem once the IS administrators saw others participating. However, this was not to be. We now have to deal with this by rethinking our methods.

## REFLECTIONS

As we said earlier, because this project is unfinished, a final evaluation is not possible. However, we will provide some tentative reflections on our experience of the work undertaken so far.

Certainly, in the distinction stage, the use of boundary critique highlighted the contexts in which choices are made, and supported the participants in exploring the ethical implications of these choices. This is something people said that they valued, and it fitted well with both the mission and strategy of the organisation (to influence wider society) and the Jesuit culture. People also took advantage of the opportunity to explore the variety of domains of action in which they participate. Again this was widely perceived as valuable, and engendered commitment to the project. We have therefore reached the tentative conclusion that our approach to the distinction stage of the work, which embodied the theories of autopoiesis and boundary critique in a synthesis of methods drawn from Critically Reflexive Action Research (Weil, 1998b), Critical Systems Heuristics (Ulrich, 1983) and Interactive Planning (Ackoff, 1981), was successful. However, we will suspend final judgement until the project is over and we have had an opportunity to evaluate it more systematically.

We have encountered some problems in the improvement stage, but do not believe that these are insurmountable: the IS administration is still talking about future phases of the project despite their lack of participation in the workshops, and indeed they have recently asked whether we can continue our involvement beyond the period when we planned to withdraw, suggesting a continued commitment to the work. In our view, the problems we have experienced do not stem from any fundamental flaw in the theoretical or methodological ideas we have used. Indeed, we can draw upon one of these ideas, the theory of autopoiesis, to produce an interpretation of what went wrong (although it is not the only possible interpretation). We should be clear that this is our own reflection and has not yet been checked with other stakeholders. At this stage we therefore advance it tentatively, with the intention of engaging others in debate before deciding whether it is an interpretation we wish to hold onto in the longer term.

Looking at the resistance of the IS administrators through the theory of autopoiesis, we can see that the theories of autopoiesis and boundary critique, together with the methods from SSM, became our own autopoietic discourse. In a sense it is rather ironic that the use of methods specifically designed by Checkland and Holwell (1998) and ourselves to overcome the negative effects of traditional, 'expert-led' IS planning methodologies were so alien to the culture of the IS administration in Javeriana University that participation beyond the distinction stage became problematic. This can be seen as a failure on the part of the research team to sufficiently appreciate the rationality of the IS administration, and we feel it is our duty to try to remedy the situation—but hopefully without resorting to the use of 'expert-led' methods that would alienate those who have actually chosen to participate in what we have facilitated so far. We are currently discussing with stakeholders a variety of possibilities for taking the work forward, and it seems that these are being positively received.

In summary, it appears that reflections on the theories of autopoiesis and boundary critique delivered some successes in the distinction stage. However, they also led us to make some mistakes in choosing methods in the improvement stage: in our eagerness to promote participation (which stemmed from our theoretical and methodological commitments), we failed to appreciate that some stakeholders were working in a completely different rational domain. Paradoxically, however, it has been our ability to reflect on the very theory that separated us from the IS administration that has enabled us to begin to identify and address this problem. We are now in discussion with stakeholders about how to move forward, still using the methodology we have outlined in this chapter. Of course, it remains to be seen whether we will be successful, so the jury is still out. Nevertheless, it would appear at face value that it is not the methodology that has been at fault, but our choice of methods at one crucial juncture in the IS planning process—and all the signs are that this can be remedied.

## CONCLUSIONS

In this chapter we have argued that uses of IT and IS in the education sector tend to make similar assumptions to the traditional methodology of education itself: that it is acceptable for an 'expert' to impose ideas on others who appear to know less than themselves. This traditional methodology of education is what Freire (1972) calls the "banking" method, where students are seen as empty vessels needing to be filled. The "banking" method has been widely criticised on a variety of grounds, and one of these is that it is more appropriate to see students as active learners building on their past knowledge and experience than passive recipients of knowledge. If this is accepted, then it makes no sense to exclude students from the IS planning process: students are the primary users and need to participate in order to ensure that information systems are appropriately tailored. Also, like all people, students participate in multiple domains of action. Education can support them in many of these domains, not just those associated with the workplace, so an effective IS planning methodology will give students (and other stakeholders) the freedom to explore a variety of meanings of education before IS are debated.

After exploring these general issues concerning education and IS planning, we went on to present two theories—autopoiesis and boundary critique—which informed the construction of our own methodology for IS planning. We then described the first application of this methodology to an IT/IS planning project in Javeriana University, Colombia. This application was partially successful, but ran into difficulties at a crucial stage. We reflected on these difficulties, and tentatively concluded that our theoretical orientation has been useful for informing the construction of our methodology and our choice of methods, and also for reflecting on problems encountered in the IS planning process (allowing alternative paths for action to be identified).

Of course, because this project is incomplete, no *final* conclusions can be drawn. However, we believe that the theories of autopoiesis and boundary critique, synthesised in the manner described in this chapter, could have considerable utility for IS planning.[12] There is obviously a long road ahead of us in terms of conducting further research, and we welcome fellow travellers who also see the potential in these ideas.

## ACKNOWLEDGMENT

We wish to thank all the participants from within and beyond Javeriana University for their collaboration on the project reported in this chapter. We particularly wish to thank the staff of the Computer Science Department who have gone out of their way to provide the resources necessary to make this project run smoothly.

## ENDNOTES

1   This chapter addresses the problem of IS *planning*, although is it believed that a similar analysis could be made in relation to the process of IS implementation and use as well.

2   This reflects the insight of many programme evaluators that 'formative' evaluation (providing on-going feedback to participants) is preferable to 'summative' evaluation (providing an 'expert' report) because the former is less negatively judgemental and more meaningful for people trying to promote improvements (e.g., Patton, 1978, 1980; Guba and Lincoln, 1989).

3   This point signals a difference of opinion between two of the authors of this chapter. José Cordoba believes that the theory of autopoiesis provides a foundation upon which to build, and the theory of boundary critique is only useful in so far as it supports the translation of the theory of autopoiesis into methodology and practice. In contrast, Gerald Midgley views boundary critique as a kind of 'process philosophy' which relativises supposedly 'foundational' theories like the theory of autopoiesis by revealing the limited boundary judgements they are based upon (see Midgley, 2000, for more details).

4   An example is the marginalised position of people who are unemployed: there is a conflict between the liberal discourse of citizenship (where all people have equal value because of their status as rational beings), and the capitalist discourse of good employment practice (which limits the responsibility of organisations to their employees alone). This conflict is not stabilised by either the inclusion *or* exclusion of the unemployed, but by their marginalisation. If unemployed people were to be fully included along with employees in the primary boundary of industrial organisation, 'good employment practice' (indeed, the whole capitalist system of organisation) would become untenable. However, if they were fully excluded, the liberal ideal of equal citizenship would become untenable instead. Both the liberal and capitalist discourses have long histories in the West, and have come to be institutionalised throughout the economic and legal systems of our societies. While on the whole the two discourses are mutually supportive (Booth Fowler, 1991; Midgley and Ochoa-Arias, 1999), there are still significant tensions, and the phenomenon of unemployment points to one of them. The key to understanding the status of the unemployed is to realise that it is only possible to maintain the dual commitment to liberalism and capitalism if people who are unemployed are neither fully included nor excluded. People who are unemployed therefore become

marginalised, but the conflict is finally stabilised when a sacred or profane status is imposed on them: when they are regarded as profane, it justifies thinking in terms of narrow organisational boundaries; when they are regarded as sacred, this justifies programmes to support social inclusion. There is rarely a consensus on whether a marginal group or issue should be viewed as sacred or profane, but there are dominant patterns of social action which come to be solidified in rituals. In the case of the unemployed, a typical example is 'signing on' which many people view as an exercise in ritual humiliation.

5   Midgley et al. (1998) link the theory of boundary critique into critical systems thinking (CST), a systems paradigm with a concern for methodological pluralism (see Flood and Jackson, 1991, and Flood and Romm, 1996, for two edited books on CST).

6   See the literature on critical systems thinking (e.g., Flood and Jackson, 1991; Jackson, 1991; Midgley, 1992b, 1997a, 2000; Gregory, 1996) and multi-methodology (e.g., Mingers and Gill, 1997) for more details of the theory and practice of methodological pluralism.

7   Midgley (1997b) argues that, ideally, both within- and between-stakeholder discussions should be facilitated, but they serve different purposes and are appropriate at different times.

8   In a way it is a pity that the opportunity to write this chapter came as early as it did. Had we had an extra six months or a year, we could have undertaken and presented a full evaluation of our work.

9   In the 17th Century, this region was called Nueva Granada and included the territories of Colombia, Venezuela, Ecuador, Peru and Bolivia.

10  The theory of synthesising methods will not be discussed here, but is covered in detail by Midgley (1997a, 2000).

11  Checkland (1981) suggests that visions of the future do not belong in rich pictures, which are supposed to represent the current situation only. Visioning the future needs to be undertaken separately, and the feasibility of visions can be tested by looking at whether proposed actions would effectively transform the current reality. However, we argue that it *is* the current situation that people are generating new visions for education, and future planning should take these into account.

12  They have already shown their utility in systemic intervention: see Bilson (1996, 1997) for a particularly interesting application of the theory of autopoiesis, and Midgley et al. (1998) for an application of boundary critique.

# REFERENCES

Ackoff, R.L. (1981). *Creating the Corporate Future*. Wiley, New York.

Andreu, R., Ricart, J. and Valor, J. (1996). *Estrategia y Sistemas de Información*. McGraw Hill, Bogotá.

Banathy, B.H. (1992). A *Systems View of Education: Concepts and Principles for Effective Practice*. Educational Technology, Englewood Cliffs, NJ.

Bertalanffy, L. von (1956). General systems theory. *General Systems Year Book*, 1, 1-10.

Bilson, A. (1996). *Bringing Forth Organisational Realities: Guidelines for a Constructivist*

*Approach to the Management of Change in Human Services*. Ph.D. thesis, Lancaster University.

Bilson, A. (1997). Guidelines for a constructivist approach: Steps toward the adaptation of ideas from family therapy for use in organizations. *Systems Practice*, 10, 153-177.

Booth Fowler, R. (1991). *The Dance with Community: The Contemporary Debate in American Political Thought*. University Press of Kansas, Lawrence, Kansas.

Bostock, S. (1998). Constructivism in mass higher education: A case study. *British Journal of Educational Technology*, 2(3)9, 225-240.

Burgoyne, J. and Reynolds, M. (eds.) (1997). *Management Learning: Integrating Perspectives in Theory and Practice*. Sage, London.

Carr, A., Jonassen, D., Litzinger, M. and Marra, R. (1998). Good ideas to foment educational revolution: The role of systemic change in advancing situated learning, Constructivism and feminist pedagogy. *Educational Technology*, January/February 1998, 5-15.

Checkland, P. (1981). *Systems Thinking, Systems Practice*. Wiley, Chichester.

Checkland, P. (1997). Rhetoric and reality in contracting: Research in and on the NHS. In: Flynn, R. and Williams, G. (eds). *Contracting for Health*. Oxford University Press, Oxford.

Checkland, P. and Scholes, J. (1990). Soft Systems Methodology in Action. Wiley, Chichester.

Checkland, P. and Holwell, S. (1998). *Information, Systems and Information Systems: Making Sense of the Field*. Wiley, Chichester.

Churchman, C.W. (1968a). *Challenge to Reason*. McGraw-Hill, New York.

Churchman, C.W. (1968b). *The Systems Approach*. Delacorte Press, New York.

Churchman, C.W. (1970). Operations research as a profession. *Management Science*, 17, B37-B53.

Churchman, C.W. (1971). *The Design of Inquiring Systems*. Basic Books, New York.

Churchman, C.W. (1979). *The Systems Approach and its Enemies*. Basic Books, New York.

Clark, R. (1983). Considering research from media. *Review of Educational Research*, 53, 445-459.

Clark, R. (1994). Media will never influence learning. *Educational Technology Research and Development*, 42(2), 21-29.

Cohen, C. and Midgley G. (1994). *The North Humberside Diversion from Custody Project for Mentally Disordered Offenders: Research Report*, Centre for Systems Studies, Hull.

Currid, C. (1994). *Computing Strategies for Reengineering your Organisation*. Prima Publishing, USA.

Davies, L.J. and Wood-Harper, A.T. (1989). Information systems development: Theoretical framework. *Journal Of Applied Systems Analysis*, 16, 61-73.

Douglas, M. (1966). *Purity and Danger: An Analysis of the Concepts of Pollution and Taboo*. Ark, London.

Douglas, M. (1986). *How Institutions Think*. Routledge & Kegan Paul, London.

Educacion XXI (1998). *Educación: La Agenda del Siglo XXI. Hacia un Desarrollo Humano*. Hernando Gómez Buendía (ed.). Tercer Mundo Editores, Bogotá.

El Tiempo. Magazin: Del Dicho al Hecho. Marzo 23 de 1999. El Tiempo, Bogotá. Http://www.eltiempo.com.co

Fischer, M. (1996). Integrated learning systems: An application linking technology with human factors and pedagogical principles". *Educational Technology Research and*

*Development,* 44(3), 65-72.

Flood, R.L. and Jackson, M.C. (eds.) (1991). *Critical Systems Thinking: Directed Readings.* Wiley, Chichester.

Flood, R.L. and Romm, N.R.A. (1996). *Critical Systems Thinking: Current Research and Practice.* Plenum, New York.

Freire, P. (1970). Cultural Action for Freedom. Harvard Educational Review, Cambridge, MA.

Freire, P. (1972). *Pedagogy of the Oppressed.* Penguin, Harmondsworth.

Freire, P. (1973). *Education for Critical Consciousness.* Sheed and Ward, London.

Friis, C. (1997). A critical evaluation of the Danish ICT strategy. *The Economic and Social Review,* 28(3), 261-276.

Galvis, A. (1998). Educación para el siglo XXI apoyada en ambientes educativos interactivos, lúdicos, creativos y colaborativos. *Informática Educativa,* 11(2), 169-192.

García, A. (1993). *Sistemas de Información: Planeamiento Estratégico y Análisis.* Universidad de los Andes, Facultad de Ingeniería, Bogotá.

Giddens, A. (1991). *Modernity and Self-Identity: Self and Society in the Late Modern Age.* Polity Press, Cambridge.

Greene, S. and Ackermann, J. (1995). Expanding the constructivist metaphor: A rhetorical perspective on literacy research and practice. *Review of Educational Research,* 65, 383-420.

Gregory, W.J. (1993). Designing educational systems: A critical systems approach. *Systems Practice,* 6, 199-209.

Gregory, W.J. (1996). Dealing with diversity. In: *Critical Systems Thinking: Current Research and Practice.* Flood, R.L. and Romm, N.R.A. (eds.). Plenum, New York.

Grid (1997). *National Grid for Learning: The Government Consultation's Paper: Connecting the Learning Society.* DfEE, London.

Guba, E.G. and Lincoln, Y.S. (1989). *Fourth Generation Evaluation.* Sage, London.

Habermas, J. (1976). *Communication and the Evolution of Society* (English ed., 1979). Heinemann, London.

Habermas, J. (1984a). *The Theory of Communicative Action, Volume One: Reason and the Rationalisation of Society.* Polity Press, Cambridge.

Habermas, J. (1984b). *The Theory of Communicative Action, Volume Two: The Critique of Functionalist Reason.* Polity Press, Cambridge.

Harré, R. and Gillett, G. (1994). *The Discursive Mind.* Sage, London.

Hegel, G.W.F. (1807). *The Phenomenology of Mind.* 2nd edition (English version published 1931). George Allen and Unwin, London.

Illich, I. (1971). *Deschooling Society.* Calder and Boyars, London.

Information I. (1996a). *Information Society Ireland: Strategy for Action.* Information Society Commission, Dublin.

Information I. (1996b). *Information Society Ireland: Strategy for Action. First Report.* Information Society Commission, Dublin.

ISC (1998). *Information Society Commission Update Bulletin* No.12.

Jackson, M.C. (1991). *Systems Methodology for the Management Sciences.* Plenum, New York.

Jaramillo, J. (1982). *Manual de Historia de Colombia—Volumen 2: Siglo XIX.* Procultura y Printer Colombiana S.A., Bogotá.

Javeriana Sistemas (1999). *Documento de Diagnóstico de la Función Sistemas.* Facultad de Ingeniería, Universidad Javeriana, Bogotá.

Kearsley, G. (1998). Educational technology: A critique. *Educational Technology*, March-April 1998, 47-51.

Kelly, G.A. (1955). *The Psychology of Personal Constructs. Volume One: A Theory of Personality.* W.W. Norton, New York.

Kozma, R. (1994). Will media influence learning? Reframing the debate. *Educational Technology Research and Development*, 42(2), 7-19.

Leach, E. (1976). *Culture and Communication: The Logic by which Symbols are Connected.* Cambridge University Press, Cambridge.

Levrat, B. (1992). Basic strategies for introducing and using informatics in education. In: *Education and Informatics Worlwide: The State of the Art and Beyond.* Unesco, Paris.

Lewis, P. (1994). *Information-Systems Development.* Pitman, London.

Lleras, E. (1995). Towards a methodology for organisational intervention in Colombian enterprises. *Systems Practice*, 8, 169-182.

Lovelock, J. (1988). *The Ages of Gaia: A Biography of Our Living Earth.* Oxford University Press, Oxford.

Lyytinen, K. and Hirschheim, R. (1987). Information systems failures—A survey and classification of the empirical literature. *Oxford Surveys in Information Technology*, 4, 287-309.

Maturana, H. (1981). Autopoiesis. In: *Autopoiesis: A Theory of Living Organization.* Elsevier, New York.

Maturana, H. (1988a). *Ontology of Observing: The Biological Foundations of Self Consciousness and the Physical Domain of Existence.* Internet publication: http://www.inteco.cl/biology/

Maturana, H. (1988b). Reality: The search for objectivity or the quest for a compelling argument. *Irish Journal of Psychology*, 9, 25-82.

Maturana, H. (1997a). *El Sentido de lo Humano.* Dolmen Ediciones/Granica, Chile.

Maturana, H. (1997b). *Emociones y Lenguage en Educación y Política.* Dolmen Ediciones/Granica, Chile.

Maturana, H. and Varela, F. (1992). *The Tree of Knowledge: The Biological Roots of Human Understanding.* Shambala, Boston.

Midgley, G. (1992a). The sacred and profane in critical systems thinking. *Systems Practice*, 5, 5-16.

Midgley, G. (1992b). Pluralism and the legitimation of systems science. *Systems Practice*, 5, 147-172.

Midgley, G. (1994). Ecology and the poverty of humanisam: A critical systems perspective. *Systems Research*, 11, 67-76.

Midgley, G. (1996). What is this thing called Critical Systems Thinking? In: *Critical Systems Thinking: Current Research and Practice.* Flood, R.L. and Romm, N.R.A. (eds.). Plenum Press, New York.

Midgley G (1997a). Developing the methodology of TSI: From the oblique use of methods to creative design. *Systems Practice*, 10, 305-319.

Midgley G (1997b). Dealing with coercion: Critical systems heuristics and beyond. *Systems Practice*, 10, 37-57.

Midgley, G. (1999). Rethinking the unity of science. *International Journal of General*

*Systems*, in press.

Midgley, G. (2000). *Systemic Intervention: Philosophy, Methodology and Practice*. Plenum, New York (forthcoming).

Midgley, G., Kadiri, Y. and Vahl, M. (1996). Managing stories about quality. *International Journal of Technology Management*, 11, 140-150.

Midgley, G. and Milne, A. (1995): Creating employment opportunities for people with mental health problems: A feasibility study for new initiatives. *Journal of the Operational Research Society*, 46, 35-42.

Midgley, G., Munlo, I. and Brown, M. (1997). *Sharing Power: Integrating User Involvement and Multi-Agency Working to Improve Housing for Older People*. Policy Press, Bristol.

Midgley, G., Munlo, I. and Brown, M. (1998). The theory and practice of boundary critique: Developing housing services for older people. *Journal of the Operational Research Society*, 49, 467-478.

Midgley, G. and Ochoa-Arias, A.E. (1999). Visions of community for community OR. *Omega*, 27, 259-274.

Mingers, J. (1995). *Self-Producing Systems: Implications and Applications of Autopoiesis*. Plenum, New York.

Mingers, J. and Gill, A. (eds.) (1997). *Multimethodology: Towards Theory and Practice for Mixing Management Science Methodologies*. Wiley, Chichester.

Murray-Lasso, M. (1992). Latin America. In: *Education and Informatics Worlwide: The State of the Art and Beyond*. Unesco, Paris.

North, R. (1987). *Schools of Tomorrow: Education as if People Matter*. Green Books, Hartland.

Orientaciones (1998). *Orientaciones Universitarias*. Documento Interno Número 10. Universidad Javeriana, Bogotá.

Patton, M.Q. (1978). *Utilization-Focused Evaluation*. Sage, Beverly Hills.

Patton, M.Q. (1980). *Qualitative Evaluation Methods*. Sage, London.

Pinzón, L. and Midgley, G. (1999). Developing a systemic model for the evaluation of conflicts. *Systems Research and Behavioral Science*, 16, in press.

PNE (1998). El Tiempo, Bogotá. http://www.eltiempo.com.co

PNI (1997). *Lineamientos de Politica Nacional de Informática*. Ministerio de Comunicaciones, Bogotá.

Postman, N. and Weingartner, C. (1969). *Teaching as a Subversive Activity*. Penguin Books, Harmondsworth.

Proyecto (1992). *Proyecto Educativo*. Documento Interno. Universidad Javeriana, Bogotá.

Reimer, E. (1971). *School is Dead: An Essay on Alternatives in Education*. Penguin Books, Harmondsworth.

Reyes, A. and Zarama, R. (1998). The process of embodying distinctions—A re-construction of the process of learning. *Cybernetics and Human Knowing*, 5(3), 19-33.

Russell, G. (1994). Valuing values: Reflections on a social value paradigm of educational computing. *British Journal of Educational Technology*, 25(3), 164-171.

Senker, P. (1992). Technological change and the future of work. *Futures*, May 1992, 351-363.

Shotter, J. (1993). *Conversational Realities: Constructing Life through Language*. Sage, London.

Spitzer, D. (1998). Rediscovering the social context of distance learning. *Educational Technology*, March/April 1998, 52-56.

Solloway, E. (1991). Issues in educational technology. *Communications of the ACM,* 34, 29-33.

Tarrago, F. (1993). Educational telecommunications services: A case study on an integrated approach. *IFIP Transactions,* 13, 3-9.

Telecomm (1997). *Plan Nacional de Telecomunicaciones 1997-2007.* Resumen Ejecutivo—Visión. Ministerio de Comunicaciones, Bogotá.

Thomas, P., Carswell, L., Price, L., and Petre, M. (1998). A holistic approach to supporting distance learning using the internet: Transformation, not translation. *British Journal of Educational Technology,* 29(3), 149-162.

Thompson, K. and Bates, T. (1998). *Knowledge, Learning and the Social Roles of Education.* Open University Press, Milton Keynes.

Ulrich, W. (1983). *Critical Heuristics of Social Planning: A New Approach to Practical Philosophy.* Haupt, Berne.

Ulrich, W. (1986). *Critical Heuristics of Social Systems Design.* Working Paper No.10. Department of Management Systems and Sciences, University of Hull, Hull.

Ulrich, W. (1988a). Churchman's "process of unfolding"—Its significance for policy analysis and evaluation. *Systems Practice,* 1, 415-428.

Ulrich, W. (1988b). Systems thinking, systems practice and practical philosophy: A program of research. *Systems Practice,* 1, 137-163.

Ulrich, W. (1994). Can we secure future-responsive management through systems thinking and design? *Interfaces,* 24, 26-37.

Ulrich, W. (1996a). *Critical Systems Thinking for Citizens: A Research Proposal.* Research Memorandum No.10. Centre for Systems Studies, University of Hull, Hull.

Ulrich, W. (1996b). *A Primer to Critical Systems Heuristics for Action Researchers.* Centre for Systems Studies, Hull.

Video Conferencia (1999). Apuntes del Seminario "La Video conferencia como herramienta de productividad", Junio 10 y 11 de 1999. Universidad Javeriana, Bogotá.

Vygotsky, L.S. (1978). *Mind in Society: The Development of Higher Psychological Processes.* Harvard University Press, Cambridge MA.

Vygotsky, L.S. (1986). *Thought and Language.* MIT Press, Cambridge MA.

Weil, S. (1998a). Our concerns as researchers. Workshop with research students, held at the School of Management, University of Hull, May 15th, 1998.

Weil, S. (1998b). Rhetorics and realities in public service organizations: Systemic practice and organizational learning *as* critically reflexive action research. *Systemic Practice and Action Research,* 11, 37-62.

Weil, S. (1999). Re-creating Universities for 'beyond the stable state': From 'Dearingesque' systematic control to post-Dearing systemic learning and inquiry. *Systems Research and Behavioral Science,* 16, 171-190.

Whetzel, D., Felker, D. and Williams, K. (1998). A real world comparison of the effectiveness of satellite training and classroom training. *Educational Technology Research and Development,* 44(3), 5-18.

Wickham, J. (1997). Where is Ireland in the global information society? *Economic and Social Review,* 28(3), 277-294.

Winograd, T. and Flores, F. (1987). *Understanding Computers and Cognition.* Addison-Wesley, New York.

Wittgenstein, L. (1953). *Philosophical Investigations*. Basil Blackwell, Oxford.
Yolles, M. (2000). Management systems, conflict, and the changing roles of the military. *Journal of Conflict Processes*, in press.

# Final Thoughts

On the commencement of this project, now over a year ago, the objective was to source a variety of global contributions, which would represent the rapidly emerging domain of human-centred information systems. That the success in this regard has exceeded all our expectations as editors is due entirely to the exceptionally high quality of the submissions received, and for this we are indebted to all contributors.

To cover such a domain in one text is, of course, an impossible task. All that can be hoped is that the book is representative of the issues currently seen to be important. In this respect, whilst accepting that we have chosen to represent information systems as a highly human-centred area, sometimes to the detriment of a more technological viewpoint, we feel content that, with the aid of our contributors, we have largely succeeded.

The final verdict, however, must rest with you, the readers, and we will be happy to receive any comments which you feel may help in furthering our understanding of the domain. At the very least, with your help, the next compilation of edited chapters on this subject, which we fully intend to produce, will be more representative of current practices and theories.

Please forward any comments to the editors:
Dr. Steve Clarke
University of Luton Business School
Department of Finance, Systems and Operations
Park Square
Luton LU1 3JU
United Kingdom          Email: Steve.Clarke@Luton.ac.uk

or:

Dr. Brian Lehaney
University of Luton Business School
Department of Finance, Systems and Operations
Park Square
Luton LU1 3JU
United Kingdom          Email: Brian.Lehaney@Luton.ac.uk

# About the Authors

## EDITORS

**Steve Clarke** received a BSc in Economics from The University of Kingston Upon Hull, an MBA from the Putteridge Bury Management Centre, The University of Luton, and a PhD in human centred approaches to information systems development from Brunel University – all in the United Kingdom. He is Reader in Systems and Information Management at the University of Luton. His research interests include: social theory and information systems practice; strategic planning for information systems, and the impact of user involvement in information systems development. Major current research is focused on approaches to information systems strategy informed by critical social theory.

**Brian Lehaney** received his MSc in Operational Research from the London School of Economics. He has subsequently specialised in simulation and soft systems methodology, which are his current research interests. He is Principal Research Fellow in Systems and Operations Management at the University of Luton.

## CONTRIBUTORS

**Simon Bell** is a Lecturer in Information Systems in the Systems Discipline, Centre for Complexity and Change at the Open University in the UK. Simon has spent the last fifteen years working as an academic researcher and consultant on scoping, developing, planning, implementing and evaluating IS projects in many different parts of the world. His books include *Learning with Information Systems*, Routledge, 1996; *Rapid Information Systems Development: systems analysis and design in an imperfect world* with Trevor Wood-Harper, McGraw-Hill, 1998 (second edition) and *Sustainability Indicators: measuring the immeasurable* with Dr. Stephen Morse, Earthscan 1999.

**Elayne Coakes** is a Senior Lecturer in Business Information Management at the Westminster Business School, University of Westminster. Her research interests lie in the sociotechnical aspects of information systems and in particular the contribution of stakeholders to the process of computer information systems development. As Vice Chair of the BCS Sociotechnical Group she is active in promoting this view of information systems development and is currently principal editor of a book of international contributions to this field, *'The New SocioTech: Graffiti on the Long Wall'*, due to be published early in 2000. She is also involved in a research group at her university, looking at Learning Organisations and Knowledge Management. She has published a number of conference papers and articles in journals such as *Information and Management, Management Decision*, as well as several chapters in books.

**Jose Córdoba** has a BSc in Computer Science from the University of Los Andes in Bogota, Colombia, and an MA in Management Systems from the University of Hull, UK. He is currently doing his PhD in the Hull University Business School. Jose worked for 6 years as a project manager, facilitating strategic information technology planning processes. He is now conducting research into the development and application of systems thinking to improve the use of information technology in the Colombian education system.

**Elizabeth Davidson** is an assistant professor in the Department of Decisions Sciences at the University of Hawaii, Manoa. Her research and teaching interests include social cognitive aspects of information systems development in organizations, the implementation of clinical information systems, and organizational implications of technology implementation.

**M. Gordon Hunter** is currently an Associate Professor in the Department of Information Systems at St. Francis Xavier University, Antigonish, Nova Scotia, Canada. He has previously held academic positions at universities in Canada, USA, Hong Kong, and Singapore. He has a Bachelor of Commerce degree from the University of Saskatchewan in Saskatoon, Saskatchewan, Canada. He received his doctorate from Strathclyde Business School, University of Strathclyde in Glasgow, Scotland. Dr. Hunter has also obtained a Certified Management Accountant (CMA) designation from the Society of Management Accountants of Canada. He is a member of the British Computer Society and the Canadian Information Processing Society (CIPS), where he has obtained an Information Systems Professional (ISP) designation. He has extensive experience as a systems analyst and manager in industry and government organizations in Canada. Dr. Hunter has conducted seminar presentations in Canada, USA, Asia, New Zealand, Australia and Europe. His current research interests relate to the productivity of systems analysts with emphasis upon the personnel component, including cross-cultural aspects and the effective development of information systems.

**Bill Hutchinson** is the Associate Head of the School of Management Information Systems at Edith Cowan University in Perth, Western Australia. He has over 20 years information systems experience in education, government, the oil industry, and the finance sector. His academic interests are information operations, project management, system failures, and methodologies.

**Jonathan K. Lazar** is an Assistant Professor in the Department of Computer and Information Sciences in the College of Science and Mathematics at Towson University. Dr. Lazar earned his Ph.D. in Information Systems at the University of Maryland. His research focuses on human factors in the Internet environment. Specifically, Dr. Lazar is interested in user error, interface design, user satisfaction, end-user training, and requirements determination for distributed populations. Dr. Lazar has taught courses on System Analysis, System Design, Human-Computer Interaction, Web Development, Online Communities, Database Management, and Decision Support Systems. Dr. Lazar is also interested in integrating community service with courses and research in Information Systems.

**Gill Mallalieu** is senior Research Fellow at the University of Sunderland, working on the RAMESES project funded by the UK Engineering and Physical Sciences Research Council under the Systems Engineering for Business Process Change. Research interests are in requirements engineering, process modelling and socio-technical systems analysis.

**Gerald Midgley** has a BA(hons) in Psychology from the University of London, and an M.Phil. and Ph.D. in Systems Science from City University. For several years he ran his own business conducting evaluations of services for people with disabilities. After this, he worked in the Rehabilitation Resource Centre at City University for a couple of years before moving to the University of Hull. He is now the Director of the Centre for Systems Studies in the Hull University Business School. Gerald has published widely on systems methodology and community operational research, and is the author of the forthcoming book "Systemic Intervention: Philosophy, Methodology and Practice" (to be published by Plenum/Kluwer in the year 2000).

**Joline Morrison** is an assistant professor in the Management Information Systems department at the University of Wisconsin-Eau Claire. She received her Ph.D. in MIS from the University of Arizona in 1992. Her current research interests include group and organizational collaboration and knowledge management. She has published widely in these areas, and has also written multiple textbooks on database and client server programming.

**Dr. Anthony F. Norcio** is a Professor of Information Systems at the University of Maryland Baltimore County (UMBC). Dr. Norcio is also the Co-Director (with Dr. Marion J. Ball) of the World Health Organization (WHO)/Pan American Health Organization (PAHO) Collaborating Center for Health Informatics. Dr. Norcio serves as an external advisor to the PAHO and to the Inter-American Development

Bank (IDB) on computing and health informatics. He is an invited member of the PAHO/IDB Health Task Force of the Informatics 2000 Initiative for Latin America and the Caribbean. He also currently serves as a Computer Scientist at the Artificial Intelligence Center of the Naval Research Laboratory; and he has also served as the Scientific Advisor to the Mathematical, Computer, and Information Sciences Division of the Office of Naval Research.

**Ruth V. Small, Ph.D.** is Associate Professor in the School of Information Studies at Syracuse University. Her research focuses on the application of motivation theories to a variety of information-based learning, work, and virtual environments. Ruth has published widely in this area, including over 50 articles and three books (two on Web site evaluation). She has won several honours for her research and teaching including Syracuse University's Faculty Technology Associate and Information Studies' "Professor of the Year." Ruth's PhD is in Instructional Design, Development and Evaluation. She is a national and international consultant and speaker on motivation and evaluation.

**Lorraine Warren** is currently a Senior Lecturer in the Department of Business Strategy at the Lincoln School of Management. She has acted as consultant to a number of public sector and commercial organisations and in doing so has assisted in the management and resolution of complex problems. Her research specialism centres around systemic approaches to organisational interventions, with a bias towards those involving success factors for Information Systems. She has taught extensively in the fields of Organisational Behaviour, History of Management Thought, Operations Management, Systems Thinking, Information Systems and Philosophy of Research. She has lectured in the UK, Spain, Australia, Israel, Hong Kong, Singapore, Japan and Dubai. She has presented papers at many national and international conferences, and has published extensively in the areas associated with her teaching and consultancy activities. She has been a Visiting Scholar at Edith Cowan University in Perth and the Tokyo Institute of Technology in Japan. She is professionally active, and is a member of the Operational Research Society and the UK Academy for Information Systems (Treasurer for the Northern Regional Area).

**Andrew Wenn** is a lecturer in the Department of Information Systems at Victoria University of Technology, Melbourne and is currently undertaking his PhD in the History and Philosophy of Science Department at the University of Melbourne. His main field of research is nexus between the social and the technical particularly in the area of global information systems. This chapter is the result of an as yet incomplete study into the way the users, designers and technology are co-constituting one particular information service. Andrew has also published in the area of internet based education.

**Dianne Willis** is a Senior Lecturer in Information and Communications Technology at Doncaster College. Her research interests include sociotechnical issues surrounding the implementation of new technology in business and social environments and gender issues in the field of ICT, particularly factors influencing participation levels in both academic and practical fields. As a member of the BCS Sociotechnical group, she has co-edited a book on international aspects of information systems development and is currently researching in the field of Computer Mediated Communication.

**Vance Wilson** is an Assistant Professor of Management Information Systems at the University of Wisconsin–Eau Claire. He researches organizational aspects of human-computer interaction, with special interests in computer-mediated communication, decisional guidance, and computer support for software development teams.

# Index

## A

abstract conceptual model  86
action research  211
action researcher  102
activation error  78
Actor Network Theory  19
analog conceptual model  86
analysing communication patterns
    127
autopoiesis  205

## B

bi-polar description  51
black-boxing  19
bottom-up strategy  64
business process  133

## C

capture error  78
change agents  68
change management  133
client-led design  7
cognitive mappings  161
cognitive policy evaluation  52
collaborative venture  124
communication flow  125
community development  211
computer-aided learning  199
computer-based information systems
    4
computer-based systems  175
computer-mediated communication
    121, 125, 145, 148

conceptual component  67
constrained variety  2
constructivist approaches  183
critical awareness  179
critical content  92
critical systems heuristics  62, 217
critical systems thinking  9, 179
Customer, Actors, Transformation
    process  5

## D

data collection  140
data collection method  15
data quality  166
Data warehousing  159
data-as-knowledge  171
data-driven error  79
debugging program code  150
deduction  62
description errors  78
distinction  212

## E

easy-to-use interface  91
efficient interactions  199
electronic mail  20, 120
emergent properties  73
enabled by information technology  1
end-user computing system  166
end-user error  76, 81
end-user training  88
error management  84, 86
error message  82